For Jock & Virginia
because I believe they
will understand

Prisulla Narman
Nov. 1982

. . . IN THE WAY OF UNDERSTANDING

'Forsake the foolish and live;
and go in the way of understanding.'

Proverbs 9 v.6

Four Generations, my grandfather, my mother, myself and my son, Simon

... IN THE WAY OF UNDERSTANDING

Part of a Life
Lantern Slides in a Rough Time Sequence

by

Priscilla Norman

Foxbury Press
1982

Foxbury Press
Foxbury Meadow, Godalming, Surrey

First published 1982
© Priscilla Norman 1982

ISBN 0 946053 00 6

Printed in Great Britain by
St Edmundsbury Press, Bury St Edmunds, Suffolk

TO ROBINA

my loving companion in our joint pilgrimage to succour the mentally ill and handicapped and to help those who fear to understand.

Table of Contents

Acknowledgements — xiv
Preface by Dr. Denis Leigh — xv
Introduction — 1

GROWING WINGS AND FIRST FLIGHT

1. Childhood — 7
2. Adolescence — 18

WINGS OF CHANGE

3. Young womanhood: first marriage: divorce — 35
4. Local Government and some other activities — 50
5. Child Guidance Council, the Feversham Committee and proposed amalgamation of the Voluntary Mental Health Services — 58

ELYSIAN FIELDS

6. Pre-marital vicissitudes — 69
7. Second marriage, 1933 — 73
8. Post-marital vagaries, Plodge and Moor Place — 86
9. St. Clere: personalities there and elsewhere — 96

STARK REALITY

10. Clouds gathering and war in 1939 — 109
11. My husband's illness, retirement and convalescence in Isle of Man and later in South Africa — 117

Contents

SOME POST WAR ACTIVITIES

12 Justice of the Peace — 129
13 National Association for Mental Health: Scottish Association for Mental Health — 137
14 First Congress of World Federation for Mental Health (1948) — 151

IN WIDOWHOOD

15 Widowed (1950), loneliness and the solace of work — 161
16 The Bethlem Royal and Maudsley Hospitals — 174
17 Two Royal Ladies — 187
18 South East Metropolitan Regional Hospital Board — 192

FRESH FIELDS AND PASTURES NEW

19 World Travels:
Introduction — 207
Switzerland — 209
Belgium — 212
North America and Canada — 215
Austria — 228
Egypt — 229
Jersey — 231
Germany — 232
Denmark — 235
Northern Ireland — 238
Nigeria — 240
France — 248
Greece — 250
The Netherlands — 252
Hong Kong — 254
Thailand — 262
The Philippines — 265
Australia and Singapore — 267
Czechoslovakia — 275
Peru — 278

Contents

	Venezuela	281
	United Kingdom	283
	The Holy Land	288
	Israel	290
	Uganda	292
	Taizé	296
	China	298
	South Africa	301
	Canada	309
	Austria	311
20	Retirement	317

Epilogue 323
Appendix 329
Index 331

List of Illustrations

facing page

1	Four Generations, my grandfather, my mother, myself and my son, Simon	Frontispiece.
2	Portrait of my father	
3	Miniature of my mother	8
4	Portrait of myself, aged 5	
5	Mother and father standing, Uncle Edmund FitzAlan sitting and myself on Aunt May FitzAlan's knee 1909	9
6	Self in cloche hat	
7	With Simon and Peregrine during L.C.C. election, North Hammersmith	50
8	The Peacock Room, Plodge	51
9	The Music Room, Plodge	90
10	With Mont, in Plodge garden	
11	On the way to Buckingham Palace, 1933	
12	Reading	91
13	St. Clere, a drawing by P. Studiati-Beini	
14	The Norman clan	
15	Moor Place, a drawing by P. Studiati-Beini	102
16	Cruising in Jamaica Lord Reith, Mont, Lena Ashwell (Lady Simson) and myself	103
17	Plodge garden in summer	
18	The de Laszlo portrait of Montagu Collet Norman, 1919	152
19	Myself at W.V.S. Headquarters, 1939	153
20	Robina Addis, 1980	
21	Statue of Mont by Sir Charles Wheeler R.A. in Garden Court, Bank of England *by courtesy of the Bank of England*	168
22	James Burton and Lilian Whitchurch	
23	Dominique, Peregrine's daughter	169

List of Illustrations

facing page

24	Simon's seven children Front row: Peregrine, Cosima, Victoria Back row: Charlotte, Alice, Baby Frances, Katharine	169
25	Bethlem Royal, 1746 *by courtesy of the Bethlem Royal and Maudsley Hospitals*	
26	My portrait by David Poole, R.A. 1973	176
27	Princess Alexandra, Eileen Skellern C.N.O and L. H. W. Paine, House Governor at Bethlem Royal	
28	Myself with Deirdre O'Connor, Head Mistress, Bethlem Royal & Maudsley Hospital School	
29	St. Dymphna, Patron Saint of mental health	177
30	Iris Marwick and self in Nigeria	
31	With Hospital staff, Singapore, 1965	
32	Planting a tree, Singapore	242
33	Nigeria: Lady Mbanefo, Eastern region, self, Lady Ademola, Western region, 1961	
34	Alhagi Sir Abubaka Balewa, Prime Minister of the Federation, with Lord Brain and myself	243
35	Group of past Maudsley students in Hong Kong, 1971	
36	Opening session, Hong Kong, self in chair *by courtesy of the Ming Yuzn Studio, Hong Kong*	262
37	Bangkok, At a Palace garden party with Dr. Estefania Aldaba-Lin, Miss Dolores Francesco	
38	Queen Sirikit	
39	With the King of Siam	263
40	Philippino half-way Housing Scheme, self and Dr. Reyes	
41	Manila group workers with Robina and myself	
42	Robina and self with Philippine Association for Mental Health Executive Board	266
43	N.A.M.H. Dinner 1962 Miss Mary Applebey, Dr. T. P. Rees, The Lady Adrian, Lord Butler, H.R.H. Princess Marina, self, Lord Feversham, Lady Butler (*London News Agency Photos*)	267

List of Illustrations

		facing page
44	Royal Tomb, Kampala, 1970	296
45	Self at Fort Gerry, renamed Fort Portal in 1900	296
46	London Congress, 1968 H.R.H. Princess Alexandra, self, Dr. Morris Carstairs, Lady Butler	
47	Peregrine	320
48	Her Majesty the Queen with Simon and Mary, 1980 *by courtesy of the Lancashire Evening Post*	321

xiii

Acknowledgements

Amongst the many people who encouraged and bullied me into writing this tale only two were willing or able to take part in the actual writing.

Deidre O'Connor, after retiring from the Bethlem Royal and Maudsley School, offered to act as a sounding board and she did just that. To me she became friend, psychiatrist, psychologist, PSW and superb teacher all rolled into one. Without her almost daily at my side I could never have found the courage or physical strength to finish the book.

Denis Leigh, a hard task master and severe critic, gave up much of his time to advise me and acted all through my long ordeal as a supporting and understanding friend. So to Deidre and Denis I give great thanks.

I am also grateful to the various voluntary and professional organisations who helped me by making available material and assistance, notably N.C.V.O., N.A.M.H. (MIND) and W.R.V.S.

To Shirley Knight I am deeply indebted for typing and retyping the manuscript, for deciphering my execrable handwriting and coping with the vagaries of the postal service as we lived far apart. S.K. was bequeathed to me by Eileen Younghusband after they had finished work on the 'Albatross'.[1] I believe Eileen would have given me active support had she not been killed so tragically in the U.S.A. in 1981. She knew S.K. was the prop I needed, someone who never wavered in her affirmation that this book would be published. So to Eileen posthumously and to S.K., her friend and now mine, I give thanks.

1 July 1982   P.N.

---

[1] Eileen Younghusband, *Social Work in Britain: 1950–1975*, George Allen & Unwin, London, 1978.

Preface

Concern for the mentally ill has never been exclusively the province of the Doctor, indeed, it is only comparatively recently that the present medically orientated approach to mental illness has become dominant. For centuries, the Church was the moving spirit and it is to the Church that we owe the first establishments for the mentally ill, here in Britain the Hospital of Bethlehem and in Spain Santa Maria de Los Innocentes. Caring laymen, such as John Howard, the Tukes and Dorothea Dix, will never be forgotten. It was Clifford Beers, a sufferer himself from mental illness, who early this century founded the mental health movement.

These three strands, the spiritual, the philanthropic and the medical, all meet in the life and work of Priscilla Norman. A doctor manqué herself, a woman of deep spirituality and one remaining to this day fascinated by the human predicament, she can truly be regarded as a modern pioneer in the field of mental health. How she came to this can be traced in the story of her life, her childhood experiences and her struggles to find her true self whilst still a young woman. Marriage, alas all too brief, to that great, and even now, enigmatic man, Montagu Norman, seems to have been the catalyst which set her firmly on her course—her goal, that mental health for which we all so much yearn. Understanding, sympathy and compassion in her have combined with a sound practical commonsense and, at times, with a forthrightness that has not pleased everyone. A quest for knowledge, too, has been her hallmark. How many octogenerians would still brave the rigours of a winter day to make their way to a lecture at the Institute of Psychiatry, located in the wilds of South-East London?

I first met Priscilla Norman in 1956 at a meeting in Berlin of the World Federation of Mental Health. From then on, together, we have visited Hospitals in many countries, never

In the Way of Understanding

forgetting the poor and neglected and always hoping that the caring professions, in their meetings and in their work, would be able to transcend national and personal prejudices. It has been an uphill struggle at times, punctuated by periods of despair. But the overall goal remains, an understanding of the other person's point of view and of the difficulties which demand sympathy rather than facile criticism. I asked her to write this book, a daunting task needing energy and, at times, a painful recollection of things passed. It is a record of a long life of service, peculiarly English in style, but of a wider significance. I hope the reader will be able to share the pleasure that my wife and I have experienced in reading Priscilla's memories.

Denis Leigh

Introduction

Into the computer of my memory
  I insert a word, a thought, a name.
  Immediately
  the silent wheels whirl
  and I remember
  past names, past happenings
  stored ready
  for the associating key,
  unrecalled for years,
  reviving the past,
  conversing with those from the past,
  resurrecting the dead
  as if present.
  Perhaps they are always present,
  just waiting
  the recalling memory,
  the remembered presence.
So now I can speak
  words of welcome and love,
  of gratitude and inquiry,
  words of pardon or apology,
  setting right the past
  in total recall,
  making the bygone past
  into the timeless present.
George Appleton, "Memory" from The Word is The Seed, SPCK, 1976.

To recall the past is not always easy nor pleasant. There is so much that I could have done that I left undone, and much that I could better have left undone. However, colleagues in the field of mental health in the U.K. and abroad, and others whose opinions I value, have pressed me to undertake the task of writing—a task about which I feel diffident and inadequate. I hope my readers will forgive me if I stray from all the shades and variations of mental illness and mental handicap, because it seems to me necessary to describe myself as I was before and during my interest in education, social work and mental health and how my work in these fields enriched my life.

The caring professions of psychiatrists, psychologists, nurses, social workers and teachers with whom I have been privileged to work have urged me to think back to try to see why I devoted most of the working years of my life to a subject distasteful to the majority of people, a subject once not to be mentioned in the society in which I lived (unless professional help was needed, when it was used but not referred to again). My professional friends (some became intimate friends) accepted me, though untrained, as an amateur professional because they felt that my interest in learning and my wish to help if I could were genuine. I was not a fair weather worker: whatever the attractions in other fields—music which I loved, theatre, family, friends—all came second to any engagement for mental health. Sometimes this was very hard and I know I missed out on many interests which in retirement it would have been a pleasure to continue.

I know many friends and relatives were wary of me because of my interest and involvement in this strange thing called mental health. Some of them felt mental illness to be a mysterious or even frightening subject. Crime or cancer could have been understood and accepted, exciting their curiosity. But I have always felt a loner throughout my life and this became clear to me when I got immersed in the little-known work of psychiatric hospitals and clinics here and all over the world, and later became a founder member of the World Federation for Mental Health. Professional workers regarded me as a colleague and at the Bethlem Royal and Maudsley Hospitals, where I served on the Board of Governors for twenty years, I felt welcome and completely at home. Later on in the South East Metropolitan Regional Board it was the same, and finally on a national and international level I knew and enjoyed the friendship of professional men and women of all races.

I travelled the British Isles, Europe, Africa, Canada, the U.S.A., South America, and the Middle and Far East, but alas never India or Pakistan. My journeys took me three times to Hong Kong and three times to Israel. Usually these visits were

Introduction

to conferences in which I was invited to take an active part and I was always much amused by the deference shown to me by the foreign professionals who must have scratched their heads to place me in a well defined category. Here was someone neither fish, flesh, fowl, nor good red herring in their field of work. Perhaps I was the herring. Personally I have always regarded myself as a queer fish (although not 'queer' as this word came to mean!). Perhaps this idea spurred me on to agree to write these memoirs in order to try to make clear to myself what made me tick. Could my background give the answer?

So readers, bear with me as I go through the length of years that brought me in the end to maturity and happiness. I feel much discomfort in doing this, rather like a woman giving birth, but I hope that what follows may encourage another travelling a similar road.

Growing Wings and First Flight

I
Childhood

Soit comme l'oiseau pose pour un instant
Sur des rameaux trop frêles
Qui sent ployer la branche et qui chante pourtant
Sachant qu'il a des ailes.[1]
(Source unknown)

The heading to this chapter was inscribed by Lady Kitty Vincent in a commonplace book I once started at the age of ten. She was one of the most beautiful women I have ever seen and was painted by Sargent in 1905. The portrait now hangs in the York Gallery. Lady Kitty was a great friend of my mother but why she wrote this rather cryptic poem for a child I shall never know, nor could hardly have known how prophetic it was to be. I memorised it and it has been with me in moments of sorrow and despair, for a bird-like spirit has haunted me all my life and Lady Kitty may well have unconsciously communicated to a child her hopes and fears of an uncertain future. Flight to and from something has dogged my footsteps, perhaps because of the very unsettled life which I led during my first 18 years, with no roots to make the home I longed for. We flitted from house to house for various reasons, as the reader will discover, which made for uncertainty and frustration, but I always managed to find a branch on which to poise myself, if at times precariously.

I was born in Brussels in 1899. The snow was falling, so I have been told, and I was only 3½ lbs. in weight. I was wrapped in cotton wool and oiled and not dressed until I was a month old. My father, Major Robert Reyntiens, was a Belgian officer in the Artillery and A.D.C. to Leopold II, King of the

[1] *Translation* from French
  Be like the bird
  who alights for an instant
  on branches so frail
  that when feeling them break
  sings nevertheless
  knowing he has wings.

In the Way of Understanding

Belgians. My mother, Lady Alice Josephine Bertie (known as Joey), always a great lady, was an aristocrat to her finger-tips and second daughter of the seventh Earl of Abingdon. Her first husband, Sir Gerald Portal, K.C.M.G., C.B. died in 1893. She met my father while paying a visit to some Jewish friends, the Leon Lamberts, in Brussels. Leon Lambert, a distinguished Belgian banker and his wife Lucie were great friends of my father. Lucie was the sister of Lady Sassoon, the mother of the late Sir Philip Sassoon and the Dowager Marchioness of Cholmondely (Sybil). Mother was a beautiful rider and went hunting with the Rothschilds outside Paris at Chantilly where she met Mme Lambert who asked her to go to stay with her in Brussels.

My father had been married before to a lovely Spaniard who died and left him with three sons and a daughter. It would have been fascinating to hear from my mother's lips just why she married my father. I doubt if it was love because I think she only loved one man who was neither her first nor her second husband. She admired and was proud of her first husband, Sir Gerald Portal, and enjoyed being the wife of this brilliant young soldier and diplomat who in 1893 opened up Uganda and Abyssinia for Queen Victoria. She enjoyed living in Zanzibar and being courted and loved by this very handsome man and by his many friends, including his brother Raymond Portal and Frankie Rhodes, brother of Cecil Rhodes. After her husband's death I suppose my mother was lonely and life was no longer as exciting as it had been in Africa. My father was madly in love with my mother and I can remember well his adoration which lasted until his death in 1913, just before the First World War. He must have laid siege to her heart and in the end she yielded and became the step-mother of three rampagious teenager boys and a girl of ten. The boys liked their step-mother but she tried to get my father to send them to school in England instead of having them at home with all the problems of tempestuous youth with Spanish temperaments. When the school reports were bad my father, who had a fiery temper, used to chase the boys round the house with a hunting crop. My mother told me laughingly that she sometimes thought she was living in a mad house, never having experi-

Portrait of my father

Miniature of my mother

Portrait of myself, aged 5

Mother and father standing, Uncle Edmund FitzAlan sitting and myself on Aunt May FitzAlan's knee 1909

Childhood

enced such fantastic behaviour, even among her family, the Berties, who were also a little eccentric.

The step-daughter, Ynes, was eleven years older than I and needed love and affection which my mother, who was on the surface rather cold and haughty, was quite unable to give her. She was not an attractive girl and had violent emotional outbursts. She was sent to school in England to a convent in Roehampton. I think she was happier there than at home but never forgave my mother for coming between her and my father.

This was the setting into which I was born and, to complicate matters, a strong-minded Irish Nanny was engaged, a "maîtresse femme" as my father called her, who ruled the nursery, looked up to my father but was jealous of my mother and of my half-sister. This nurse adored me and possessed me completely.

I don't think my mother wanted a child; sex to her was something rather disgusting which one had to endure. It was never mentioned to me and my mother shied like a horse if any questions on the subject were ever raised. But she was fond of me in her way and I was as fond of her as my possessive nurse would allow. There was a continuous battle between my mother and my nurse, and father usually took my nurse's side as she had all the qualities my father admired—punctuality, the ability to make decisions and a belief that his "little Puss' (me) could do no wrong.

As I grew older I suffered very much from this jealousy in my nurse for I loved her and was afraid of her and of hurting her feelings if I ever admitted I liked mother best. When she went for a holiday—two weeks in the year—I cried bitterly and was ashamed of myself if there were moments when I enjoyed myself in her absence. I always slept in her room and there was a terrible scene when mother insisted that, at the age of eight, I should have a room to myself. I feel pretty sure now, looking back, that my nurse was the root cause of a stutter that has dogged my life. I began to try out my wings and my bird-like spirit came to my assistance. I struggled to get free from so much possessiveness and to be loyal to my mother and my nurse, and from a shaky twig I watched hoping that the battle could be happily resolved, but it never was. It was not until my second marriage that I found security, both physical and spiritual, and lost my hesitant way of speech—though even now, during any difficulty of expression or shyness, it comes back. I was a self-conscious and shy child and this was made worse as my half-brothers 'ragged' me. I was devoted to Guy, the eldest—later on a dashing young officer in the 'Guides', a Belgian crack regiment—who took me driving in his dog cart to the 'Bois' on Sundays when I was dressed up in a white rabbit fur coat, hat and gloves. I was then made much of by his friends and brother officers.

My mother and nurse both discouraged me from forming any relationship with my half-brothers. They thought foreign boys most dangerous as regards sex and I was told to keep away from them. Even if this were true it might have been healthier had I been warned by explanation instead of by mysterious hints, for these only made me curious. Ynes, my half-sister, ignored me or laughed at me for my deference to my nurse. She only tried to make friends with me when wanting to annoy her step-mother and my nurse. This may all have contributed to my being a delicate and puny child with crushing headaches or migraines once a week when my head throbbed and I was sick and ate nothing for twenty-four hours. The only thing that soothed me was a rhythmic beat from someone's hand on my body—my mother was splendid at it. As soon as I was better I craved for scrambled eggs. Aspirin was never tried until I was sixteen and then it worked a miracle. I grew out of these headaches when the war came in 1914 and I have never had the same kind of sick attacks again.

The Belgian doctors thought I did not eat enough and by their standards I suppose it was true. Mercifully, neither mother or father nor my nurse, who distrusted all foreign doctors, forced me to eat more than I wanted to. Curiously enough, but understandably in these days of psychology, I ate enormously when I was away alone with my nurse at the sea in lodgings or staying with an aunt in Derbyshire—pork pies, shrimps, oranges—all the things of which my mother disapproved.

My first conscious recollection—and it is very clear to

Childhood

me—is of when I was three years old, in my nurse's arms at the top of the grand staircase at Wytham Abbey, Oxford, the then home of my grandfather, the Earl of Abingdon. My mother's old nurse took my little hand and called me 'Ladybird' which thrilled me and pleased my Nanny no end. It was a name that stuck for a time, although my mother's family called me 'Pris' and my Belgian family 'Lilla'. Later, my Belgian girl friends who could not understand my extraordinary name called me 'Pré salé', a delectable dish of lamb reared on salt marshes.

I never discovered that my name came out of the Bible[1] until I gave up the Roman Catholic faith and read the Authorised Version with intelligence and great pleasure. There is certainly not much recorded about Aquila's wife but her name is enshrined in the book of all books.

My nurse taught me my letters—'Cat sat on the mat', etc., not without tears and I was always told how stupid I was. This gave me an inferiority complex as I was a proud child. When I finally learned to read I devoured books secretly and there was always trouble about bedside reading and forbidden books. But nothing stopped me and I lived in a dream world of my own. *The Scarlet Pimpernel* by Baroness Orczy was my favourite and I was Lady Blakeney for years and had many children, nurses, governesses and a whole household of servants in my dream world. My half-sister gave me books my mother did not approve of and there were rows over this for her and for me.

Being virtually an only child I was much alone and lonely among adults so that I made my own world in which I was the adult, was happily married, and had children and servants. All this was real to me and I talked to myself out loud and sometimes, when heard, was teased unmercifully.

But when I was a child I took everything for granted,
Including the stupidity of older people . . .
They lived in another world, which did not touch me.[2]

---

[1] *Corinthians*, Chap. 16, v. 19.
[2] T. S. Eliot, *The Family Reunion*, Faber & Faber, Ltd., 1939, p. 55.

In the Way of Understanding

My mother was very religious and her Roman Catholic faith meant a great deal to her, but when she married Sir Gerald Portal, a Protestant, and lived in Africa, she became more broadminded. When married to my father, an easy-going Catholic, she once again took her religion very seriously. When we lived for a time near Maestrict, on the Dutch border, she built a chapel and worked hard to get it going, firstly, by getting the Bishop to approve, and then by finding a chaplain. She herself embroidered vestments and bought holy statues and chalices. Only the most beautiful were good enough. It must have cost my father a lot of money. He was not very well off, only acting at that time as agent to his step-father, Monsieur de Brouckère. This old man was shut up in a separate part of the house. Two psychiatrists, in those days called alienists, came to see him once a month. He had a male nurse, and a delightful woman secretary whom we called Manelle who taught me French because, except for prattling to servants, I never spoke French. He also had three pairs of horses so that he could drive alone daily for three hours in a carriage, insisting on closed windows. It was only years later that I realised that he was a mental case and it is curious, looking back, to think how early I had been subjected to madness and its problems. No one, as far as I knew, thought the situation unusual. It was all part of caring in a family setting for an old relative who was financially able to cope with the problem. I was discouraged from talking to him. There was never any fear of violence but no one seemed to have the courage to break down the barriers which he put up and that is the way he wanted it. He was lonely and today would have received treatment and been encouraged to mix and have physiotherapy and occupational therapy.

Mother's chapel was a subject of immense curiosity for this old man because he was an agnostic. During his morning peregrinations on the estate he would always go in to see what was going on. Mother's days were filled with work for the chapel and when in Brussels she consulted her Confessor and brought back new ideas after every visit. My father smiled and I suppose if it amused his darling he was happy. He took no part himself but went to Mass on Sunday.

Childhood

The chapel craze brought my mother and Nanny closer together but I rather rebelled at the part I had to play. It was in preparation for my first Communion that, as is usual for Roman Catholics, I had to ask forgiveness of all my family, servants and friends living near at the time. My mother thought this a grand occasion to get me to go and kneel to the old mad step-father and ask him to come to my First Communion service. I was very shy about going to bother him but did as I was told as if in a trance. He was sitting in the kitchen garden under a tree and as I got on to my knees and asked his forgiveness in French, he jumped up and shouted to my mother in French: "Madam, how could you make this poor child do such a thing? No! No! Go away!" And he walked off. Mother said he was possessed by a devil and I was sad that I had failed in my mission.

My catechism lessons were a nightmare and all the names of the different vestments and what they all meant appealed to my sense of the ridiculous. I see that even at that early stage I was protesting. The ritual and all the fuss that went on irked me and when, aged eight, the day of my First Communion arrived, I was in a kind of a dream. However, I thought I was very religious and this pleased my mother. I said that God spoke to me, and I believed it. The beautiful white silk dress and veil, the incense, the lovely choir especially brought from Brussels, the beautiful presents—a walnut and silver crucifix, a white and gold tooled prayer book, a mother-of-pearl rosary, a red enamel and pearl watch and pearl chain—all served their purpose and made me feel the chosen of the Lord. Later, a sense of humour brought me back to earth and the intenseness of my mother's religion began to irk me again.

The next phase of my life was in Brussels after the death of the old mad step-father, Monsieur de Brouckère. I had a governess whom I loved dearly and who came daily. She was a saint but I treated her very badly and my nurse aided and abetted me in this. Nevertheless I respected her and she was a true educationalist and knew how to teach. She was very old-fashioned, badly dressed and very poor but most lovable. She persuaded and never ordered and this made me furious but I always did what she asked. My mother laughed at her and my

In the Way of Understanding

father called her "Mademoiselle Ennui" (her name being Hennuy) and this made me cross and angry with them. Later, my mother wanted me to go to a modern day school run by a Parisian who used all the latest teaching methods. It was probably, on the face of it, a much better education for the ordinary child with a normal family life and brothers and sisters, but for me, a funny little half adult, very spoiled, very advanced emotionally, this old governess was the right person. When I raged and refused to go to the school, this dear old Mademoiselle persuaded mother to allow her to stay on and guide me through the school's written course of instruction at home and for us to work with the school by correspondence. Mother agreed and I was persuaded to conform, much against my will. This Mademoiselle must have been a remarkable woman to make peace between mother and daughter.

This peaceful curriculum was interrupted when my father developed tuberculosis and had to spend his winters in the south of France where we took a villa. For me this was all rather exciting and a new life started on the fashionable Côte d'Azur. However, I was more lonely than ever as there were no children of my age and I watched the grown-ups, listened to them and kept silent, as was required of a child in those days. Mlle Hennuy remained in Brussels because she had to care for an ailing mother so I had another governess, fashionable this time, who came daily but I don't think she checked with Mademoiselle in Brussels as to what stage I had reached. We read a lot together and I remember her delicious French accent, so different from the harsh Belgian accent, or dialect, called "Marolien". She taught French to the various Milords and Miladys and told me fascinating stories of their private lives, a truly liberal education of which I took full advantage.

We went to Cannes, Mentone and San Remo, so my teachers changed every winter and my education was interrupted and never consecutive. It was fun, or I thought so, but of course my nurse was always there and jealous episodes continued.

My poor mother must have been very worried about my father whose health was deteriorating. I was, of course, forbidden to kiss him and all the evidence of tuberculosis was distressing. In the summer of 1911 he went to a santorium in

Childhood

Switzerland. During that time we sold our Brussels home and moved to Waterloo where father joined us after a time and an English hospital nurse arrived to look after him. A Polish-German governess was engaged for me and because I disliked her and my Nanny disliked her a new war started.

I had never got beyond the 16th century either in English or French history, but now I suddenly found myself steeped in the battle of Waterloo and the life of Napoleon. Wellington became very real to me. I learned to act as guide to the battlefields and the then new panorama was most thrilling. I used to drive my pony trap to the scene of that historic battle with numerous guests. Life was pleasant, except for the shadow of father's illness and my hated lessons with the Polish-German governess who was no teacher—although I own I must have been a difficult pupil. Nothing was made to come alive; learning was dry and seemed to me useless. Things never made sense and again I was told how stupid I was. But my imagination continued to run riot and I dreamed up love affairs and children. This imaginary life became more and more important and I felt the grown-ups must never know about it because they would not understand. My loneliness continued and the death of my father at the end of 1913 was over-dramatised by me. I was sad, but having been kept away from him so much for many years he had not really come into my life although we lived under the same roof.

During our stay in Waterloo, Cardinal Mercier, who had a cottage close by, often came to see us. He became very famous during the 1914–18 war for his fight against the German Army of Occupation, and later as a great friend of Lord Halifax and a first protagonist of the ecumenical movement. He was a very saintly and simple person. He talked and listened to me, and was very understanding to my mother. He said Mass in a room in the house which had been turned into yet another chapel. I always remember him as one of the few Roman Catholic prelates I looked up to. I never knew my godfather, Cardinal Vaughan, though he carried me up the tower of Westminster Cathedral as a baby while it was being built.

After my father's death in October 1913 mother hurried me back to England. And to my joy, the Polish-German gover-

In the Way of Understanding

ness left but, of course, Nanny was still there. We moved into a lovely Regency house in Regent's Park, London, where I had a bedroom and sitting room of my own. This was perhaps the first chance I had of freeing myself from the possessiveness of my Nanny, but even then as housekeeper she played a considerable part in my life. I had struggled in my bird-like fashion consciously and unconsciously to get free, but I knew how she had cared for me as a delicate baby and child and how deep was her love for me. Thus, a guilt complex stayed with me until she died many years later. My mother too would have been happier without her, but for much the same reason hesitated to dispense with her services. She retired during the war (1914–1918) when we left York Terrace.

Mother was usually full of courage except in this case. In Africa and in Brussels she lived in advance of her time and conventional people were surprised by her. As the great aristocrat she could of course afford to be unusual and play at what we now call "Women's Lib." Her pet name of "Joey," short for Josephine, was used by her step-children and she went on bicycling holidays with them which astonished her Belgian friends. She also did much social service and took an interest in the activities of voluntary organisations, especially "La Protection de la Jeune Fille", a society to protect girls (particularly foreigners) who were travelling or arriving at railway stations, from being molested and taken for prostitution—a real danger in those days. She lived a full life, was interested in art and music and was one of the earlier pioneers to visit Bayreuth, for she loved Wagner's music, especially *Parsifal*. My father took a box at the opera for her special enjoyment and her friends were in the avant-garde or artistic set and not the socialites of Brussels society.

So it was that we two came to live a very different life in England, mother a widow again amongst her own people, much changed perhaps by her past experiences in Africa and then in Europe. She was happy to be at home again: nevertheless I think she was irked by the insularity of her country, having tasted the thrill of the wide open spaces as well as the political intrigues going on in Belgium, France and the Austro-Hungarian countries where she had many friends. However

Childhood

she was able to carry on her Jewish friendships and these meant a lot to her. I tried to settle into my new role amongst my English relations, still an only child and now in a one-parent house. I felt a little scared!

2
Adolescence (1914–1918)

> ... education in the past has been radically infected with inert ideas. That is why uneducated clever women, who have seen much of the world, are in middle life so much the most cultured part of the community. They have been saved from this horrible burden of inert ideas.
> Sir Richard Livingstone, *The Future in Education*, Cambridge University Press, 1941

Mother and I had been just over a year in England when the First World War broke out. During that time I had various governesses, went to classes and even as a boarder to the Cavendish Square Convent, London, for a brief while. This was my first taste of boarding school. I hated it, sensing how much I had missed out and how much better educated were my class mates though emotionally they had missed many of my experiences. I felt terribly lonely. The dear nuns, though meaning to be kind, had no understanding of my background or upbringing and treated me like an ordinary school girl. I found myself amongst a herd of children with ordinary backgrounds, many of them being friends outside school. My mother, thinking she had parked me safely, had let our Regents Park house and was staying with various relations and friends whilst searching for cheaper accommodation as money in Belgium was frozen because of the war. I felt trapped and decided to run away. I knew it would be useless to try to express to my mother or the nuns my feelings of despair so I flew to the one person that I knew would listen. This method of dealing with a difficult problem set a pattern which has recurred throughout my life, i.e. immediate action.

I went to my mother's cousin, Cosmo Gordon Lennox, who had a luxurious and beautiful home in Manchester Street, not far from the Convent. He and my mother were more like brother and sister and he had often visited us in Brussels and fitted in with all the foreign relations and friends. He was a comfort to my mother in the new world she had adopted. He

Adolescence (1914–1918)

had been my hero from the earliest days so it was not surprising that I turned to him with my tale of woe. He had never approved of my being sent to a convent school and, being a lapsed Catholic, disagreed with mother though they were on the whole tolerant of each other's views.

Cosmo sensed that here was a desperate young adolescent on his doorstep and took me into his bizarre establishment, all male except for one housemaid. He talked to me as if I were an adult in his avant-garde drawing room with glorious flowers and signed photographs of all the leading artists of the day, male and female, in the theatre and the ballet. Cosmo himself was leading a bachelor life, being divorced from his wife, the famous actress Marie Tempest. He was not a good looking man; he was of medium height and stocky but always beautifully dressed and well-valeted, rather a dandy of the Oscar Wilde variety. This was obviously not the milieu my mother would have chosen for me. His house was quite exceptional for those days, modelled much on the Diaghilev Russian Ballet style. My room had a black carpet, gold walls and Chinese red lacquer furniture and a bed with Chinese shaded lamps. The rest of the house was also very modern, pale colours on the walls with pictures by artists like Bakst and Picasso and those who painted the scenery for the ballet. He was catholic in his tastes because he also incorporated antique furniture, and many icons, pictures and drawings, showing that what is good in all centuries can merge in harmony.

My sudden arrival in his male-dominated society must have been a shock for my host and caused his friends much amusement. We talked as "man to man" and decided I should go to school daily. I felt very pleased with myself and somehow the nuns and my mother must have been placated for I do not remember any acrimony. My nannie's sister, whom we called the "Dolt" came to chaperone me and walk me to and from the Convent. Life in Manchester Street was a curious experience but I remember so well now how very much at home I was in this milieu of professionals who treated me as a normal human being, allowing me to express myself as well as to listen. They were all very busy and I was at school all day, but there was gaiety in the house, much laughter and much use of the

In the Way of Understanding

affectionate term "darling" amongst the guests. Cosmo had a nice young male secretary who lived in the house and I became accustomed to male company and, unlike in my aunts' and grandfather's houses, here they treated me as one of themselves. Cosmo was my friend and accepted me in this way. How early in my life my preference for older men manifested itself, men with whom I could be myself! Cosmo was an only child and therefore understood intuitively my need for companionship and so became my first real male friend.

My mother had a deep affection for Cosmo and would I know have much enjoyed herself in his set had she ever been able to escape from her conventional family connections and religious convictions. She was in so many ways ahead of her time and in advance of her generation but at that time was fearful of stepping into an uncharted world.

Mother's continued search for cheaper accommodation ended in finding rooms in a convent in Harrow where her Aunt Evie Bertie was a nun. It was not a school and we used it as a comfortable and inexpensive lodging. I had a French governess daily and again led a most unnatural life, now amongst adults, this time celibate women. It was a tremendous contrast to Cosmo's house but I was quite contented as I rode a bicycle and so got about, feeling emancipated in a divided skirt. It was easy to get to London so we kept in touch with friends and relations.

Pre-war I had lived in an exciting political atmosphere; ultra Conservative in my Aunt May Talbot's[1] milieu and midst the Liberal Opposition with my step-Aunt—Goonie Churchill[2]. It was fascinating to be like a fly on the wall as the various views and arguments were expressed. I found myself an adolescent in a political setting, just watching and listening and even at that time understanding both sides most clearly. This propensity for seeing the other person's point of view has never really left me, although I got much involved in politics later on.

In the Conservative setting I saw many interesting political figures at my Aunt May's house. She was a J.P. and in many

---

[1] Wife of Lord Edmund Talbot, M.P., Chief Whip of the Conservative Party, later Viscount FitzAlan of Derwent and the last Viceroy of Ireland.

[2] Lady Gwendoline Churchill, wife of Jack Churchill, Winston's only brother.

Adolescence (1914–1918)

ways progressive in her views on women, social work and education. Besides politicians, some famous historical personalities appeared at her lunch table; for example Mary McArthur, a leading woman Trade Unionist, and Gertrude Tuckwell who led a strike of the grossly underpaid chain makers. This gave me my first glimpse into the lives of the underprivileged and a taste for social work, sometimes called "dogooding" then.

Education was also much discussed and I met Sir Robert Morant, Permanent Secretary to the then Board of Education, who was the first to sponsor Nursery Schools. I also met Rachel McMillan and Margaret McMillan, pioneers in this field who did valuable work in Bradford and Deptford and in which I was to have a part later in life. Sir Robert was a very remarkable man. In early life he had been tutor to the heir of the King of Siam (now Thailand) and wrote the first primary grammar for Siamese children. He was a great friend of my Aunt May and I saw a good deal of him and his wife, and also of his daughter Margaret, now Mrs. John Bailey, who is still one of my oldest and closest friends.

In the Conservative circle the Irish Home Rule crisis was uppermost and the real possibility of war with Ireland was freely discussed. A European war was only discussed in Liberal circles and was ridiculed by the Tories.

In the Liberal setting I met many controversial figures, especially Winston Churchill, then First Lord of the Admiralty. Once at a luncheon party I felt drawn to him because he was very taken with a little Italian greyhound which my mother had given me, a delightful, gentle and obedient little animal of which I was extremely fond. She crept close to Winston and he was much attracted to her. He took her on his knee and calling to his wife in his lisping way said: "Clemmie, theeshe are very nishe little dogsh, we ought to have shome of theeshe dogsh."

Meeting and listening to so many leading figures of the day was all very exciting and dramatic for me and my political education was built on a cross-section of ideas and my imagination was well fertilised.

The European war came on August 4th 1914, a date indelibly imprinted in my mind, just as 1066 is imprinted in any

In the Way of Understanding

British child's mind, and I was made conscious for the first time of good and evil as a reality. During the fatal week prior to August 4th my mother and I had been staying with my Aunt Goonie at Pear Tree Cottage, Overstrand, Norfolk, where Clemmie and Winston Churchill had a holiday house. I not unnaturally got caught up in the war fever. I remember an incident which perhaps added to my growing up. Jack Churchill, Goonie's husband, had inadvertently on the beach let his bathrobe slip open, thus exposing for a split second his naked body. The shock to my till then complete innocence of the male form was electric and got inexorably mixed up in my mind with war, destruction, and male aggression. What Freud would have made of this I don't know. But my mother had instilled into me a sense of the comic and warned against indulgence in what she called foreign hysteria so I kept my mixed-up feelings to myself. As it was, I learned something and the episode slipped away like water on a duck's back into my unconscious, only to surface now as I write.

The euphoria engendered by the declaration of war was terrifying, but there was a thankfulness for what we thought the right leadership and courage by the Government. Later, after a Scottish visit, travelling home by the night train I remember vividly the carriages filled with young boys, some called up, others voluntarily flocking to join the services—some perhaps to escape a humdrum life for a life as they thought of chivalry, a chance perhaps to perform deeds of valour for a beloved country, in short to find some fulfilment in life. Young as I was then, my heart was full of foreboding. The more they sang their patriotic songs and cheered and were cheered in return at each stop, the more tears welled up in my eyes as I wondered how many of them would live to tell their stories. Happily I could not foresee the drawn-out horror of four years of hell. While crossing the Forth Bridge and seeing the battleships in the fading light, looking like great proud sentinels of security, I felt the full force of deceptive emotion envelop me and a longing to give of my best to help in the war effort in however humble a capacity.

I felt angry that I was too young to take any active part. As Belgians we were very restricted and, to her disgust, mother

Adolescence (1914–1918)

had to register weekly at the local police station. However this was soon ended as influential persons helped her to regain her British passport and, being a minor, I automatically became a British subject with the option of taking back Belgian citizenship on reaching the age of twenty-one, something which I never did.

During this time mother was deeply involved in a secret service operation organised in Brussels by Myriam, the wife of one of my half brothers, Jack Reyntiens, who was then fighting in the Belgian army. Hugh Gibson, who later married my half-sister, Ynes, was First Secretary at the United States Embassy and he motored weekly to Holland and allowed Myriam to stuff the tyres of his car with messages for the Belgian troops fighting on the Belgian Front. These messages came to my mother who, with helpers, sorted them out, reducing and deciphering them as necessary, before sending them on to the troops whose answers were sent back to her to be similarly treated and relayed to the families concerned in the Occupied Zone. It was very difficult and exciting work and took much time to give the letters a coherent and understandable form before forwarding to their destinations.

As the work grew to an almost unmanageable size I begged my mother to allow me to help her, for I considered learning, except for the "three Rs" which I believed I had mastered, a complete waste of time. I felt history to be a dead letter, geography a list of names, and literature just a frill. The war which was supposed to end all wars to me meant action, even by children. I was intent on playing some part, however humble, and giving up everything to the war effort. I felt this intensely, I suppose because I was among adults devoted to the war effort and never saw youngsters of my own age group. Mother finally agreed and I was allowed to help, much to the disgust of my then governess. But this useful work came to an end fairly soon as things were tightened up in occupied Brussels and Hugh Gibson was very suspect after his tragic failure to rescue Edith Cavell[1] from the firing squad.

Reading autobiographies written by women contempor-

---
[1] Edith Cavell, 1865–1915, British nurse, Matron of a Brussels hospital, shot by the Germans for helping Allied soldiers to escape into Holland.

In the Way of Understanding

aries I am shocked to see how little some were affected by the whole human tragedy taking place all over Europe and in many other parts of the world. Except for recording the terrible casualty lists and death in battle of their men friends and relations, lately their dancing partners, they tell merely of light war work in hospitals for officers, or canteen work at stations, with week-end parties, dinners and dances to cheer those on leave going on as usual. There were exceptions like Lady Iris Capell who escaped her sheltered Edwardian background and, like others of her social class who rarely travelled without a maid, drove an ambulance at the Front and nursed in the trenches. Many other girls did the same but then they were not usually "out of the top drawer" where it was not even considered by the girls themselves, let alone their fathers, that their womenfolk could rough it among the troops. This straight-laced outlook, or perhaps I should call it the protective care by their parents of girls of the privileged classes, was still so strong in 1914 that it was considered out of the question for young ladies to know, let alone face the horrors of war or to take any part in it. Had it been otherwise it might have made a real difference to the lives of the future aristocracy that their womenfolk had shared more closely in the hell to which their brothers and lovers were condemned. It certainly did this for Iris Capell and must also have done so for many others who have not written their stories. Vera Brittain in her book *The Testament of Youth*[1] gave us a true and dramatic account of how war affected her upper-middle class family during 1914/18. She writes firstly of her fight for a university education and then of how she left it for life at the Front, sharing unbelievable hardship with the soldiers as a nurse. The B.B.C. in their wisdom serialised the story on T.V. which, to those who saw it, will have illustrated vividly my theme. It took another war to make a real change in attitudes.

The following is an extract from a letter written by Captain Norman Leslie of the Rifle Brigade, shortly before he was killed in action. It was written to his mother Lady Leslie, sister of Lady Randolph Churchill (Winston's mother).

[1] Victor Gollancz Ltd., 1934.

Adolescence (1914–1918)

Try and not worry too much about the war, anyway, units, individuals, cannot count. Remember we are writing a new page of history. Future generations cannot be allowed to read of the decline of the British Empire and attribute it to us. We live our lives and die. To some are given chances of proving themselves men and to others no chance comes. Whatever our individual thoughts, virtues, or qualities, maybe matters not, but when we are up against big things, let us forget individuals and let us act as one great British unit, united and fearless. Some will live and many will die, but count the loss naught. It is better far to go out with honour than survive with shame.

I felt passionately moved by the letter and longed to take up nursing and join the V.A.Ds who were doing such magnificent work overseas and at home. My mother would not yet agree and I was whisked off to Paris to stay with her uncle—Sir Francis Bertie, later Lord Bertie of Thame, then Ambassador in Paris. This was, I presume, to show me another side of life and to divert me from the idea of taking an active role in the war effort, for I was then only seventeen. It was certainly fun living in ambassadorial grandeur in those days with nice young Secretaries dancing attendance, gossip about the war, wrangles between our Government and the French, and squabbles among Generals. I was not allowed to go down to dinner when French politicians were present for fear of their conversation not being proper for a jeune fille's ears, but once at a big dinner party given for Lord Robert Cecil, later Viscount Cecil of Chelwood, I was allowed to make the fourteenth at the table to avoid the unlucky number of thirteen, especially in war-time. Lord Robert was a most delightful companion at dinner and talked to me as if I were an intelligent adult and I warmed to him, losing all my sense of shyness. He asked my opinion about all sorts of things which was unlike any of my family and in my astonishment, during the soup course, I swallowed a whole boiling spoonful and can almost still feel the agonising pain of it.

During this stay in Paris, as I insisted on doing some war work, I went daily to a lace shop selling priceless lace made by slave Belgian labour under the occupation. These professional lace-makers were organised by a voluntary Committee in Belgium and a corresponding Committee ran the shop in Paris whose job it was to sell the lace at proper prices to ensure decent wages. I took this work seriously and worked every day learning about the different exquisite laces made by these professional workers for sale to the rich Parisian ladies for their underclothes. It was interesting work and I enjoyed it. The only drawback was that I was not allowed to walk in the streets of Paris alone and someone always had to accompany me to and from work.

I went to several French plays and I especially remember Yvonne Printemps, then wife of Sacha Guitry, singing enchantingly in *Le Petit Mozart*; also the famous Lucien (Sacha's father) in *Pasteur*, and a matinée of *L'Aiglon* with poor old Sarah Bernhardt. The plays I went to were carefully vetted for me, but even so the bits about sex were incomprehensible and passed me by, nor did they seem as funny as they were meant to be. This, of course, was before I learned about the facts of life which was to come later, during my hospital career. In one play the fact that a lady came running onto the stage drawing-room from her adjacent bedroom with her skirt undone, to the amusement of the audience, left me perplexed. Why was it funny? Of course, not wishing to show my ignorance, I never enquired!

On returning from Paris we were on the move again as the Regents Park house was sold and we moved to a much smaller house in South Eaton Place, Chelsea. Soon the Zeppelins found us and a bomb fell opposite our house on the same night that bombs fell in various parts of Chelsea, doing much damage to the Russian Embassy. Our damage was not serious but inconvenient. It made us sleep most nights in the basement where our poor Belgian refugee cook was terrified lest the Germans should arrive and take her away. I found the droning of the engines and the sight of the cigar-shaped Zeppelin in the sky a horrible and uncanny experience. Perhaps that was why a great fear of planes and bombing came back to me in World War Two.

Cosmo had by now shut up his house, disbanded his staff

Adolescence (1914–1918)

and together with his secretary gone to France with a Red Cross Ambulance Unit. His friends were in one way or another doing war work, either entertaining the troops or helping to keep up morale at home. It was in this climate of opinion that I at last persuaded my mother to agree to my joining the St. John Ambulance Brigade as a V.A.D. This was not too difficult as mother had been offered the job of Quartermaster at the Winchester General Hospital where her cousin, Lady Portal, was Commandant. This meant that she was in charge of linen, stores, blue hospital uniforms worn by the wounded, pyjamas, splints, etc.—a responsible job which she did very well and much enjoyed. There were three large huts, administered by the Red Cross and St. John Ambulance Brigade and purpose-built to receive military patients, standing in the grounds of the General Hospital. We were a mixed bag of V.A.D.s from various backgrounds and all wore the appropriate uniform and badges. I wore the St. John uniform—grey cotton dress and white apron with the Maltese Cross, black stockings, laced shoes and a handkerchief type of veil cap which suited me and kept my wavy hair tidy. Nearly all my colleagues were senior to me and wore stripes according to their years of service. The Staff Nurses and Sisters were professionals and came from the hospital staff and were responsible to the Matron. The V.A.Ds were responsible to the Matron and her staff for their medical work but discipline came under the Commandant. We all shared the same Mess but the Commandant and Quartermaster sat at Matron's table with the Sisters. The nurses had their own tables and we small fry, the V.A.Ds, were suffered to sit with the youngest probationers. The food was insufficient and nasty but I had a huge appetite and never seemed to have enough. One horrible pudding was glutinous and tough but always quietened my tummy, so many girls who couldn't face it would say: "Pass it down to Reyntiens, she eats anything!"

The V.A.Ds lived in a hostel and at last I had got my wish and was completely happy and satisfied. My delicate health improved, with no more headaches, and I threw myself into nursing which I think, on looking back, I did most competently. I should have taken it up as a profession but, alas, in those days it was considered below my station in life and I had not

In the Way of Understanding

the necessary courage to fight this ridiculous idea, nor did I have the spirit, education or intelligence of a Florence Nightingale.

The work was hard and, at times, heartbreaking as the hospital trains came straight from Southampton Docks and many of the worst wounded came on to us at Winchester, the first port of call after Southampton. Some of the work was unpleasant and dirty, because the many facilities of today, such as automatically cleansed bed pans, washing machines and soluble dressings and bandages were then unknown.

As V.A.Ds we had passed through First Aid and Home Nursing tests, but like so many all over England and at the Front we were completely untrained medically. As such we were suspect by the professional nurses who kept all the V.A.Ds in their place and gave us the most menial jobs. Some staff nurses were nasty but the Sister of my hut and the Matron of Winchester Hospital recognised the need for pairs of hands to help cope with the rush of hundreds of wounded being sent home daily from the slaughter and horror of the Western Front. I soon learned the facts of life, until then carefully withheld from me. For example, when I had asked my mother the meaning of venereal disease, she had said that this was a subject which must never be mentioned. I was seventeen and did not know how babies were born or anything about sex. This ignorance I tried to keep from my colleagues who were all very knowledgeable. They adopted me and, in the nicest way, educated me. The wounded too sensed my innocence. They were respectful and very helpful when the professional nurses were beastly to me. Even the tough Aussies seemed to look upon me in a kindly way as something unusual, for when I was in charge of a hutted ward on night duty, one of them crept back to his bed after paying a visit to the forbidden domestic hostel not far from his hut and delicately explained to me what he had been doing and asked me to overlook his lapse.

The V.A.Ds were responsible for a sluice room in the main hospital across the way from the three large Red Cross huts, accommodating about thirty beds each. Tonsil and adenoid operations were performed in a little surgery next to this room and large tin hip baths full of blood and the discarded tonsils

Adolescence (1914–1918)

and adenoids had to be disposed of by the V.A.Ds and the baths left clean and ready for the next morning's operations. Children were brought in by their mothers and their tonsils and adenoids were quickly ripped out. The children were only slightly anaesthetised and their whimpering and misery were there for all to hear and see. Bandages full of pus and blood had to be washed, sterilised and carefully rolled up again on a small hand-rolling machine. Bathrooms had to be cleaned and were then inspected by the staff nurses. Woe betide the wretched V.A.D. who had skimped her work. Cleaning meant scrubbing floors on hands and knees and then polishing them and, of course, at that time no electric polisher had been invented. This work was over and above our duties to assist in and watch the dressing of wounds and the preparation of the doctors' trays. We stood respectfully behind the staff nurse on the doctor's round, but the doctors were sympathetic to the V.A.Ds and often willing to explain what they were doing. Not so the professional nurses who took it out of us if ever we made a little slip through forgetfulness or ignorance. I was certainly thrown in at the deep end, for during my first week on duty, because of a heavy operation list, I was sent up with a young boy who had to have his leg amputated. I don't know which of us was the most nervous. In the theatre the surgeon, perhaps tired, or thinking he would see what kind of stuff this young, rather pretty nurse was made of—or he may just have thought he would explain the operation—told me to come along and watch carefully. I steeled myself not to faint and I shut my eyes, but I could not prevent my ears from hearing the grating noise as the bone was severed.

By far the worst part was the dressing of wounds. Some were gangrenous, always pouring out pus and smelling foul. The agony in the men's faces and their efforts not to cry were to me unbearable. As the trolley was wheeled to the bed we knew and they knew what had to be endured. The great gaping wounds in the back or in the stomach caused the greatest agony for they had been packed with gauze. Now it all had to be removed bit by bit and most of the gauze would bring flesh with it. One incontinent patient in his agony got rid of most of his impurities in the bed and all over me as well, as I was trying to help by holding him in my arms. As I was covered with filth from my neck to my legs I decided not only to change my clothes as best I could but also to get into the large sink with plenty of hot water and Lysol. Matron happened to be passing on a visit and looking into the sluice room was not a little shocked to see me in a not very respectable position! She said: "What do you think you are doing nurse!" in a kindly way so I explained that I hoped to escape catching some unpleasant disease. This happened on night duty when one's spirits were always low and one's thoughts turned to the worst possible.

If a patient died, the V.A.D. took the body to the mortuary—a grim place in the general hospital. I was once accused of taking a long time over the job but I remember being fascinated by a room alongside and having disposed of my sad burden I had a good look at the bottled specimens the room contained, including tiny babies.

A less gruesome but unpleasant task was to fetch our nightly meal from the larder next to the kitchen where, on switching on the light, one would see the floor black with cockroaches on which one had to tread. I have visited Winchester General Hospital since and believe the cockroaches has been eliminated, but otherwise the hospital seems to me to be much the same as in 1918, despite its face-lift and so-called improvement.

During the final months of the Great War, as if the carnage and destruction were not enough, a plague or epidemic swept through Europe which was called "Spanish 'flu". It was world-wide and took a huge toll in death and misery. We were lucky in Winchester and not badly afflicted although I personally succumbed for a week or two, feeling dreadful. One of the symptoms of this Spanish 'flu was serious nose bleeding and in my case this was very difficult to stop. Not before I had filled nearly a basin with sticky blood, with the use of many impregnated towels and ice, did the flow cease. I believed I was dying and though I was, and still am, accustomed to seeing blood shed accidently, a nose bleed, however small, makes me want to faint or be sick. With psychological hindsight I believe that the First World War took a greater toll of me emotionally than I had anticipated. Every nose bleed I witness today brings

Adolescence (1914–1918)

back a feeling of impending doom and the horror and dramatic experience of war and violence. I recovered from the so-called Spanish 'flu in a fortnight, or at least sufficiently to be able to go to London to take part in the jubilations and hysteria which marked the Armistice on November 11th 1918. I was young and resilient and extraordinarily happy in the discipline of my nursing world. I entered into the celebrations of the Armistice by sitting on top of a taxi, singing, crying and shouting, and a gang of us hilariously let ourselves go as we toured London at night. Here was I, normally a loner, giving vent to pent up feelings and believing like many others that the world had purged itself of sin, that brotherly love was born and Christianity had triumphed. After four years of misery we were celebrating the end of the war to end all wars! No wonder that in 1939 my disillusionment was complete and my courage failed me.

After the war I wanted to go on nursing and not get caught up in the coming-out racket or "marriage market" as some people called it. Alas, this was not to be. I was allowed to do a little "do-gooding" in a nursery but hated this because runny noses and wet pants were not my idea of nursing and when I brought bed-bugs home mother objected and I gave up the struggle to continue my nursing career.

Wings of Change

3
Young Womanhood: First marriage: Divorce

I do not wish him back
Save when the sun, regained,
Illumines East to West
Where long it rained.

I do not wish him back
Save when the river blue
Swirls to a golden sea,
The sea he knew.

I do not wish him back,
Yet when the birds rejoice
From night to morn their trills
Break as his voice.

And cherries turning ripe,
Sweet Mirabelle White-heart,
Like his dear rosy cheeks
And his white heart.

And summer dowers peace,
Drugging our quick alarms
By colours, scents—I weep
My empty arms.

Millicent, Duchess of Sutherland, "A Memory".

Although the end of the war came as a great relief, undoubtedly there was a feeling of anti-climax. The emotional strain, as well as the set working hours, rules and regulations which had become part of hospital life, were suddenly relaxed and once again I felt very much a loner with no raison d'être. However, I became involved in politics once more because my Uncle Edmund Talbot was a Member of Parliament and Conservative Chief Whip. I went electioneering with him and I heard arguments for and against hanging the Kaiser, amongst many other issues of the day. I found these fascinating and heard many of the famous speakers of the time, such as Asquith, Lloyd George and Curzon. Their eloquence stimulated me but deep down I was often suspicious that their speeches were political propaganda.

Back in South Eaton Place the seemingly endless and futile life of a debutante continued, with balls and parties—not on such a grand scale as formerly—but big enough and boring, at least to me. There were few big houses where chaperones were invited as in the pre-war days, but hostesses gave dinners for about twenty men and maidens who then went on in pairs to dances. Somehow I never found a man I really liked or one who was the least interested in me. I adored dancing but few partners came up to my standard and I thought the talk between dances was dull and laboured. My peers seemed to be having a good time and this made me self-conscious and unhappy. Why, oh why, was I so different? Sometimes I would even slip into the "Ladies" and have a nice chat with the maid in charge of the cloaks. I was not alone in this because a certain royal figure, now nationally and internationally beloved, was at times my companion. As I was not allowed to go home alone with a young man, a brougham from a respectable livery stable arrived at midnight to fetch me. I cared about the horse and the driver and rarely kept them waiting but my friends would be enjoying themselves until the early hours and were then accompanied home by their male escorts. It seems strange to me today that neither my mother nor anyone else challenged my restlessness. My energies could have been diverted into further education or group activity such as the Bach Choir, art classes or lectures. The L.C.C. Education Committee must have had all sorts of extra-mural classes which could have coped with my dangerous boredom.

One escape route was not barred for I spent a lot of time at the ballet, usually by myself, although occasionally with like-minded friends. Pavlova was dancing with her company at the Alhambra and as often as I could I would buy a rover ticket for matinees for 2/6d (12½p). I forgot myself in the glorious music and exquisite dancing of such ballets as *Les Sylphides*, *The Dying Swan*, *California Poppy*, etc. It was supposed to be a risky business for a girl alone or even with other girls to use a rover ticket, which meant being able to walk about—not a set

Young Womanhood

seat—but I never had any trouble. Perhaps I was so intent and wrapped in the luxury of what was a new world to me that men with a roving eye saw that I was not good for a pick-up. Here I longed to dance, to express myself through movement, to steep myself in dancing—just as I had longed to nurse! Knowing this could never be I watched avidly, living for a while in the atmosphere of the ballet and trying to absorb the personality of this supreme actress/dancer. The Diaghliev Ballet was yet another enchantment, different but exciting and colourful and I was captivated by the new ones such as the *Fire Bird* and *La Boutique Fantasque*. I saw Nijinsky give his famous leap in the *Spectre de la Rose*, "a leap in the air from which he came down, landing as softly as a deer clearing a hedge onto snow."[1] However, Tamara Karsavina, Lydia Lopokhova and Liubov Tchernicheva were the great ballerinas of that time. In those days the male dancers, except for Nijinski, provided more of a supporting role to the ballerina and did not, at least for me, attract the enthusiasm they do today. They may have had their fans but it was the female dancers who held us spellbound by the beauty of their movements.

All this stemmed of course from my early initiation into the artistic world when I stayed with Cosmo during the war. I still kept as close to him as I dared, but mother, perhaps rightly, did not encourage me to mix with what she called the Bohemian set. Enid Bagnold in her autobiography vividly describes these people who lived "violently and uniquely for themselves, who breathed freely on the top of the world"[2]. Enid was a friend of Cosmo and of Catherine d'Erlanger[3] who entertained lavishly in her home at 139 Piccadilly (now destroyed) where she attracted "fashion, brains and wit and much that was outlandish at the moment"[4]. Cosmo, having given up Manchester Street, had a studio flat at the back of this house, with a door leading into Park Lane. I was attracted by all this like a butterfly to a candle but I was shy and not a little shocked.

[1] Rebecca West's review of Richard Buckle's *Nijinsky*, Widenfeld & Nicolson, 1971, in the *Sunday Times*.
[2] Enid Bagnold, *Enid Bagnold's Autobiography*, Heinemann, 1969.
[3] Wife of Baron Emile d'Erlanger (German banker).
[4] *Op. cit.*

In the Way of Understanding

Catherine d'Erlanger had befriended my Belgian sister-in-law, Adrienne, wife of my favourite half brother, Guy Reyntiens, when Adrienne came over as a refugee from Belgium in October 1914. Guy had been shot through his spine which partially paralysed him, but he escaped via Ostend before being captured by the Germans. Adrienne was a pretty woman and Catherine liked to have beautiful well-dressed women in her ménage. Her house was exotic, much more so than dear Manchester Street, with much laughter, smoke, drink and maybe much more. Chaperoned by Adrienne and Guy, who after the war became military attaché to the Belgian Embassy, I did go to these parties but found them frightening because the pace was so fast and furious. Though I now knew the facts of life the sometimes outrageous behaviour bewildered me. It was exciting, but I was not happy in this milieu any more than at the dull balls and parties I have already described. What was I looking for, why so choosey? Maybe it was a profession, something real, a caring profession such as I had met in the hospital. Even though the trained nurses had despised me I admired them, likewise the doctors, the ancilliary workers and even the administrators. They all had a worth-while job dealing with real people. Whereas I was a play girl with no purpose in life and I knew it.

On a visit to Brussels one winter to meet my Belgian relations I danced and flirted in a very unreal atmosphere. I was a sophisticated British girl compared with Belgian girls in their restricted lives and I suppose I enjoyed myself. Adrienne and Guy escorted me to mixed parties because as a jeune fille I should have kept to the "Bal Blanc" for unmarried girls. Adrienne, still looking back nostalgically on her war and post-war experiences at Catherine d'Erlanger's, was disgruntled and Guy's health was visibly deteriorating. There were terrible quarrels between them and my heart bled for Guy who seemed so dear, so very helpless but beloved by everybody, full of gaiety and happy to be back in his own country. I had many admirers, all older men and mostly married. I enjoyed the conversation of these foreigners with European manners and still more their dancing, for here I found partners who could whirl me round in the perfect rhythm and music of the

Young Womanhood

Viennese waltz. It was bliss for me, and a much safer and saner world than 139 Piccadilly. I had a wardrobe of rather exotic and lovely dresses of gold brocade woven into various colours; also black tulle—to the despair of my mother, who wanted me in white chiffon with sashes. I made friends with the wives of my dancing partners and they always welcomed me to their dinner parties, knowing that I could fit into male company with ease.

Leaving Brussels behind we motored to Paris via Lens, right through the war zone where the devastation was horrifying. We visited the trenches, only lately vacated, and the scene of squalor, dirt and mud gave me a picture of the unbearable lives of the men who had lived and died in them. The memory and the smell came back to me with a sickening feeling when once again war seemed imminent in 1939, and I remember it still. When in Paris, life was again very unreal yet exciting; going to plays and night clubs, learning about vintage wines and drinking brandy in coffee—still made with acorns.

Back in England our social life continued, and mother and I were invited to many week-end parties which I enjoyed. But my happiest memories are of the yachting season and I went to Cowes with my mother on several occasions. These yachting expeditions thrilled me as I had, and still have, a great love of the sea. I felt I had something in common with the older men with whom I came into contact on these trips and with those *that go down to the sea in ships, that do business in great waters; these see the works of the Lord, and his wonders in the deep.*[1] The Royal Yacht Squadron at Cowes was something of a Holy of Holies and I well remember the notice at the entrance gate "No dogs or ladies". As the guests of Sir William Portal, mother's cousin, a senior and respected member of the Squadron, we were privileged. We sailed in his yacht down the Solent and along the South coast and besides our dear host there was always Sir Henry McMahon[2], who became a very dear friend of mine, as did his wife.

[1] Psalm 107, v. 23–24.
[2] British High Commissioner in Egypt—author of the McMahon letters and negotiator of the McMahon Line which defined the frontier between Assam and Tibet, and the 1915 McMahon Declaration concerning Arab Independence.

In the Way of Understanding

On one fateful occasion mother accepted an invitation from a gorgeous young man, who sailed and skippered his own yacht, to join him on a trip. (How careless of my mother not to realise the emotional risks that might be involved for a daughter like me!). We sailed slowly from Cowes along the South coast and up the West coast to Fort William, arriving on an unforgettable evening in August when the sun was setting and the moon rising—heady stuff for a romantic girl and a young, attractive, good-looking and war-weary Scottish aristocrat. It was late in the evening when we anchored and during the night I heard much rumbling and talking. The others were fast asleep but I slipped on deck and found the drifter attached to the battleship H.M.S. *Queen Elizabeth* trying to contact us. This famous battleship, the latest, fastest, most powerful and beautiful in the Royal Navy was the one which led the assault on the Dardanelles in 1915 and which four years later watched the surrender of the German fleet at Scapa Flow. The officer in charge of the drifter asked me if our yacht would allow her to tie up alongside in order to avoid having to drop anchor. They, like us, had to make an early start next morning and, knowing that our yacht needed a tow through the Caledonian Canal, I bravely suggested to the nice young officer that next morning he might discuss things with the owner of our yacht and give us a tow: meanwhile, he could tie up.

So from Fort William we were towed through the canal and across the lochs. Unfortunately, while I was alone in charge of the wheel during lunch I ran our bowsprit straight through the drifter's deck-house, mercifully hurting no-one! Even this disastrous exhibition of poor navigation did not dull the ardour of my host.

From Inverness we went by car to Tongue, as far north as it is possible to go, and we enjoyed the glory of a Scottish autumn. The little grey-slated house where we stayed, with its walled garden going down to the sea, was like something in a fairy story. We played three-handed bridge in the evenings, entertained our host's friends and relatives and had a happy and domesticated time. My mother seemed to be completely unconscious of the obvious consequences. I fell deeply in love and I believe was loved in return. Maybe I was a very different

Young Womanhood

girl from any my host had previously come across. He had made a hurried war marriage and was regretting it and these few weeks of peace were perhaps what he had been seeking. Although he had had the pick of all the most eligible girls in London he seemed curiously to care for me.

On our return to London, however, we both came down to earth with a bang. He was the heir to an historic Scottish title and I was a Roman Catholic, born and bred. According to the conventions of those days marriage was an impossibility and he was urged to return to his wife and to try to produce an heir. This he did but a daughter was born and soon afterwards he died.

We had not the guts to fight our families and maybe he did not care enough; certainly my heart was scarred and took some years to heal. We never saw each other again. I saw the child once when I took my two boys to a dancing class and, even now, when I read about her, my heart misses a beat.

About this time my Aunt May gave a coming-out dance for me in her house in Buckingham Palace Gardens. Besides the boys and girls she invited many of her own friends, such as Mrs. Keppel, the friend of Edward VII, Lady Salisbury, and others of her own generation. The Prince of Wales (later Edward VIII) came to this dance and spent most of the time sitting, or rather lolling, on my aunt's golden sofa bed with a lovely girl, the daughter of a Scottish duke. He could so easily have married her if the royal conventions of the day had not made it impossible, since she was not of royal blood. Who knows how this might have changed history for I believe his heart was deeply involved at this time. Later in the evening, after nearly all the guests had left, my wise and very dear Cosmo said, prophetically, to me: "Mind you, I don't believe that young man will ever be King".

I saw as much of Cosmo as I could. He had acquired a house on the river at Cookham near Maidenhead and made it most attractive with many of his things from Manchester Street, but especially with gay chintz furnishings and bright colours. He also took to gardening and made his guests work hard during their weekends there. Mother and I went on river parties with the usual gay theatrical set in boaters and white flannels.

In the Way of Understanding

It became clear to me at this time that I must lead a life of my own. The only way to do this for a girl in my position, or at least for a girl of the kind of family into which I had been born, was marriage. With hindsight, I see how immature and wrong this idea was: however, no attempt was made to dissuade me from my choice. This was a young man in the Irish Guards, Alexander Koch de Gooreynd, of Belgian descent and son of a banker in the City. He had been to Eton and was a Roman Catholic, therefore acceptable from a conventional angle. We were both in our twenties and only the redoubtable Lady Helmsley (sister of Lady Londonderry, the friend of Ramsey Macdonald) warned me not to become a young man's slave. She said it was better to be an old man's darling; advice which was not appreciated at the time but oh, how prophetic! I doubt if either Alexander or I ever realised the seriousness of marriage. We thought it would mean just friendship and a good time and I wonder how many young couples have made the same mistake. With the greater freedom nowadays for getting to know one's partner before marriage it is easier to discover an incompatibility of temperament before it is too late. Going to the church on my wedding-day I already had doubts; perhaps the first of my hunches which I so rarely obey.

The wedding was a big society affair in the Brompton Oratory, a Roman Catholic church, with just a short Mass arranged so that the majority of the guests who came to the service and who were not Roman Catholics would not be bored. My grandfather gave me away and I wore a really lovely off-white velvet dress with long sleeves and a train flowing from the waist, a tulle veil and orange blossom. As at my first Communion I was in a dream though I distinctly remember someone saying as I was led up the aisle "they're off" and I was wondering where to!

The honeymoon was the usual one—a Claridges suite for the first night, then Paris with its gorgeous theatres and restaurants. With my beautiful clothes to match the occasion I was kept busy changing and getting dressed with the help of a French maid who also valeted my husband. Then we travelled by train to Marseilles and by boat to Cairo. As fate would have it, on board were the brother and sister-in-law of the young man of my yachting experience. It came as a shock to me to meet them face to face. Maybe they had guilty feelings, although it is possible that they were glad to see me safely married. We were icily polite to each other, and behaved as if nothing had happened, but out of the corner of my eye I watched their every movement. This seems to show that my emotions were by no means dormant.

In Cairo Alexander and I stayed at the best hotel and met some Egyptian Pashas to whom we had been given letters of introduction. We were lent a couple of horses for a trip into the desert. A fearful storm broke out and I took my mare into my tent because I was afraid that something adverse might happen to her. What my husband was doing I don't remember! Later we went to Luxor on donkeys to see the great work being done there on the tomb of Tutankhamen. All this was beautiful and thrilling and is now a glorious memory except for what I felt was an incomplete companionship, a lack of intimacy of thought.

On our return home I found that I was pregnant and this was a source of great rejoicing for my mother and family. They thought that at last I would find a purpose in life. We lived for a time in my mother-in-law's house in Belgrave Square where Simon was born. The waiting period seemed a long one to me. It was a very hot summer and in those days one was encouraged to rest and take great care which did not suit my restlessness. After Simon's birth we had a house of our own in Cadogan Square and my mother had sold South Eaton Place to help us buy it. She came to live with us and took over part of the home, thus reversing our previous roles. I wonder now if this was a wise plan but circumstances dictated it at the time and financially it was a great help to us as my husband was not earning anything.

We also had a house in Kent although I was not cut out for the role of a country-house hostess, nor for the hunting and racing which my husband enjoyed. He was indolent, staying in bed late because of course he had nothing much else to do except on hunting or racing days. He would not go into his father's banking business, saying that money-making was not his line. I fear I aided and abetted him in this as I wanted him to

In the Way of Understanding

take up a profession more in keeping with my outlook on life. It might have been wiser had he stayed in the Army, for during the General Strike he was called up and the military discipline was just what we both needed. In order to give him a job my Uncle Edmund appointed him as extra A.D.C. in Dublin during his Viceregal reign. This interested me and I found scope for mental activity, meeting many fascinating personalities and hearing the problems of the day discussed by the extremely able permanent civil servants, such as Sir Stephen Tallents[1]. There were also what we now call moles, who went down the drain and communicated with what was known as the enemy. On looking back I wonder if the problems could have been resolved satisfactorily had the discussions been left to the able men on both sides, equally devoted and loyal to their causes. However, the politicians had the last say.

Something that inadvertently may have helped to prolong this illsorted marriage was the death of Cosmo in 1922. It was sudden and occurred after an internal emergency operation. He had told no one of his illness, but the surgeon and his nurse told my mother after his death that he had not wanted anyone to know and had said that should the operation prove that he had a terminal illness he did not wish to be kept alive. His death was a great sadness but certainly the beginning of a new chapter both in my life and in that of my mother. She now found herself the sole beneficiary of the Worsthorne portion of the Towneley Estate, Burnley, Lancs, which Cosmo had inherited from his mother, Lady Alexander Gordon Lennox.

Cosmo was buried at Cookham and though mother and I were much distressed we were also mystified when we met Cosmo's lawyer and agent for the reading of the contents of the will in Cosmo's house after the burial. In some ways it was a comic experience which Cosmo would have enjoyed because owing to all the secrecy there were few friends present and only the funeral staff, lawyer and resident agent—all solemn in black clothes—who took charge of us and introduced themselves.

[1] Sir Stephen Tallents, K.C.M.G., 1884–1958. Imperial Secretary, Dublin, 1922 –26.

Young Womanhood

The agent was Mr. Fraser, a dour Scot who had a wary look on his face and was probably anxious about his future relationship with the new owner, my mother, obviously a very different personality from Cosmo. She was a great lady and doubtless would take things more into her own hands, whereas Cosmo had been an absentee landlord. The solicitor was Mr. Oliver of Hempson, very correct in his manner as were the undertaker's staff and there was an icy atmosphere that we did our best to break. Death and all its trappings were no part of Cosmo's life and we found ourselves in an extraordinary situation. At no time had Cosmo discussed this side of his life with my mother though she knew vaguely of his interests in part of the Towneley estate in Lancashire. It comprised about 5,000 acres which included Burnley and much of the Todmorden valley immortalised in the stories of the Lancashire witches.

On the invitation of Mr. and Mrs. Fraser, mother and I went north soon after the funeral to stay in the house called "Dyneley" which he had built for the resident agent. We were both disappointed to find a suburban villa erected on a bleak hillside. Mother had imagined and hoped for a good stone Lancashire farmhouse. Instead she found a mansion with a gable roof which was to cause trouble when it snowed and still does! The one bright spot was a grave-faced but efficient and welcoming butler called James Burton, to whom we took at once. After much discussion and many heart-searchings on both sides Mr. and Mrs. Fraser and their family were prepared to move to another house. Mother moved into Dyneley and redecorated the house with good taste and imagination, taking with her much of her lovely furniture, and making as homely an atmosphere as possible under the circumstances. Alas, James went with the Frasers, but he left Dyneley with a heavy heart as his roots were there. He had been born and brought up in the stable cottage close by and his brother and sister-in-law and their family still lived there.

Mother coveted James and he hankered after Dyneley and badly wanted to be mother's butler. It was all very difficult, but with much tact on both sides James eventually came to take charge of Dyneley and remained in the family as a friend and devoted servant for about 50 years.

In the Way of Understanding

Mother had now acquired a house of her own and inherited James. He was a most interesting character and a beloved man. Deferential and an upholder of the "establishment", he was devoted to mother and later to me and my sons. He was of humble origin, born of parents who had lived in the stable cottage at Dyneley where his father was coachman to Mr. Fraser. James often told me stories about how he and his brother Archie, later to become my mother's chauffeur, had to doff their caps and always keep out of Mrs. Fraser's way. James joined the Army in 1912 and the new life must have been an eye-opener to this shy and gentle man. He was, I am sure, a superb batman although by nature retiring—or as he would say, "keeping himself to himself". He had a sense of humour and could be made to laugh by my children or by people of whom he approved but they had to be "out of the top drawer". He was badly gassed in France and invalided out of the Army, becoming Mr. Fraser's butler-valet. The war experience must have been a nightmare to this sensitive man and the gassing left him permanently disabled as far as his lungs were concerned. He gradually improved in health but always liked fresh air and plenty of it—sometimes to my discomfort when years later he came to work in my London flat. Alas, he would smoke and this did not help his trouble or my nose, though no one ever saw him with a cigarette except when off duty or washing my car. He never married, which is a pity, as for the right woman he would have made a good husband and a fine father. He was a perfectionist. His silver was always immaculate, the furniture and floors polished so that one could see one's face in them – even if one could easily break a leg! His manners were perfect: perhaps this is why some people nicknamed him "the Archbishop" but all loved him. His pantry was his domain and woe betide anyone who entered it without being asked! This was de rigueur in most large houses and James had been through the professional servants' mill—as hall-boy, third footman, second, first, and so on, in establishments of the aristocracy.

Mother made her home in Dyneley and despite her disappointment with the house she took on all the responsibilities of a chatelaine and found herself a real role in life. She got

Young Womanhood

immersed in local problems and voluntary social service and for her generation was in many ways a remarkably progressive woman. She was appointed a magistrate and was also active in Guiding, becoming County Commissioner for Lancashire. She took an interest in national and local politics and an active part, as I did, in the 1931 election. It was an exciting contest in Burnley because Liberals and Conservatives joined together to unseat the then sitting member, Arthur Henderson, Labour Foreign Secretary. Mother was a respected and beloved lady, always a great aristocrat but interested in people and entertaining the local middle-class with old-fashioned courtesy, sometimes to my embarrassment. She was a friend of Lord Derby—the so-called King of Lancashire—Lord Lieutenant of the County Palatine of Lancashire. She would have been happy could she have known that her grandson, my elder son, is now privileged to carry on the Towneley tradition of service to the State as the present Lord Lieutenant.

When my husband and I came to stay with Mother at Dyneley we were amazed to find how she had put down deep roots. It was almost as if she had lived her whole life in Lancashire. However, her early experience in Africa and Europe gave her a wide vision and ability to mix on even terms with men and women of all walks of life. She was unfettered by bonds of class, yet she clung to traditional values in religion and politics. Like the man in Kipling's *If*, she could walk with kings and not lose the common touch. Alexander, my husband, had already thought he might like to go into politics so now with our Lancashire connection we both thought it a good idea. It would give him something to do if he looked for a Lancashire constituency. However, we also felt he would have a better chance if he had a less foreign name. (This shows how fashions change because today it might even have been an advantage!) Mother and I would have liked the name of Towneley but the old relations at that time did not smile on this suggestion so the other name of Worsthorne, a village on the estate, was assumed by Deed Poll in 1923. Unfortunately it did not help Alexander in his political ambition. He lost the seat and we were back to square one despite a lot of hard political work which I had enjoyed. My second son Peregrine was born about this time but I became more and more convinced that the life I was expected to lead was not for me.

My husband, I believe, loved me in his fashion, though he was completely unable to relate to me or talk of life in depth and so we just made surface chat. He was irritated at my inability to express what I was looking for. He had no antennae and needed direction, being emotionally insecure himself. This was something I could not give him. I should never have married him as I needed an older man with wisdom to guide me. I married this man of my own free will simply to escape, to fly somewhere, and my wings took me to this disastrous experiment. I was not made to be a perfect wife for Alexander nor do I ever consider myself to have been a perfect mother.

Perhaps our first real communication was when we decided to separate; he going to Africa ostensibly to shoot big game and I staying in London with the boys. The boys had very different characters. Simon was more malleable and establishment-minded, very caring for me. Peregrine was independent, always questioning and nearly always antagonistic. We struggled even during the breast-feeding days! Simon in later life became much attached to Towneley and all that that great name stands for in Lancashire, especially in its Roman Catholic connections. In 1945 he was to assume by Deed Poll the additional surname of Towneley and by Royal Licence, in 1955, the Arms of Towneley, relinquishing the surname Worsthorne. I handed over Dyneley and the estate to him when mother died. He enlarged the house and lives there with his dear wife, six daughters and one son called Peregrine, this name appearing both in the Towneley and Bertie families. My younger son, who also married and has one daughter, remains Peregrine Worsthorne, a name he has made famous in journalism.

After two years of separation Alexander and I decided to divorce, despite what the Church and our relations might say. Mother was broken-hearted, though she had quite enjoyed the period of separation as we had worked closely together and she loved the boys and we shared them. She was never reconciled to the divorce. Incompatibility was, alas, not recognised as grounds for divorce then, nor did the merciful two

Young Womanhood

years' waiting apply and we had to go through the sordid and horrible business of the Divorce Court as the A. P. Herbert Act did not become law until 1937. Even up to the time of her death Mother was always begging me to come back to her Roman Catholic faith. This gave me pain because I loved her and her objections—so deeply felt—meant much to me but I was never convinced by her arguments. The Roman Catholic faith was secure certainty to her but never to me, and even as a child I was silently protesting. During my life I had been thrown amongst people of different religions, and some with no religion at all. Mother had even encouraged me to mix with them, and we had strict and not so strict Roman Catholics in our own family, especially amongst the Belgians. I never felt guilty, as some people had predicted, and as time went by I became more personally interested in religion and closer to God. I was no longer bound by rules of iron made by churchmen and I was sad that my beloved mother remained behind her prison bars and kept my children with her in spirit. In due course I joined the Anglican Church and became an ardent and active supporter of the Ecumenical Movement and of the World Congress of Faiths.

4
Local Government and some Other Activities

During the time of separation from my husband and after my divorce I had the chance of leading my own life again. With the help and advice of my mother's cousin, Wyndham Portal[1], I went into local government politics and was elected a member of the London County Council for North Hammersmith. Wyndham was another of my older men friends. He was supportive to me and saw intuitively that I needed a job, but he realised I was untrained for anything and therefore advised my getting some experience in local politics. He took me to what was then called the Municipal Reform Headquarters (Conservative), who were prepared to give me a constituency to fight at the next election. Wyndham took a lot of trouble to guide me. He rehearsed my speeches and shepherded me during my campaign. The last three weeks before the election were hectic. There was much canvassing and there were many meetings, for in those days there was not much local coverage by the media. One had to meet the electors face to face. However, I got good publicity coverage and the boys enjoyed coming round the constituency with me.

Wyndham's solicitude for my career was in no way altruistic. He was in love with me in a fierce, possessive way. I am not proud of this part of my life. It was selfish because I was content to receive with no intention of giving. He gave me a good time—theatre outings, first nights, racing and week-ends at his home in Hampshire. I was included in his shooting expeditions to Scotland in which he also included the boys, who enjoyed it. Rosemary, his wife, was on the large side like

---

[1] Wyndham Raymond, later 1st Viscount Portal, P.C., G.C.M.G., D.S.O. Died 1949.

Self in cloche hat

With Simon and Peregrine during L.C.C. election, North Hammersmith

The Peacock Room, Plodge

Local Government and some Other Activities

Wyndham himself. She was an intelligent woman and interested in all the things I was interested in; education, social services, and she was a member of the Hampshire County Council. But we never became friends. She tolerated me and looked the other way as far as my friendship with her husband was concerned. She realised that he wanted it that way and she was devoted to him. I certainly lived dangerously at that time, with a moth who was attracted to my candle, and I enjoyed this new experience.

Mother continued to keep an eye on me while I lived at Cadogan Square in a house bought after my marriage. She kept rooms here even after she inherited Dyneley, so I was chaperoned, and Mother and Wyndham got on well together. Rosemary was very fond of mother and protective of her.

After my election I became a member of the Education Committee and its three important sub-committees. I also became a member of the Public Health Committee and the Maternity and Child Welfare Committee. I was made Chairman of one of the first open-air schools for pre-tubercular children on the Old Oak Estate in my constituency near Wormwood Scrubs. It was at that time that I came in contact with the Rachel and Margaret MacMillan Nursery School in Deptford and was elected Chairman of its Management Committee. It was a full life and I enjoyed the companionship of many interesting people who became my friends and mentors. A fellow L.C.C. member was Lady Lawrence, the wife of Sir Herbert Lawrence who was Chief of the Imperial General Staff during the 1914–18 war and who later became Chairman of Vickers Armstrong. Lady Lawrence (Isabel was her name but as she was a much older woman I would never have dared in those days to use her Christian name) taught me so much for she had an active brain and a quick wit. Both her sons had been killed in the war. They had enlisted under age and now their mother was trying to drown her sorrow in an active life. She may have realised that I wished to do the same, but for different reasons. Sir Herbert was one of the first of the older men I got to know well and we enjoyed each other's company.

This was the golden age of the L.C.C., when it was served by men and women of considerable stature. Besides Lady Lawr-

In the Way of Understanding

ence there was Mrs. William Wilson Phipps, the subject of a striking portrait by John Singer Sargent. She was a friend of Lord Rosebery, Prime Minister and first Chairman of the L.C.C. Mrs. Phipps was a very able Chairman of the Education Committee. She always wore a hat and black kid gloves. These she only removed when eating, and even at a dinner party I missed seeing her bare hands, for she quickly put her gloves on again after the dessert. Other well-known personalities were Herbert Morrison, later Lord Morrison of Lambeth; R. C. Norman, that wise and handsome man, later to be my brother-in-law and Chairman of the B.B.C.; Ishbel Macdonald, daughter of the Prime Minister, Ramsay Macdonald; Evelyn Emmet, later Baroness Emmet of Amberley, and Thelma Cazalet, a future Member of Parliament. There was also Susan Laurence, a Fabian and Socialist politician who, while in the chair at an all-night sitting, rebuked me for knitting in the Council Chamber—this was against the rules. These were all outstanding colleagues. Sir George Gater and Sir Frederic Menzies were brilliant Chief Officers of Education and Public Health who also became personal friends.

In Council meetings debate was fast and furious and all-night sittings were frequent. Mob violence was not unknown during the General Strike, and then we had police protection. The fine horses of the Mounted Constabulary were stabled in the County Hall quadrangle. I had two constituencies during my nine year connection with the L.C.C. The first was North Hammersmith, covering all the Old Oak Estate, Wormwood Scrubs and Hammersmith Post-Graduate Hospital and the race track at the White City Stadium. It occurred to me that it might be fun to own a racing greyhound, so I bought and shared one with an Irish man friend. The dog's name was Hammy and he won the North Hammersmith Stakes but I lost the next election through the strong disapproval of the non-conformist voters! However, Norwood, then a safe seat for my party, adopted me and I represented this genteel area until my retirement from politics in 1935. As for Hammy, he had unfortunately strained a leg badly so he had to retire. He lived happily at Dyneley until he died.

It was the exciting time of the reorganisation of the Poor

Local Government and some Other Activities

Law and the taking over of their schools, plus a training ship for boys moored in the Thames. This was a huge piece of work, involving complete reconstruction, including the setting up of new committees to replace the Poor Law Guardians. These were often elderly and were also nearly always politically orientated. There were, if I remember rightly, about twenty-six such large residential schools accommodating about 1,500 children in each school. Some were cottage homes with children going out to school and some had schools in the home building. There was an amusing incident when, as Chairman of the Committee taking over the Poor Law schools, I had to inspect a training ship which was run on nautical lines by a retired Admiral. He was disgusted at the thought of being taken over by the London County Council and even more so when he learned that the Chairman to whom he would be responsible was a woman! I was piped on board and, to his dismay, I asked to see the "offices"—a polite word for ablution quarters and toilets. These I discovered to be a relic from the time of Nelson!

I was also a member of the Chelsea Borough Council during this period, as I was living in Chelsea. This was an amusing activity because the Council was entirely Conservative, so about a dozen of us young ones, led by Mrs. Walters (later Dame Flora Macleod), whose husband was connected to *The Times*, formed ourselves into an opposition group of Young Conservatives. We carefully checked agendas and met regularly in order to be able to reject the Resolutions to be taken by the Council of which we did not approve. Our elders and betters must have cursed us but it taught me much of the democratic way of doing things.

The interest I developed at this time in Nursery Schools continued right through to the 1939/45 war and I worked hard to promote them in the education system. The idea of Nursery Schools, a School Medical Service and a School Meals Service stemmed from Margaret McMillan's view of education. This saw the development of the whole child as the main object, and not merely how much learning could be crammed into one small head. She and her sister Rachel were the pioneers of Nursery School education and were supported by the Indepen-

In the Way of Understanding

dent Labour Movement. These sisters were friends of George Bernard Shaw, William Morris and many Fabians. From 1893 onwards Margaret devoted herself to the alleviation of one particular evil—what might in those days have been called the sordid sacrifice of the child. Infant mortality in Bradford for example was 1 in 5. I was inspired by Margaret, a truly great reformer and a genius in her understanding of children. She also inspired Nancy Astor[1] whom I met in Deptford and with whom I worked eventually to found the Margaret McMillan Training Colleges in Deptford and Bradford, set up to train Nursery School teachers.

Nancy Astor was in many ways a lovable figure. She was always beautifully dressed and most soigné with the simple taste of a rich woman. Her stockings, shoes, gloves, hats, jewellery, and so on were thought out by her and executed, I presume, by excellent designers, coutouriers and milliners. All these things were handled with care by her devoted maid. On one occasion when I visited her by appointment at 10 a.m. about the question of the cutting down of Nursery Schools, I was ushered into the great house in St. James' Square by a perfect butler (her friend as well as servant). The house was full of gorgeous flowers from Cliveden, her country home. She was in her boudoir on a chaise longue being attended by a manicurist. Her face was covered with grease in preparation for the small amount of make-up she used. She was most welcoming but naturally unable to shake hands. We discussed our common problem of how to keep Nursery Schools away from the educational cuts proposed by her Conservative Government. We were, as usual, in a financial crisis – one of the many to dog me all the time I worked in politics and mental health. She suddenly said, fiercely and loudly "You care deeply about this and so do I, but don't ask me to speak on the subject in the House. Get someone else because they hate me (meaning the Tories) and will not even listen." She clenched her hands, thus ruining all the polish the manicurist had so carefully put on, but what she said was true and she knew it. If the Nursery

---

[1] Viscountess Astor, 1879–1963, Nancy Langhorne of Virginia, U.S.A. First Woman M.P. 1919–1945.

Local Government and some Other Activities

School movement, in which she took so prominent a part, was to benefit from an advocate in the House of Commons, it should not be Nancy Astor. At this point Lord Astor came in to bid her good morning but she spoke harshly to him for she was in an emotional state. She was very concerned, as was I, about young children being once again the target for financial saving.

In 1951 it was the centenary of Margaret McMillan's birth, and the Nursery School Association, now the British Association for Early Childhood Education, gave me a miniature of the Margaret McMillan medal in recognition of my long years of service promoting Nursery Schools. I was happy to receive this as a reminder of my admiration for this great woman, and of her sister.

Another remarkable figure in the educational field at that time was Madame Montessori whom I met during one of her visits to London. She was a delightful woman with a very obvious love for children, but not just in a sentimental way. In the schools where her methods were used one immediately sensed a freedom to learn and the concentration of the little pupils. They were absorbed in their learning toys, and the three Rs were fun to learn in a peaceful atmosphere. This was in contrast to the noisy atmosphere in ordinary schools where School Visitors were sometimes mobbed by the children. Teachers using the Montessori method told me how much more quickly the pupils grasped the 3 Rs through not being bound by desks or strict rules and being able to roam about. The more intelligent children quickly moved up to accomplish higher standards of study through good play material. This method was considered by some teachers to be suited only to the mentally handicapped and was therefore not taken seriously by the education authorities. Madame Montessori hotly denied this and I certainly believe her ideas, now adapted and improved upon in our progressive system, permeate all infant teaching. They benefit clever as well as duller children alike so that each can advance at their own pace. I was involved for a short time in helping to set up a Montessori Training College, for I had a real admiration for this born teacher who devoted her life to learning through play.

During this part of my life my own two boys went to a

In the Way of Understanding

private nursery school in Kensington Square, having graduated from Nannies. Alas, I never found the real, cosy proverbial Nanny who might have been the mother figure they so much needed. There were always those who disliked my progressive ideas on bringing up children, and here I am sure I left undone many things I ought to have done and did things I would have better left undone. The boys had no father at home: I was all they had and yet I let myself become immersed in local government and my own amusements. I had many friends and went out a lot in the evenings to many exciting first nights at the theatre, when the audiences were in full evening dress and the whole house looked glamorous. I often went to concerts and to the opera but especially to the ballet at Covent Garden. These were lovely occasions, and seated in the boxes were beautiful women covered with jewels, vying with the brilliant and spell-binding ballets produced by Diaghilev and conducted by Sir Thomas Beecham. The earlier education I had given myself in ballet proved fruitful during this period and my visits to Covent Garden were a delightful ending to my busy days of local government work. I also entertained at home a great deal, having considerable domestic staff. I suppose we were a one-parent family, but without financial or housing difficulties we had a few advantages.

The boys after nursery school had a short trial run of a governess, called Miss Hart, who was a vegetarian with many advanced ideas of teaching, but somehow it didn't work out. They then went to a Roman Catholic boarding school at Seaford. Simon had already tried a term at Ampleforth prep. school. But both were unhappy at Seaford, so they went to Abinger, a new school with a nice young headmaster with progressive views and I think they were as happy there as they could be. Neither of them ever liked school. Later, however, Perry ran away in company with another boy, but unlike me when I had done this he had a home to run to nor did he run for the same reasons as I did. He had, I think, good cause, but like many children was not able to divulge it to me at the time. His headmaster had even more of a shock than I had for he did not know of the boys' absence until I rang him up! He came post-haste next morning and perhaps this action on Perry's

Local Government and some Other Activities

part made for a happy ending because Perry and his friend returned to the school feeling they had made their point and had been listened to by parents and teachers.

5

Formation of the Child Guidance Council and Clinic: the Feversham Committee and Proposed Amalgamation of the Voluntary Mental Health Services

> *During the second decade of the present century a small band of pioneers was spreading the idea of "child guidance". By means of this new form of team-work involving doctors, psychologists and social workers based on 'clinics' they hoped to arrive at a total understanding of the difficulties of problem children. Such understanding, they believed, would lead directly to appropriate therapy and better management, since root causes rather than superficial symptoms would be dealt with.*
> Olive C. Sampson, "A Dream That Is Dying?",
> *Bulletin of British Psychologists*, Sec. 28 (1975)

During the year 1927, while I was a member of the London County Council, my attention was attracted by a remarkable report in my Education Committee agenda paper. It was signed by the Education Officer, George Gater, whom I have already mentioned, and who at this time had come to London from Lancashire with a reputation for his progressive views. Later he was appointed Clerk to the London County Council by Herbert Morrison under the first Labour administration.

This report which so greatly intrigued me gave details of a psychological service for children as practised in America, especially in Boston at the Judge Baker Foundation. It was called "Child Guidance". Alas, the original report was lost through enemy action, and therefore it has been impossible to trace who first brought the idea to George's desk. Anyway, with his brilliant mind he saw at once what such a service

Child Guidance Council and Clinic

could do to help those children who found themselves either unable to adapt to normal methods of learning, or who were unwilling to fit into the rigid discipline practised in schools at that time with sixty children to one teacher. It sparked off in me a flame of enthusiasm which was not shared by the other members of my party. No doubt they must have had some difficulties in their childhoods themselves, but unlike me they were apparently oblivious of the fact. A few of those concerned with delinquency gave some luke-warm support to the idea and the educationists saw some sense in it for tiresome misfits in school. The public health people had more understanding, for they believed debilitated children might need more than physical aid. My colleagues would have been surprised had they realised my hopes were simply for the misunderstood and purely unhappy child.

The report gave me food for thought and was the germ that eventually developed my life-long interest in mental health amongst children and adolescents, and through adulthood to old age. So 1927 was crucial in my pilgrim's progress. This concern grew, like Topsy, over the years despite opposition, misunderstanding and miserable frustration. My interest was of course motivated by personal childhood experience. My memory flashed back to my early feelings of guilt about my Nannie whose possessive love I could not return; it also recalled my inability to enjoy the company of other children which led eventually to my school refusal. In my education there had been only one exceptional teacher and her influence remains with me today. I began to realise I was not alone in being a sort of misfit in what some would call normal surroundings. It was comforting to realise that many other children had shared my plight, and that there was a scientific explanation which the experts in this child guidance business were beginning to unravel. I learned from a social worker (later to become a dear friend and travelling companion) that child guidance was not an institution, but a function concerned with the emotional well-being of children. It includes elements of psychiatry, psychology and psychiatric social work. The team approach is its basic principle, and is used in diagnosing and treating problems in children and their families. Such problems may be in the field of psychiatry, education or society and can be dealt with by the full team, or by individual members of it representing the different professions involved. As a non-professional even at that early stage I realised that the involvement of the parents was essential.

The report on my agenda paper was hotly debated in Committee and in Council on party political lines. The Municipal Reform Party (Conservative) was deeply suspicious of this new approach to learning, especially since it came from America, but the Labour Party immediately saw the importance of such an approach for use in our schools and for children coming before juvenile courts. With pressure from George Gater and the approval of the then Medical Officer of Health for London, Sir Frederic Menzies, a team of experts composed of doctors, psychologists and social workers went to the States to survey their methods of handling emotionally disturbed children and their parents. These pioneers returned quite satisfied with what they had seen and heard at first hand in Boston and elsewhere. After further discussion but much delay the decision was taken to support the first child guidance training centre and clinic in Canonbury, Islington.

Mrs. St. Loe Strachey, a juvenile court magistrate, who had been in Boston with her husband St. Loe Strachey, Editor of *The Spectator*, had also seen the work of the Judge Baker Foundation. She was another enthusiastic supporter who saw the possibilities of dealing more adequately with problem and delinquent children. Other progressive magistrates, doctors, psychologists and social workers, in true British style, formed a committee. Dr. Mapother of the Maudsley Hospital (who taught me to spell psychiatry!) and Professor Sir Cyril Burt, the L.C.C. psychologist, both gave me an understanding of what psychiatry and psychology were about. I certainly got hooked, and in my passionate way was determined to do something about promoting child guidance (shades of my 1914 nursing enthusiasm all over again!). When the Child Guidance Council (C.G.C.) was formed in 1927 I became an active member. Besides professionals it had many influential lay members, like Isabel Lawrence, a County Councillor and magistrate, and Ishbel Macdonald, daughter of the P.M., who always ready to

Child Guidance Council and Clinic

help by lending No. 10 for meetings or fund raising concerts.

The Commonwealth Fund of America (Harkness Trust) was the great supporter of the child guidance movement in the U.K. for it not only financed the team of professionals that visited the States but also for many years supported on a generous scale the C.G.C., the first London Clinic and the Mental Health course at L.S.E. The Director of the Clinic, the late Dr. William Moodie, F.R.C.P., and his staff, worked valiantly in its establishment. This country, and especially those working in the now recognised field of child guidance and child psychiatry, owes a great debt to the few persistent volunteers backed by American financial support.

It was at this time that I first met Evelyn Fox, later Dame Evelyn, who was Honorary Secretary to the Central Association for Mental Welfare, the important organisation concerned with helping mental defectives, now known as the mentally handicapped. To me she was always the Florence Nightingale of the mental health movement. We worked closely together in those early difficult days. She also became the indefatigable Hon. Secretary to the C.G.C. and faced with courage the growing pains of establishing the service in the U.K. It was a thrilling experience for me, and I shall always be grateful for having been privileged to play a small part in this great enterprise and to have come under the influence of Evelyn Fox, who was to make such a lasting impact on the future of mental health. She came from Fox Hall, County Longford, was related to Charles James Fox[1] and exhibited not a few of his characteristics. Her Irish sense of humour carried her through many difficulties and her smile and the quizzical light in her grey eyes were always disarming.

My work on the C.G.C. and the Executive Committee of the Canonbury Clinic brought me for the first time into the world of psychiatry, albeit at that time only child psychiatry. On reflection it seems curious that I had shunned the mental hospital committee of the L.C.C. despite being repeatedly pressed to join by the late Dr. Adeline Roberts, a psychiatrist,

---

[1] Charles James Fox 1749–1806, the first Lord Holland and indulgent father of Charles Fox, Pitt's formidable opponent.

In the Way of Understanding

and the late Miss May Wallas, sister of the late Professor Graham Wallas, the distinguished Professor of Politics and one of the first Fabians. Education and public health were then my main interests. I had felt that there was something sinister in the name "asylum" (which has only just been dropped). It gave me a feeling of despair – I wanted to work where I could see quick results for my efforts.

Looking back, I wonder how much we so-called 'educationalists' achieved: I believe now that we were not 100% successful. Perhaps the cause was lack of money, but it is likely the large classes played a part, as did the apathy of the public and of those who should have known better. There was little understanding of the importance of education until the Butler Education Act of 1944. However, I struggled on, but gradually without noticing it I became immersed in the large problems of mental health.

At that time the field of mental health in England was covered to a large extent by four voluntary organisations:

1. The Mental After-Care Association, the oldest, started in 1879 and catering for patients discharged from mental hospital by running hostels – a function which they still perform:
2. The Central Association for Mental Welfare, caring for mentally defective patients, founded at the time of the Mental Deficiency Act 1913. Evelyn Fox, the Secretary, with her unusual lucidity of mind had entrée to most ministries and departments, especially the Board of Control. The permanent officials were in considerable awe of her while holding her in the greatest respect. The Association's objects were to "promote, watch, support or oppose any legislation or amendment of existing legislation". Its President and active Chairman was the late Mr. Leslie Scott, K.C., M.P., later Lord Justice Scott.
3. The National Council for Mental Hygiene, formed in 1918 to study preventive methods in nervous ill health, to educate the public in mental health problems and to further the establishment of special clinics for early treatment. It coped with the discharge of shell-shocked patients from the ser-

vices and endeavoured to secure a more important position for psychiatry and a closer association for psychiatry with general medicine. It tried to educate the public by lectures, because problems of psychological neuroses had been thrown up after the war and no organisation, official or voluntary, existed to care for mental conditions which lay outside the borders of certifiable illness. The positive aspect of mental health lay hidden until voluntary effort brought it into the light. The late Lord Southborough, G.C.B., G.C.M.C., G.C.V.O., was the presiding genius of the N.C.M.U. and its Treasurer.

From the efforts of these societies came the Royal Commission of 1926 which made useful recommendations.

4. The Child Guidance Council was the latest organisation to enter the field. Its aims were "to further the practice of child guidance by encouraging the provision of skilled treatment for children showing symptoms of nervous disorder". Lord Alness, P.C., became Chairman of the C.G.C. (He had been a former Lord Advocate and Secretary of State for Scotland.) It rendered valuable service to mental health by introducing psychiatric social work into the U.K. and its educational and training scheme was administered firstly by the C.G.C. and the London School of Economics and Political Science.

It is interesting to note that three of these voluntary organisations were closely connected with the law through their respective chairmen.

As time went on many members on the committees of these societies began to think that all four should work together more closely. In the early 1930s Dr. J. R. Rees, C.B.E., a far seeing psychiatrist at the Tavistock Clinic, discussed with me and with various other people how such an amalgamation could be brought about. Anybody who has ever contemplated an amalgamation of this sort will know that the emotion and hostility immediately engendered are very strong. This time the antagonism was intense and dear Evelyn Fox's explosive temperament did not make matters any easier! She saw things

In the Way of Understanding

clearly from her point of view, but the three other organisations saw this move as a swallowing up of their identities by this dynamic personality.

I took an active part in all these negotiations, by trying to be a go-between and get some sense of urgency into each group. I tried to persuade them that one entity for mental health could exert greater influence on government departments by speaking with one voice when considering legislation for the defective and mentally ill. It could also demonstrate the need for child guidance in our educational system.

At last, in 1937, after ten years debate a committee was set up to try to break down barriers. It had representatives from all four voluntary organisations and from the Home and School Council, and was under the chairmanship of the Earl of Feversham, a Yorkshireman and a young man of great humanity and understanding of the problems of mental health. He had been trained as a probation officer and with his position in the House of Lords as Parliamentary Secretary to the Ministry of Agriculture and Fisheries we had a great ally and leader. Dr. James Mackintosh, Professor of Preventive Medicine at Glasgow University, was appointed Secretary and Rapporteur. We worked hard, all in a voluntary capacity, meeting fortnightly on Fridays in the late afternoon or evening in a private committee room in the House of Lords. In the winter it was sometimes quite dark when we finished our work and it was most eerie to have to find one's way out by night light and hear policemen call "Who goes there?". Debate was often heated, but the Chairman and the Secretary guided us delicately and succeeded in persuading even the most vocal to listen to the wise counsel of less emotional members. We heard evidence from all over the country—from hospitals, local authorities, doctors, nurses and social workers: all came to put their points of view. We had, of course, psychiatrists and psychologists on the Committee and Miss Fox was always there to champion the patients.

Finally, in the summer of 1939, the report was ready for publication[1], beautifully and clearly written by Professor

[1] *Report of the Feversham Committee on the Voluntary Mental Health Service*, 1939.

Child Guidance Council and Clinic

Mackintosh, with only the Mental After-Care Association dissenting. When it was published it looked like a Blue Book, a formal government report, and was I believe entirely financed by our Chairman. It arrived on the desk of every local authority and mental hospital in England, Scotland and Wales on the day the second world war was declared. Obviously, these authorities now had to deal with the still more important subject of facing war; the problem of mental health became but one of many.

The proposed amalgamation was part of a wider movement in industry and elsewhere towards the consolidation and pooling of resources of manpower. Alas, the outbreak of war prevented the consideration of the report by the authorities concerned and the move towards full amalgamation was delayed until the war was over. However, nothing daunted Miss Fox: she immediately formed an Emergency Committee for Mental Health and I became its Chairman – but more of this later.

When I look back to my youth and adolescence, I am sure that if child guidance been in existence at that time and if my mother been willing to accept the help of a child guidance team, my growing up might have been easier for us both. I think the same could be said of my mother-in-law, (Mrs. Norman,) and her non-conforming and difficult elder son. It might also be said of Queen Mary and her relations with her young family, especially the Prince of Wales, later the Duke of Windsor!

It has saddened me greatly over the years to watch those of the aristocratic and privileged social classes shunning the help of child guidance when facing problems of backwardness or deviant behaviour in their children. These classes, with no lack of money, and able to secure the best professional advice, have put their heads in the sand. I have seen the often tragic outcome of such stupidity—eventual certification and even suicide on reaching adolescent and adult life, not to mention broken marriages and much unhappiness for children and parents. I wish I could see the younger generation today having a more enlightened attitude but, alas, they too shun clinics. They prefer to seek all sort of advice from qualified and unqualified

In the Way of Understanding

professionals who have been recommended by all kinds of caring 'darling' friends. So they visit innumerable psychiatrists who, because they sometimes give a true picture of what is going wrong, are discarded for another opinion. Dear Dr. Moodie once told me about a friend of mine who had consulted him about her son at his Harley Street consulting rooms, "Your friend suffers from being too rich. If she were poor I could do something for her son with my team but her inability to face facts makes this impossible."

It is true that child guidance clinics are mostly in the poorer boroughs or in psychiatric hospitals, and this is off-putting to this class of parent, though Chelsea, Kensington and Hampstead have excellent facilities. Adolescent units, too, tend to be housed in psychiatric hospitals and this is a complete barrier to the parents to whom I refer. A school psychiatric service is acceptable, but child psychiatry in a psychiatric hospital is not for those full of fear and guilt. Perhaps the Royal College of Psychiatrists might consider this question when discussing the merits of child guidance as against child psychiatry, and if adolescent psychiatry ever evolves as a speciality it must consider the privileged as well as the under-privileged.

In these democratic days we are all supposed to be equal, but I believe that the poor little privileged children do not get equal opportunity. This has sometimes made me sick at heart because I have sensed the danger and yet no effective action has been taken by those concerned.

To end this chapter, I now believe that if my boys had not been such survivors and had my mother – to give her her due – not been their mother substitute, I might have had to call on some colleagues in the child guidance team!

Elysian Fields

6
Pre-marital Vicissitudes

*Hector will greet this stranger to all fears
And aged Priam, with a courtly grace,
Will teach proud Agamemnon to give place,
When in the Elysian field his wraith appears.
Deep-eyed Casandra, smiling through her tears,
Odysseus, too, whose guile was never base,
Will run to meet his rival face to face,
And blind Teiresias, the prince of seers.
What other age or clime, of men what race,
Could muster him a company of peers?
Alas, alas, Troy burns: The insensate flame
Soars up to the highest heaven; but now as then,
Above the dust, the horror and the shame
Shines out, supreme, the splendour of such men.*

Arthur Goidel "Montagu Norman", an article in
Alphabet for Odette, a Miscellany privately published 1946.

In the first chapter I have mentioned my mother's first marriage to Sir Gerald Portal, whose parents lived at Laverstoke in Hampshire. The Portals (de Portal) were Huguenot refugees who became famous paper-makers, using the lovely clear water of the Test to manufacture, among other things, Bank of England notes. This has gone on at their mills for over two centuries. Although my mother married again after the death of her first husband, her Portal in-laws kept in touch. As a child, I spent many happy times at Laverstoke through Wyndham Portal and continued to do so as generations came and went.

All the Portal family were welcoming and affectionate to me, saying laughingly that it was only by chance that I had not been born a Portal and that they therefore treated me as one of the family.

It must have been in the late Twenties that I first heard the name of the then Governor of the Bank of England, Montagu Norman, for whom Wyndham Portal had a considerable admiration. The Governor, as he was always called, took a

In the Way of Understanding

keen interest in the mills and paid periodical visits to see the making of the bank-notes and to talk to the directors and staff.

In 1926 I read two interesting appreciations of the Governor in *The Banker*, a periodical then published by Eyre & Spottiswood Ltd. It intrigued me greatly and I became more and more anxious to meet this unusual man. In the issue January 1926, of this journal, (pp. 18–19) the Rt. Hon. Sir Robert Horne, G.B.E., K.C., M.P., (formerly a Conservative Chancellor of the Exchequer) wrote:

> *Some weeks ago I was talking with a very distinguished banker in the United State of America. Our conversation turned for a moment to the Bank of England and its Governor, and my friend said, with obvious fervour and admiration:* "Norman? Ah! Yes—Norman is a Crusader!'
>
> *To most people this romantic description may sound incongruous when applied to a man whose life is spent in the financial vortex of the City of London, and whose activities are chiefly connected in the popular imagination with the fluctuations in the bank rate. But nobody who knows Mr. Norman will feel startled at the use of the image which the American banker employed. The Governor's appearance belies every preconception which one would form of a man who, through long experience of commercial men and financial affairs, had risen to the eminence which this great post confers. Anyone who expected to find in him the signs of a nature taught to be suspicious, trained to be calculating, and compelled by experience to be hard, would be greatly disillusioned on meeting him. When he confronts you he presents the aspect of a philosopher rather than that of a man of business. Put the velvet cap of the scholar on his head and he would recall to you an old print of some medieval teacher. His air is detached; his brows are wide and thoughtful; his face refined and sensitive; his manner gentle, and his eyes those of a visionary, but of a cool visionary. His hands are nervous, but they are also strong, and behind the more amiable qualities which I have described he possesses a gift of courage and resolution which carries him, in a spirit of cheerfulness – and sometimes of gaiety – into any combat*

Pre-marital Vicissitudes

which his decisions may involve. These are characteristics not unworthy of the heroes of the old Crusades.

The second appreciation, which appeared in the February, 1926 issue of *The Banker*, (pp. 160/162) was written by the Rt. Hon. Philip Snowden, M.P., a former Labour Chancellor of the Exchequer, who wrote:

> I had not previously met Mr. Norman, but I had a vague idea of what a Governor of the Bank of England ought to look like. I had seen caricatures in the Socialist Press of the typical financier – the hard-faced, close-fisted, high-nosed individual, whose active brain had worn off every trace of hair from the summit of his head. I wondered if the Governor of the Bank of England—the autocrat of international finance—the man who in these modern days had usurped the powers of Czars and Kaisers, and who held in his hands the destinies of the millions of a far greater Empire, would look like that!
>
> But there came into the room a man so different. He might have stepped out of the frame of the portrait of the most handsome courtier who ever graced the court of a queen. And it took but a short acquaintance with Mr. Norman to know that his external appearance was the bodily expression of one of the kindliest natures and most sympathetic hearts it has ever been my privilege to know.
>
> . . .
>
> It was said of a great statesman of the Victorian Age that he had the 'international mind'. How truly that may be said of the present Governor of the Bank of England. To him, more than to any statesman of Europe, is the credit due for the partial restoration of the economic condition of Europe in the last few years.
>
> . . .
>
> Even if I regretfully differed from Mr. Norman I admired the force with which he presented his views, and the tenacity with which he held to them.

In spite of the eulogistic and rather charming parts of the

In the Way of Understanding

appreciations which I have quoted, the Governor was a very controversial figure. There were those who considered him the devil incarnate, but there were many more who considered him a man in whom they had complete confidence and in whose leadership they trusted during these times of financial crisis in Europe. One of these was Wyndham Portal, the man who had done so much to shape my life by giving me an interest in local government. Now, quite unconsciously, he began to influence my emotional life by lending me *The Banker* and other city periodicals and newspapers containing many articles which were concerned with the views of the Governor of the Bank of England. Wyndham was quite unaware of what he was doing to me and it was a cruel irony of fate that he organised a meeting that was to prove so disastrous from his point of view but was to be so happy for me!

I listened to and read about the controversy concerning the return to the gold standard. It was passionately discussed, but it was all far above my head because I was only interested in the man who seemed to have a magnetic influence on those with whom he came in contact. My chance to meet him came in 1929, and we were married in 1933. Of course there is a story between these four years. In 1960 it occurred to me that younger generations of Normans might like to know how our marriage came about. It might also be of historical interest to others entering the banking profession who would undoubtedly encounter the name of Montagu Norman. I therefore felt moved then to write my portrayal of the very human side of an internationally famous man, as seen through the eyes of a young woman entering a new world. The events are still vivid in my mind but I repeat the account I wrote in 1960 unchanged, and it is given in the next section of this book.

7
Second Marriage, 1933.
(Account written in 1960.)

It was during a week-end in the summer of 1929 that I actually met Montagu Norman, though I had heard a great deal about him from my friends the Portals, who were relations of my mother through her first husband, Sir Gerald Portal.

Sir William and Lady Portal lived at Laverstoke, Whitchurch, in Hampshire and their son, Wyndham, lived some few miles away at Kingsclere. Wyndham was head of the family paper business that had made the notes for the Bank of England ever since the Portals had come over to England as Huguenot refugees.

The Governor paid an annual visit to the paper mills lying picturesquely on the river Test. Sir William and Lady Portal, "Aunt Foff" and "Uncle Willy" to me, were always anxious and ill-at-ease with the Governor. She was a hunting woman and full of small talk, very dogmatic on all sorts of matters, whilst he was artistic and a yachting enthusiast and also full of small talk. Neither of them had anything in common with the Governor—not even the business, because Uncle Willy left it all to his dynamic son, Wyndham.

A fairly large party was assembled on this particular occasion, made up of directors and their wives and members of the family. We dined late, because the Governor only arrived by car about 8 p.m. and changing for dinner was considered de rigueur. He was all I had been told to expect, and came in with that curious gait I was later to know so well, gravely courteous yet aloof and forbidding. He listened to everybody's name as introductions were made in Wyndham's boisterous manner. It was rather a stiff atmosphere in which the Governor tried his best to thaw the assembled guests. Drinks were served, and then dinner was served at which the Governor sat on Lady

In the Way of Understanding

Portal's right. He was quite at his ease and joked, but poor Lady Portal found it an ordeal as she was never able to dominate the conversation.

After the men joined the ladies the Governor, for some unaccountable reason, came over to sit by me. Of course he put me through my paces by question and answer, and soon he had the problem of the education of the children of London at his finger tips. I was on the L.C.C. and on its Education Committee at the time, and so, having such a highly intelligent and interested questioner, I soon lost any shyness I may have had and the time passed only too quickly.

The ladies retired and much teasing went on. I was the subject of much envy, mingled with relief because I think that the ladies present would have been embarrassed at having to keep the famous Governor amused or interested for nearly an hour. I remember that Uncle Willy, as he kissed me goodnight thanked me for making the party go. This only goes to show how afraid they were of this "handsome courtier of the Middle Ages".

Next morning, while I was pouring out my coffee at the sideboard, a hand was laid on my shoulder and a delightful, beguiling voice said: "Allow me, Mrs. Worsthorne, to serve you and please let me sit next to you." I was overwhelmed with embarrassment, especially when he brought not only my coffee but also two boiled eggs, one of which he peeled for me and the other for himself. He asked me to butter his toast, and with all the eyes of the other astonished guests on me I became overcome with shyness. However, he again used that extraordinary power which he kept for those who interested him, and drew me out and made me completely forget myself. He was whisked off to the mill after breakfast and I think must have lunched with the Directors.

The next thing I remember is breakfast on the following morning. He adopted the same ritual with bacon, and asked me if I would care to drive up to London with him after dinner, in order not to have to travel by the usual early train on Monday. I dared not refuse, yet wondered what on earth I was going to talk to this god about for two hours! In the event it was easy, and, of course, he got my life history out of me—

Second Marriage, 1933

something he loved doing for he was interested in people. Gravely and courteously, as if I were a princess and he an ordinary mortal, he said goodbye to me at my door. I must own to his having made a deep impression on me.

About a year later Sir William died, and the Governor came to the funeral. He sat in front of my mother and me and sang quite beautifully that favourite hymn of his—"O Love that will not let me go. . . ." The mourners walked from the Freefolk Church down a glorious avenue of limes to the little chapel in the park where the Portals are buried. There he gallantly went over to Lady Portal, bent and kissed her hand and shook hands with other members of the family.

He came over to me and we walked back to the house where he asked me if I would "relieve his loneliness and drive back to London." I was with my mother and reluctantly declined.

It must have been nearly a year later when I was again asked to meet him, but this time at Kingsclere. The day before we were due to arrive a telephone message came from the Bank to say that if I were willing the Governor would call for me about 6 p.m. to drive me down to Kingsclere, as he had ascertained that I was to be a fellow guest. He must have regretted his kindly action, for when he arrived to pick me up at nearly seven o'clock he looked ill and almost dead to the world. However, with his kingly manners uppermost, he excused his lateness and in my turn I said firmly: "Please sit back in your corner and forget me and don't let us talk." This was a very obvious relief and he sat with closed eyes until we got to Staines. Then he asked me to talk about what I had done during the week. With gentle promptings I was able to answer him, and by the time we reached our destination he had recovered and was the life and soul of the party.

It was easy with the jovial young Portals, and the champagne and good food helped a lot.

Saturday was, I suppose, taken up by another visit to the mill but I know that on Sunday the Governor at breakfast announced that he was going to take Mrs. W. up the Kingsclere Downs! This he did on a glorious summer day and we walked and talked for over two hours, the first of many long and arduous excursions. He decided we should drive up to

In the Way of Understanding

London before dinner and sup at "Plodge" (nickname for Thorpe Lodge, Campden Hill). He sat me down in the Peacock room and went to bath and change, leaving me alone with a book. The food was excellent, beautifully served, but the many kinds of knives and forks of silver and wood were confusing and I watched my host before beginning. The contemporary furniture and panelling were something new to me and peacock blue was not my favourite colour, so I was very much in unfamiliar surroundings. At ten o'clock the car was announced and he took me back to my home in Cadogan Square.

After this we met fairly often, either at Plodge or in my house and our friendship grew. One week-end we went to St. Clere in Kent, the home of Sir Mark and Lady Collet, Mont's uncle and aunt. They welcomed me warmly and Mont was at peace with them and more like a brother to Mark Collet than the nephew he really was. Another week-end Mont took me to his cottage at Moor Place, Much Hadham, Herts. We motored down with Tom, his chauffeur, in the white-topped Lincoln car and took Amy, the housekeeper, with food for the week-end. The cottage was sparsely furnished, very comfortable and simple, but without luxury. MN would never spend any money on the cottage and even after we married I had the greatest difficulty in getting him to buy new curtains or covers to replace those which were worn out. There was an extraordinary peace at this cottage in the walled kitchen garden and I have never known anything like its restful atmosphere, with the exception of Plodge. I was doubtful as to what sort of reception I would get from his sister-in-law, Lady Florence Norman, who lived at the big house at Moor Place, made over to Ronnie Norman, his only brother, by Mont. But at breakfast she came over and gave me the kindest of welcomes, and the obvious devotion between Florrie and Mont was very moving. All she wanted was Mont's happiness and she always gave him unstinted love and devotion. I already knew Ronnie on the L.C.C. and he was the dearest of men, very handsome and intelligent and with lovely manners. Ronnie and Florrie loved Moor Place, their beautiful Georgian home (built 1779)— "the Nest", as Mont called it—and anything old or of historical value to the family

Second Marriage, 1933

he would deposit in the Nest, to the amusement and at times embarrassment of his brother and gentle sister-in-law. He loved Ronnie and had something like veneration for Florrie. He was devoted to their children but in no silly or uncritical way. He always spoke his mind in no uncertain terms if they did things or held views with which he was not in sympathy. Nevertheless they respected him and took note of his opinions.

During the year 1932 I saw more and more of Mont, dining with him at least once a week and going either to St. Clere or the cottage, or sometimes spending a week-end at Plodge. We were always alone together, talking in complete harmony about everything under the sun. He opened a new vista for me and in accepting me as a woman with a mind worth cultivating, I felt stimulated and free. He set a very high standard in conversation and often read to me in his beautiful voice with its clear enunciation. I remember how moved I was on hearing Oscar Wilde's *De Profundis* for the first time, and I have kept it as a bedside book ever since. To have heard "Where there is sorrow there is holy ground" recited as the light faded on the verandah at Plodge is an experience for which I give thanks.

I think I was the first to realise how deep our friendship had become and I knew that I was sincerely in love. Mont, I think, refused to face up to what he was doing to me. This is curious because he enjoyed facing facts and never tolerated make-believe or sham. But I believe that he refused to consider that our relationship was anything out of the ordinary—he persuaded himself that as I was so much younger than he there was no danger of playing with fire and that he was master of the situation. What happened was that he found that he could not do without me. I made no demands. I was there when he wanted me, and I had my L.C.C. work and family and friends to occupy me when he was busy so that I was never a worry to him. He was terribly lonely and needed at that time one person, preferably a woman, to occupy those few hours when he was not immersed in his work with the Old Lady of Threadneedle Street. I thus learned something that stood me in good stead after my marriage—that the Old Lady must come first and that no home tie must interfere with the task to which he had dedicated his life.

In the Way of Understanding

During this period, my half-brother, Guy Reyntiens, died in Brussels and I went over for the funeral with my mother. When we arrived back at Victoria I found to my astonishment that Mont was on the platform to greet me and take me back to my house in Cadogan Square. My mother was taken aback at seeing the Governor of the Bank of England, the Station Master and various other officials waiting for us, and this shows again how carefree Mont was about gossip. He expected people to react as he did himself and never pry into other people's private lives—it was something one did not do. To him gossip was an abomination not to be tolerated, and so it became to me. Whenever I hear gossip, or participate in it, I always feel ashamed, and in a way unclean, even today.

Another episode took place in a Nursing Home, when I had my appendix out. On about the fourth day some lovely flowers came with a card on which was written: "From G. B. SURE"—a reference to those delightful letters of Ellen Terry to G. B. Shaw which played a part in our courtship, as did Charles Morgan's novel *The Fountain*. MN charmed the nurses and was soon paying me visits not unnoticed by them or my friends. We were, of course, putting our heads in the sand. Although I myself realised this, Mont was, I believe, completely unaware of what was happening—he ignored the situation and expected others to do the same.

In July, 1932, Mont was planning to go to America to visit his "American mother", Mrs. Markoe. We went to St. Clere and I could see that he could hardly bear to contemplate being alone on this trip. He looked terribly ill and was in a deep depression. At this time I was working closely with the Commonwealth Fund of America (Harkness Trust) in establishing the first Child Guidance Clinic in this country. The Trust was nobly pouring money into this scheme and had already invited officers of the L.C.C., doctors and social workers to go over and inspect the work in the U.S.A. I was considering going over as a member of the British Child Guidance Council and I suggested to Mont that we might travel together.

At first this was strongly resisted, every argument being used to discourage the idea, but at St. Clere at the week-end Mont's despair was so intense that all obstacles were removed. He

Second Marriage, 1933

decided that I must make my trip to the United States at the same time as he took his holiday. He arranged that I should travel on the same ship but see nothing of him in the States, as the light of publicity would be on him and the Old Lady must have no breath of scandal! This was easy for me as I should be fully occupied.

We sailed in August, and as luck would have it I was as good a sailor as he was, and the crossing with a V.I.P., the most delightful of companions, was perfect. Mont took some days to "unwind", as he called it, and was at first on edge, but gradually he relaxed and by the time we reached Boston he was well and active.

He was going up to Bar Harbor by train and I was going to New York. We spent the morning in Boston together, becoming more and more unhappy at the thought of parting. I cried all the way to New York and was never so lonely in my life as when arriving in that city on a Saturday evening. However, on Sunday, early in the morning, I had a telephone call from Moreau Delano, one of Mont's best friends in America. He said he had received a cable from MN asking him to call on Mrs. W. Moreau Delano came to fetch me in his car and I spent a heavenly day and night in his delightful house at Orange, New York. His old English butler, who knew Mont, taught me to eat corn on the cob and introduced me to soft-shell crabs. Years afterwards, Moreau told me that he had had no doubt about Mont's dilemma and of the way in which it would be solved!

On the Monday I was back in New York. I heard from Mont that he was coming down at the end of the week on business and that Mrs. Markoe had asked me up to Bar Harbor for the week-end. This was an important step on Mont's part and a clever one, because if I had not pleased that great lady and not fitted into her milieu, I doubt if Mont could have allowed himself to continue wandering along any road, even with me.

I was considerably mystified and, of course, flattered by this invitation, and not a little nervous. However, the visit was most successful; the old lady approved of me. The three of us talked happily together and I took care to leave Norman, as she called him, very often alone with her. I went to bed early so

In the Way of Understanding

as to leave them alone for I was really sorry that I had come between this able, witty and intelligent old lady and the comparatively young man whom she adored and had been so fond of over many years.

We sailed back again in early September from Canada. Reporters met us and were out to question me but I escaped and Mont was very nasty to them. On the boat, as the days passed, he got more and more depressed and one night said: "After tomorrow, things will never be the same again". I was very distressed, and begged him to say what this meant. All night I wondered, and only the next morning did he say: "This is my birthday: I am sixty."

On our arrival at Liverpool the press were impossible. Reporters came into my cabin at 6 a.m. My mother had sent her car to meet me, as I was going to see my children at Burnley. I smuggled Mont out of his cabin by telling him to go to the Gents. and not to return to his cabin but to slip out from the Gents. another way. The stewards entered into the fun of it. I went and said "Goodbye" loudly to Mont and took some of the reporters with me and then went with the head C.P.R.[1] man to the car. A compartment on the train was reserved for MN and the reporters went to await him at the train. I drove away in another car to return to a pre-arranged place at the side of the ship. Mont came through the hold on one side of the ship and I got down under a rug while Mont opened the door and slipped into the car. We drove away quickly to Warrington and awaited a train there. While sitting miserably on the station platform a flight of swans flew over, much to Mont's pleasure. I don't think he noticed much else but never forgot this episode, although the memory of the press and little difficulties of that kind faded.

I was depressed, although highly stimulated in some ways. However, I doubted how long I could keep up the pace and how long Mont would expect me to go on in this extraordinary fashion. Little did I know that it would be for another four months, with everything getting more and more complicated.

Life in London went on much the same. I was busy with my

---

[1] Canadian Pacific Railway.

Second Marriage, 1933

L.C.C. work and with the Child Guidance Clinic in Canonbury. My family, and especially my uncle, Lord Fitzalan, a Roman Catholic, were beginning to hear rumours of my friendship. I was given all kinds of advice. Re-marriage for someone who was supposed to be a Roman Catholic was impossible, yet my cousin, the son of Lord Fitzalan, wrote me a sweet letter. He said that the City was humming with rumours and that he, for one, hoped I would pay no attention to his father, or those who expected me to remain single.

Christmas came and Mont decided we should spend it with the Collets at Costabelle in the south of France. It meant leaving the boys, but my mother said she would take them to Cumberland Lodge with my Fitzalan uncle. Poor mother—she too suffered over all this but I think she thought marriage was out of the question.

Sir Mark Collet was Mont's uncle, his mother's step-brother and about ten years her junior, and they had always been very close friends. Violet, his second wife, had also been a close friend of MN as, for a while, she had been his grandmother's companion. When his grandmother died, Mont encouraged Violet to go to America and earn a living growing irises. She became a successful professional iris grower and only came back to England when Mark, after his first wife died, went over and asked her to marry him.

We were a merry party, including the old French couple who were the gardener and cook, and retainers of all kinds who adored "le Capitaine" as they called Mont. Lilian, (now my housekeeper), the housemaid at St. Clere, was also there, and nothing could have been more pleasant. Without anyone saying anything outright, both Mark and Violet made it plain that a marriage ought to take place and that they would welcome it.

Mont was gay and relaxed and quite unconcerned. The press came to the door and Mark despatched them in fluent French.

A few days after Christmas, we all motored up into the hills behind Marseilles. In the evening MN and I and Dick Crockford (Mont's valet) joined a P & O ship sailing to Tilbury. In those days the élite from India or Australia left the ship at

In the Way of Understanding

Marseilles to go home by train, thus avoiding the week's sail through the Bay of Biscay. We therefore each had a suite of cabins and travelled in luxury, and were able to sit out on the Captain's deck. At Gibraltar we got a cable: '"If it were done, then t'were well t'were done quickly." ViMar'. Mont asked me what it meant. I said that I knew and that he must surely know too. But I refused to be drawn any further.

That night he was unusually quiet and our conversation was restrained and rather formal—for the first time we were shy of each other . . .

Next morning, as I left my deck chair to go down to my cabin, Mont followed me. As I opened the door, saying: "I won't be long" he pushed me inside and, taking me in his arms, said: "I can't go on like this; will you marry me?" I burst out laughing, because a more unromantic moment could hardly have been chosen, and I only record it because it is so typical of Mont's unconventionality and unselfconsciousness.

From then on he was gay and relaxed: we joked and laughed and he teased me more than ever.

On our arrival at Tilbury we were met by his car and he dropped me at my house while he himself went to Plodge.

So far I have not mentioned Mont's mother, but he had taken me to see her and I had dined with them at The Red House in Hornton Street in Kensington. She was then eighty years old, very upright, tall and thin, beautifully dressed for her age in soft colours of pale blue and dove grey. She wore hand-printed materials of wool and silk. Her mind was active and forward looking and was very quick for her age. She disliked looking back and reminiscing and only once did I get her to refer to her being on her pony "Moscow" with Queen Victoria at Aldershot at a parade of troops on their return from the Crimean war.

She had had an unhappy childhood. She lost her mother when she was still a baby and she was brought up by a stony-hearted aunt. She married young and was, I think, only twenty when Mont was born. He must have been a very difficult little boy, and maybe his feeding as a baby had something to do with his being a sickly and puny child. Being a very intelligent and intuitive woman, Mrs. Norman would

Second Marriage, 1933

have benefited by, and even enjoyed, what is known today as "Child Guidance" with its psychological insights into the bringing up of children. We often talked about it and there is no doubt that if she had had expert help with her problem child, Mont's childhood would have been healthier and happier and his mother would have been less worried.

Mrs. Norman herself suffered from depression and migraine. The psychological approach to this problem instead of a purely physical one would, I am sure, have been understood and even welcomed by this intuitive woman.

My first lunch party at The Red House scared me a little. I felt in a very awkward position, but Mrs. Norman—or "Madella" as I afterwards called her—was kindness itself. On our return from Costabelle Mont told his mother of our engagement and almost at once I had an official call from my future mother-in-law. She was welcoming to me and took me in her arms and said she was happy and thankful that Mont had at last found a woman he could love. She was broad-minded enough to overlook my first marriage, but anxious to know about the boys and my mother. She said she believed that a wife should be able to reverence her husband—something I had not thought of but increasingly believe to be true.

I was relieved and very happy, because at her age it must have been a great shock to find another person becoming close to her beloved Mont. Their friendship was very real; she idolised him and leaned on him for many things and was always advising him about health foods, new medical methods and new thought in religion and medicine.

She spoke her mind easily with him and he kept her abreast of affairs in the world, and their companionship was easy and almost gay. Knowing this, I was determined not to come between them. Mont and I agreed that his weekly dinners with her should continue. This was not always easy for me, because as the years went by he used to be more and more tired at night. I would gladly have kept him at home but to The Red House he went as a sacred duty.

Ronnie was at Plodge when Mont got home from Costabelle—he and Florrie made Plodge their London home. Both he and Florrie were, I think, thankful that Mont had made up

In the Way of Understanding

his mind, although Florrie was acutely conscious of my divorce and was unhappy about it. However, she became the best of sisters to me and I loved her very deeply. She was a most generous friend and loving person, a lovely woman full of grace; she meant much to me because she loved Mont and was loved by him. She came to see me and said that she wanted Mont to be married in a church, and that she would do her best with her many clerical friends to arrange this. To her sorrow she failed.

We were married in Chelsea Registry Office on January 21st 1933. Florrie whispered to me that Mont told her he had cleaned his ears that morning and therefore was taking a personal pride in his appearance! This was a great joke between them. He may have thought about cleaning his ears but he had not thought of a ring. When asked by the Registrar if he intended to use one, he barked "Of course", undid his tie and took off the lovely old ring of his father's—gold with two pearls—that he always wore on his silk tie and put it on my finger. After that his necktie was disarranged but again, in his unselfconsciousness, he never worried.

The press behaved disgracefully over our wedding arrangements; they even camped outside my house in Cadogan Square. I therefore left the house in the dark by the back way and went to sleep at a friend's house, walking down the King's Road to the Registry Office at 7.45 a.m. on my wedding day. Meanwhile, Mont, Ronnie and Florrie went by car, the car being smuggled into the old workhouse building from where there was a corridor leading to the Registry Office. We returned the same way and so eluded the press who were waiting at the front entrance.

After a gay wedding breakfast at Plodge we tried to leave for Moor Place cottage by car, but again photographers and reporters surrounded the front gate. Mont, with a twinkle in his eye, said: "Come on, Honey" and we jumped over the adjoining wall into the garden of Moray Lodge next door. We walked out of their garden entrance into Campden Hill, but the press saw us from our garden gate which they had also been watching. From then on there was a chase and I thought I had married a madman!! Mont walked on one side of the road and

Second Marriage, 1933

I walked on the other and we made for the Underground separately. He was followed, but mercifully I was allowed to go alone. As arranged, I was to go to the house of Freddie and Gertrude Balfour, (Mont's only sister), supposedly to be introduced to them as we had not yet met. I arrived alone, and was asked who I was. Half an hour later Mont rushed in, kissed Gertrude and said to me: "Come on, Honey, we must be off before those bloodhounds find me." Poor Gertrude! The car and Tom were waiting and off we went on a cold, snowy morning.

We arrived at the cottage, only to find that photographers were in the wood-shed. Poor devils! They had been there all night but Mont sent for the police and they were turned away. Mont's battle with the press was perhaps silly and undignified and he nearly always came off worst, but it was sincere and sprang from a strong, personal belief that a man's private life was his own affair and should not be of any interest to the public. He disliked people making money out of what amounted to gossip—something he considered devilish. He knew it in America, and deplored it. He considered that whereas for a young country with no standards or traditions it was perhaps inevitable, in an old country with traditions and standards such vulgarity was unpardonable.

8
Post-Marital Vagaries—
Plodge and Moor Place

Oh, the comfort, the inexpressible comfort of feeling safe with a person, having neither to weigh thoughts nor measure words but pour them all right out just as they are, chaff and grain together, knowing that a faithful hand will take and sift them, keep what is worth keeping and then, with the breath of kindness, blow the rest away.

(Source unknown.)

After my marriage to Montagu Norman in 1933 I continued my active work on the L.C.C. but I did not stand again at the 1935 Council elections. My husband considered himself a servant of the State and took no part in party politics and I therefore found it difficult to be associated with any political party, even at local government level. I was sorry in some ways to give up this interesting work, and especially the Education Committee, as it brought me into contact with the teaching profession, including Home Office Approved Schools.

However, after my visit to the Commonwealth Fund of America I had gained much insight into the work of the child guidance multidisciplinary team work there. This helped me when working for the London Child Guidance Council and its clinic, housed in the lovely house in Canonbury. Nominally I was trying to raise money—a thing that I hated as it meant organising charity balls, dinners, garden parties and so on. But from my office in the clinic I was often invited to attend case conferences, where I was treated as an "amateur-professional". It was here that William Moodie, the first director of the clinic, and his understanding staff gave me a real insight into child psychiatry, educational psychology and psychiatric social work—a profitable experience for me in view of my future concentration on the problem of mental health in the world.

I was much encouraged by my husband's intuitive understanding of the work and his enthusiasm for the proposed amalgamation of the mental health services. We worked hard between 1933 and 1939 in getting the various factions together, and this was no easy matter, as many obstacles, real or imaginary, had to be overcome.

Thorpe Lodge, our lovely home on Campden Hill, previously referred to as "Plodge" (its telegraphic address), played no small part in the formation of the future National Association for Mental Health. Lord Southborough, a friend of my husband and a near neighbour, Chairman of the National Council for Mental Hygiene; Mr. Justice Scott (later Lord Justice Scott), Chairman of the Central Association for Mental Welfare; and Lord Blanesborough, another Scottish judge, between them helped me pour oil on the troubled waters. On one occasion my husband and I lent the house for an important dinner party for the warring parties, and our devoted staff cared for the guests' welfare. At midnight, when we returned home from an engagement, discussions were still going on so we crept to bed unseen. It may have been at this dinner that the idea of the Feversham Committee was born.

Although my husband took an interest in my mental health work he had intended to keep me quite separate from his banking world. However, his colleagues decided differently. They took counsel together and asked the then Deputy Governor, Sir Ernest Harvey[1], to see me secretly. I was then invited to the Bank on a certain Thursday after a meeting of the Court. He told me that the directors wanted to meet me, as they wished to congratulate the Governor on his marriage. It all sounded very charming and I agreed to keep it a secret from Mont. On the appointed day I was driven to the Bank by our chauffeur, Tom, in the white topped Ford Lincoln and ushered into the Governor's room. This had two doors, one leading into the passage and the other into the Court room. I was alone for what seemed a long time. Suddenly I panicked and I had a feeling that this episode might ruin my marriage. I was making for the exit door when the other one opened and Mont came in alone. He stopped and said "What the devil are you doing

---

[1] Sir Ernest Musgrave Harvey, Bart. (1867–1955). Deputy Governor, 1929–1936.

In the Way of Understanding

here?" My heart missed a beat! The Deputy was close behind him and said "Mr. Governor, I am responsible for this. Your colleagues want to be introduced to Mrs. Governor." He took me kindly by the arm and led me into the room to meet the directors, who were all standing in a circle. Mont then took me by the hand and introduced me to each one, giving an amusing thumb sketch of each. I remember one rather aged director bursting into tears. Of course this set me off, and Mont too had tears pouring down his cheeks! Looking back, it was an extraordinary emotional scene and one that only Mont's personality could have evoked. Like me, the directors were all a little apprehensive, wondering if they had been wise to take this secret step. However, it was a tremendous success. The ice was broken and I had got into the Old Lady's parlour. I was offered a glass of sherry and then courteously dispatched home. I returned to a lonely lunch but felt very happy, although overwhelmed by the ordeal. Wives were kept very much 'in their place' during my 'governorship'. Later this all changed and wives became a part of the life of the Bank— something that I should so much have enjoyed. However, years later, after Mont's death and after the 1939/45 war, succeeding Governors included me at times in farewell dinners for old friends I had known. On one special occasion I was invited to Lord O'Brien's[1] retirement party, at a dinner given by Mr. Edward Heath at No. 10 when he was Prime Minister. In his speech, to an audience which included many Governors of European and Commonwealth Banks, Mr. Heath referred most gallantly to me as the widow of a famous Governor whom so many round the table would have known. I had not been to Downing Street since Ramsay McDonald was Prime Minister. His daughter Ishbel used to help me raise money for child guidance. The farewell party for Lord O'Brien took place in a beautiful setting, with furniture and furnishings of exquisite colour and with many lovely old and modern pictures on the walls. The dinner was simple, well cooked and served. There were some delightful choristers from the Abbey who

---

[1] The Rt. Hon. Lord O'Brien of Lothbury, G.B.E., P.C., b. 1908, retired from Bank of England 1973.

sang madrigals during coffee. Mr. Heath was a perfect host and most courteous and solicitous to me. Not unnaturally I enjoyed the evening immensely.

Besides being world-famous as a banker, my husband was known also as a many-sided personality, with interests in the artistic world, especially in music. Few, however, realised the depth and quality of his interests and how original and creative was his mind. He had an especial knowledge of rare woods and delighted in working with his hands, having a keen personal interest in experimenting in designing furniture, metal work and panelling.

Mont had bought Plodge in 1904 as an almost derelict building with a large, neglected garden. He wished to fashion a "shell", as he called it, like various snails and aquatic creatures who grow their own shells and then discard them to go on to grow still bigger shells ad infinitum. He developed an interest in timber and liked using fine, wide boards, both for walls and floors. The staircase of Plodge was in solid baulks and among the woods he used were English oak, cherry, walnut, purple heart, tulip, holly with many others. None of the wood was stained or French polished and he hated paint, veneer and especially barbed wire, saying that he hoped their inventors were sizzling in hell! Trunks of trees were purchased on his various travels in the U.S.A., Tasmania and many other places and the trunks would then be towed home in convoy behind tankers.

Mont was a member of the Art Workers' Guild, and many fine metal pieces could be seen in Plodge—fire-dogs in lily pattern, electric light fittings, lamps, etc. Among the craftsmen whose work appeared in the house were William de Morgan (fine blue tiles), Henry Wilson (statuettes) and Omar Ramsden (a beautiful Mazer bowl).

As Sir Gordon Russell wrote in his article in the March 1955 issue of *The Banker*: "Had Norman used his unique influence to encourage bankers to become patrons of the work of their own day—a role for which they were eminently fitted by education and prestige—he would have performed a service of incalculable value to British industry, which might well have been set on the road to the world leadership in design."

In the Way of Understanding

My husband was inspired by the work and wisdom of William Morris, not only as an artist but as a rebel and hater of shams. An architect who worked with my husband was W. K. Shirley, who later became Lord Ferrers, and between them they must have known and admired the work of Ernest Gimson and the Barnsley brothers (the famous furniture designers). The construction of nearly all of the furniture and joinery at Plodge was executed by J. H. Wakelin, a builder in Sunningdale who employed superb craftsmen. The Music Room was beautifully described in a letter (May 31, 1907) written by Janet Ashbee, wife of C. R. Ashbee, architect designer:

> I am sitting by a great beech fire for it is wintry cold still. It smoulders orange under a heavy Italian stone mantel, with the Pelle of the Medici upon it, grey and velvety like moleskin. The room is vaulted in white plaster and nearly cruciform, and gives you the spacious ease of soul that you express in a contented sigh. The floor is of mottled and shining elm, partly overlaid by raisin- and plum-coloured Persian rugs. The electric light glows unseen above a cornice, or glints through mother-of-pearl shutters. The scarlet lacquer screen and the dull bluish discs of old Worcester plates are the only decoration. But the beauty of the room is in its panelling, carried high up to the spring of the vaulting in unpolished wood. It is impossible to describe the warm, gentle, caressing feeling given by this wood or to say definitely what its colour is. The nearest I can get is smooth, sunburnt flesh and the delight it raises is almost the joy kindled by the touch of such warm, naked, wholesome flesh.

This beautiful room was the setting for two memorable visits by Kathleen Ferrier when she came to sing to help my fund-raising activities for child guidance. These were truly inspired musical evenings with that unequalled voice soaring to the rafters. The last gay encore of *The Keel Row*, with Gerald Moore fading out the piano and letting her sing unaccompanied as she taped her foot on the platform, is a memory which I treasure as an exquisite moment in my life. She wore a very

The Music Room, Plodge

With Mont, in Plodge garden

On the way to Buckingham Palace, 1933

Reading

Post-Marital Vagaries

simple, all-gold dress. One night Ruth Draper[1] was my guest and on Kathleen's insistence she also gave one of her inimitable performances, using one of my silk shawls and a fan as her props. On another occasion her nephew Paul came with her and danced to the music of Bach and other classics.

If rooms could speak the Music Room at Plodge would have many tales to tell of the interesting persons who appeared there. The varied discussions that took place within Plodge's walls would be also fascinating to recall. The veranda was the setting for conversations between famous international bankers and political figures who came to talk with Mont and seek his wisdom. It was an enchanting experience to sit out late after dinner on summer evenings, and then turn on the electric light bulbs hidden among the vines. If there were no wives for me to entertain I would retire early and leave the men to their discussions, but the smell of good cigars would waft up to my bedroom and the occasional laughter would tell me that things were going well.

The foregoing describes some of the shell Mont wished to fashion and in it were those devoted servants and friends who ministered to their "Captain", as they called him. They welcomed me most kindly: perhaps they had watched our courtship with curiosity and not a little apprehension! Firstly there was a well-trained, rather formidable housekeeper, Amy, who had been with my husband for many years. However, she was not too happy at my arrival on the scene as she thought that I might upset the regular pace of a bachelor establishment. She stayed several months after my advent but then wisely retired to a house Mont found for her. We never quarrelled, but were over-polite to each other, and as a household we were more free and happy when she left.

Then there was Mrs. B.—a splendid character and an excellent cook; in fact, a very colourful personality and a very good actress, prominent in local amateur theatricals. I loved her and we got on well together, and she successfully dealt with all the kitchen problems. A dear little round, black-eyed parlour maid called Nellie efficiently took charge of our lives,

---

[1] *Ruth Draper, Her Art and Characters*, Oxford University Press, 1960.

as did an excellent housemaid. They were all well-trained professionals who cared for their employer and were now willing to cope with a wife who was more out of the house than in it. Later, I imported a lady's maid to replace the housekeeper. She had been a slave to Dame Nellie Melba, the great opera singer. She looked after my clothes and valeted my husband now that the housekeeper had gone.

Dick Crockford was the gardener and he travelled with my husband on his many journeys, acting as courier, valet and friend. They had been brought up together at Moor Place, Much Hadham, my husband's home in Hertfordshire. They had played together as boys and still quarrelled as men but were always reconciled in the end.

Tom, the chauffeur, another old servant, was a splendid fellow who taught me to drive a car. He strongly disapproved of women at the wheel and especially of the fact that I often drove my husband down to the Treasury and to other places where he, Tom, had friends among the porters and policemen. In time these latter became my friends too. They gave me tips as to which VIPs, foreign and others, might be at No. 10 or the Treasury and they told me when they thought the Governor might be coming downstairs.

There is one member of this household whom I find difficult to describe fairly. This is Miss Roomes, affectionately known to Mont and then to me as E.R. She was his perfect private secretary who came daily from 10 a.m. to 4 p.m. She kept the accounts, paid wages and bills, and recorded the contents of each room in her beautiful handwriting. She noted the prices the item were bought, or if it was a gift she recorded the name of the donor and the date on which it was given. I still have the book in which she recorded each item of furniture that came to Plodge, and the English and Latin names of the various woods which Mont bought for it, with their country of origin.

She was a quiet little middle-aged woman, very neat in appearance. Her short, grey hair which was rather curly, was cleverly arranged with a ribbon which kept in place any curls which tended to stray. Her eyes were dark grey and piercing. At times they held a mocking smile, but they were always enigmatic.

Post-Marital Vagaries

She welcomed me, and I think she approved of me because I was connected with social work and with helping the underprivileged! Mont had trained her to his requirements and so they had a fixed routine, and worked happily and harmoniously together. Punctually every Friday at 10 a.m. Mont went through the accounts with E.R., signed cheques, briefly discussed the weather, and listened to any problems she might have to tell. As she was a deeply philosophical woman, there were never any difficulties! I once asked him how he had acquired this extraordinary little lady and he answered that he had inherited her from a friend who was in trouble. I never enquired further, and together with the family and friends I accepted her as an endearing mystery. I believed she lived alone somewhere beyond Edgware. I only discovered her address during the war, when I insisted that we must be able to communicate with one another in case either of us were bombed. She had no telephone and did not wish to have one. She was in some ways lovable but she was not a cosy person. She had a strange aloofness which seemed to say "Thus far and no further". E.R. was teetotal, a vegetarian and a homeopathist, so my connections with doctors and hospitals were anathema to her, but she did once overcome her scruples when she came to see me in St. Mary's hospital just after the war, bringing me some flowers. I was very fond of her and I relied on her. She was extremely efficient and helped me with my paper work and of course she dealt with the financial side of running the house as well as Mont's work. The Bank and Mont's accountants and solicitors greatly admired her, and this side of her work was efficiency personified. After Mont died, his trustees and I gave her a cheque for £1,000. This she firmly refused, saying that she knew that I would understand . . . She kept in touch with me for many years. I always had a letter-Christmas card from her, until one day a nephew wrote to say that she had died peacefully and that she had asked him to inform me of this when the time came.

E.R. practised her socialism and lived out a faith which she rarely mentioned. Somehow I failed to get inside her curious little shell—perhaps I never tried enough . . .

And now, what about this man who married me so late in

In the Way of Understanding

life and whom this little band served so loyally? What was he like to live with, and what did he look like?

He was very handsome and distinguished-looking, as has already been mentioned in my quotations from Sir Robert Horne and Philip Snowden. He was courteous to a fault to everybody, regardless of their class or colour. His temper was quick and passionate and, as one of his bank colleagues said to me: "You could not have made him more lovable, but you have made him more liveable!" He was unpredictable, and therefore exciting to live with. He was always either up in the heights or down in the depths. I shared both these experiences with him, realising that to go up to the heights one must first experience the depths. He was also full of fun when in good health and on holiday, and he was a great tease. He never found it easy to explain or to justify himself. He made an ideal subject for cartoonists, and he took pride in his appearance, which revealed evidence of old-fashioned personal valeting. The author of *Lord Norman*, Sir Henry Clay, says in his last chapter:

> to all this, the one great exception was his hat, and even his hat need not have attracted any particular notice on a hat peg: an orthodox black felt, somewhat wide in the brim but quite at home with its neighbours. Yet, when he put it on, it suddenly became vocal. To say that he put it on is to give a false impression of what actually happened. He would sling it into the air somewhere in the neighbourhood of his head and it would land miraculously as in a juggling trick but at any sort of angle; and so he liked to leave it as though to illustrate his principle that responsibility should always lie where it falls. His hat gave him the appearance of reckless irresponsibility—of Bohemian eccentricity—which helped to foster the common belief that he was more of an artist than a banker, and inevitably it caught the eye more readily than other features of his outward appearance.[1]

---

[1] Sir Henry Clay, *Lord Norman*, Macmillan & Co. Ltd., London 1957.

Post-Marital Vagaries

Mr. E. H. D. Skinner[1], who worked so closely with my husband, once told me that Mont's obsession with orderliness had a philosophical foundation, order being one of the aspects of creation. Happily, orderliness was also part of my upbringing, for my mother was very strict on this point. Tidiness therefore, to a point of obsession, came naturally to me and caused me no hardship.

---

[1] Ernest Harry Dudley Skinner, C.B.E. (b. 1892), Assistant to the Governor 1927–1945.

9
St. Clere: Personalities There and Elsewhere

Before I go on, I think that I should attempt to describe the two beautiful houses, St. Clere, Kernsing, Kent and Moor Place, Much Hadham, Hertfordshire, with which my husband had such close ties. He was, however, quite uninterested in owning stately homes and he was much relieved that I was of the same mind.

I believe there had been a house at St. Clere for as long as England had existed. By sequestration, by marriage and by sale the property finally passed in the reign of Charles I into the hands of Sir John Sidley, who, it is said, was responsible for the building of the present house in about 1633. There have of course been additions, alterations and maybe even rebuilding on the same site, but the Aldham (meaning "homestead" in Anglo-Saxon), took the name of St. Clere from the 14th century owners. It is a plain two and a half storey mansion built of mellow red brick, laid in English bond. It resembles Chevening, another well known house in Kent. St. Clere was bought by my husband's grandfather in 1882. It is spacious inside, with a lovely curving staircase rising from a big square hall, now panelled with scraped pitch pine. The proportions are good, the rooms are large and the building tapers to the third floor, where the servants had their quarters. From every room there is a glorious view over the Weald of Kent. My husband loved St. Clere in many ways, having been there a good deal as a child with his grandfather and grandmother. He was devoted to them, and they treated him more as a son than a grandson. Their relationship was curiously close, although I believe the old man was far from easy to get on with. He also had been Governor of the Bank of England. To me, and I believe to Mont, it was not a cosy house or one with a peaceful

St. Clere: Personalities There and Elsewhere

atmosphere and it could never have been our home. The present owners, Sir Mark Collet (Mont's uncle) and his second wife Violet were considerable gardeners and she had grown irises professionally in Massachusetts, U.S.A. The grounds are therefore filled with rare plants and trees.

By contrast, Moor Place has great charm and a warm and welcoming atmosphere. Thanks to the shortcomings of the railway service, Much Hadham has retained a rural atmosphere and the village has a life of its own, despite cottages now owned by commuters. It lies in the vale of the river Ash, midway between Ware and Bishop's Stortford. There are many beautiful "gentlemen's houses" but I believe that architecturally Moor Place is the most important. Certainly I fell in love with it on my first visit to the cottage before our marriage, when Mont took me to look at it late one night on our way back from a big official party at County Hall. There was a full moon, the night was dead still, and even at that hour it was very warm. We sat for a while under the very old oak tree on the lawn, perhaps a relic of the days of Hatfield Forest. It was like being in a fairy story. The beautiful rosy brick of the Georgian house, with the date 1779 over the front door, was very attractive. There was a lovely fanlight over the front door, and on the South side, as we wandered about, I saw an even more lovely fanlight, above a graceful branching staircase which led up to French windows in the drawing room.

Later I found Moor Place to be as beautiful inside as it is outside. The rooms are perfectly proportioned, with high ceilings in the reception rooms. My mother-in-law, Mrs. L. S. P. Norman, told me that she had persuaded her husband to buy the house because of the glorious white marble chimney pieces in all the reception rooms. The friezes in all the main rooms are of the Adam style. They are very beautiful—neither vulgar nor too ornate. To me Moor Place is a lovable and beloved house with a happy atmosphere. It always gave Mont much happiness to watch his brother Ronnie and his family in "the Nest" as he called it. The Nest still goes on, with many fledglings having fled the nest but with others still arriving. The old oak has weathered much since I first paid it my respects, the copper beeches and the cedars have grown immeasurably, the

In the Way of Understanding

garden cottage has gone, and a garden house has taken its place. The kitchen garden with its old mulberry is now a well-planned formal garden. Toby, Mark's wife, is rightly proud of her "improvements" but I feel that some of the old charm and atmosphere has disappeared. It is perhaps difficult for a younger generation to realise the love Mont and I felt for the little old cottage. "Plus ça change mais plus ce n'est pas la même chose" is how I would see it.

Now to the personalities referred to above. I have earlier mentioned the Collets and their home, St. Clere, where we often spent weekends when we were not going to Mont's cottage in the gardens of Moor Place. May I stress that Mark Collet and Mont were more like brothers than uncle and nephew. Mont and I were completely happy with the ideal arrangement for the use of the cottage at Moor Place, but Mark was not happy about this. He felt worried and anxious because we had no country seat and because Mont had made over Moor Place and the farm to his brother Ronnie long before his marriage. We ourselves felt that we had all the advantages—a London house with a small domestic staff, and a country cottage in lovely grounds for exercise and interest. We were free of responsibility at weekends, in a place where we could cast out all cares and enjoy family life, friends and a village community. But it was not to last.

Ronnie and his wife Florrie accepted the fact that Mont and I were completely happy with the arrangement, which included Ronnie coming to Plodge during the week for his B.B.C. and L.C.C. work, and Florrie for her occasional visits to London. Mark Collet, however, grew more dissatisfied and anxious.

He was getting on in years and was keen to shed his considerable responsibilities, which included his work for Kent County Council and the onerous task of being Chairman of the Education Committee in this large county. He conceived the idea of handing over St. Clere to Mont, with its extensive acreage of park and woodlands, while he himself moved to the Isle of Man, the home of his forbears. He discussed these matters with Mont in secret, not even telling his wife. Mont discussed them very vaguely with me and I

St. Clere: Personalities There and Elsewhere

never really realised the full implications of the arrangement until after it had become a fait accompli.

I was greatly shattered, because, as readers may already have surmised, I am not the stuff of which chatelaines are made. A big staff of indoor and outdoor servants was not my idea of pleasure. I realised too late that I should have queried and discussed this proposal much earlier, to see whether another solution could be found. Now we had St. Clere with all its problems, legal and otherwise; a burden that Mont, at his age and with his commitment to the Bank of England should never have been asked to bear. It meant that at weekends, when he was tired and had a brief-case full of work, he also had to face his agent, farm manager and head gardener, all of whom had problems to discuss and were asking for decisions to be made. I too had problems, for now, instead of simply enjoying the Moor Park cottage at weekends I had to face staff queries, weekend parties and the rest, without the kind of understanding and devoted staff I had in London. This was because St. Clere staff were new to me and I was unknown to them, having so recently come into the family.

Mark Collet jokingly referred to me as the "new circumstance", for if Mont had remained a bachelor the decisions taken about the future of St. Clere might have been different. The neighbours were very welcoming, and thought it would be useful to have the new circumstance take part in local affairs, but the new circumstance thought otherwise. At the time I was heavily involved with the future of the mental health service and spent much of my time in London.

Our move from a cottage to a big house duly took place, and life was now all too full of responsibilities. But there were compensations for this on our week-days in London, where I met many interesting people who were to make history in world affairs. Though what would be called social life in the beau monde was an anathema to Mont and to me, we often did go out, as our duty, into that world, and we occasionally entertained important personalities at Plodge in a modest way.

I met the Prime Minister, Stanley Baldwin, on several occasions and this was always an enjoyable experience. Sometimes, if he and Mont were lunching at the Athenaeum, I would join

In the Way of Understanding

them after lunch for a chat. Mont admired his integrity and had a deep affection for him. He was certainly ponderous, perhaps lazy, but he understood the British people and his heart was always with them, even in the General Strike. They too knew his worth, and it was only the intellectuals and the snobs who could not understand him. Recently it has given me much satisfaction to read a biography[1] written by two completely unbiased historians who had examined the facts on which history must ultimately judge Stanley Baldwin. There were many references to Mont in this book, showing the admiration and indeed love, which he and Baldwin had for each other. There is a splendid chapter on the Abdication of Edward VIII a little of which sad story I knew from Mont and Sir Edward Peacock.[2] It shows clearly the delicate way in which Baldwin saved the monarchy. To have kept the country from revolution at the time of the General Strike—as I still think he did—and to have saved the Crown would have been enough good work by any Prime Minister. But in my humble opinion he did much more for the workers of this country, and one day this will be acknowledged. I found his dear lady rather trying, and she obviously thought I was a silly young thing who had just caught the Governor. I never got as close to her as I did to her husband, but undoubtedly they were devoted to each other, and walked about arm-in-arm when we saw them at Chequers. Poor lady, she and her family must have suffered infinite distress when the British people to whom he had given his life treated him so shabbily during the Second World War—a war for which he was much less responsible than many others on whom no blame has been laid.

A very happy occasion was when we were bidden to dine and sleep at Windsor Castle during the reign of George VI and Queen Elizabeth. As on all the royal occasions in which I have been privileged to take part, the household staff acted as perfect hosts, making it all seem straightforward by explaining the proper procedure, and the etiquette that was expected of us. The Prime Minister, Stanley Baldwin and his lady were

[1] Keith Middlemas & John Barnes, *Baldwin*, Weidenfeld & Nicolson, 1969.
[2] Sir Edward Peacock, D.C.V.O., b. 1871 20 years a Director of Bank of England.

St. Clere: Personalities There and Elsewhere

there, also the Italian Ambassador, and his lady, with various other VIPs. After dinner, when the ladies retired, I was led up to sit with Queen Mary. Either she had been well briefed or had briefed herself, for she seemed to know all about me. She also knew my Aunt May and Uncle Edmond Fitzalan who were now living at Cumberland Lodge in the Great Park. She knew of my interest in education and expressed her own strong views on the subject of bringing up children, including her grandchildren. She felt that the present day trend was far too permissive, although she did not use that word, and hoped I agreed.

Later I sat for a while on a sofa and talked to Queen Elizabeth, who so lately had joined the Royal Family. She was the charming lady we have all come to love over the years, with her fascinating smile and quick response. She much admired the parrure of semi-precious stones which Mont had designed, and which had been made up for me by that superb craftswoman, Sybil Dunlop of Church Street, Kensington. She asked to handle the brooch and to write down the name and address of the maker. She half rose to get a pencil and paper and then suddenly remembered that she should summon a Lady-in-Waiting. Her Majesty laughingly told me that not to be free to do things for herself was one of the hardest lessons she had yet to learn. I was puzzled by her request, saying that my humble but lovely jewels could not compare with the magnificence and history of the royal gems. She smiled that lovely smile, saying—"Ah yes, but they belong to the Crown and I like to have things of my own."

My turn then came to be taken to sit with the King, and I was tremendously impressed by his intimate knowledge of current affairs, both international and domestic. He had already read all the happenings in the House of Commons that afternoon. His stammer was beautifully controlled and except for a rather slow way of speaking one would never have guessed that he suffered so grave a defect for a king. He impressed on me that Mont should not work so hard, but take more time for relaxation. This was very thoughtful of him, considering how hard he worked himself and the obvious time he had already taken to brief himself on the interests of his guests.

In the Way of Understanding

The next morning I was taken on a personally conducted tour of some parts of the castle which are not normally seen by the public, and to meet the royal children and dogs. It was a fascinating visit, the memory of which I cherish.

Perhaps the King's remarks made me take the problem of relaxation seriously, so with Ronnie Norman's help a cruise to the West Indies was arranged. He suggested that we include Sir John and Lady Reith, but Mont and I were dubious, as the then Director General of the B.B.C., though an intellectual stimulus, could be a formidable personality to cope with for three weeks! However, Reith jumped at the suggestion and Ronnie, then Chairman of the B.B.C., was wickedly thankful to be rid of this "turbulent priest" who so enjoyed overworking, and therefore made everyone else suffer the consequences of his own overstrain and depression. As it turned out, Lady Reith would not come. (I suspect she needed a rest from her demanding husband). I therefore invited a great friend of mine, Lena Ashwell, the widow of Sir Henry Simson, the royal accoucheur who had also brought my Peregrine into the world. She had been a well-known actress and was therefore much interested in the arts, had a considerable wit and sense of humour and was a good conversationalist. In fact, she was the ideal companion to help me deal with these two unpredictable lions!

Dinner got off to a sticky start on the first night because Reith—who we were to call Walsham, his second name—liked to conduct a conversation by question and answer, never listening to the answer. It was an infuriating habit which Lena and I resented, and said so! As we needed to have a quiet and peaceful holiday the Captain kindly arranged for us to have our meals in the Officers' Mess, away from the rest of the passengers who, not unnaturally, called us the untouchables.

Lena, (whom Mont now called "No P", because when asked her name, would say "Lady Simson without a P") had had much experience in leading theatre and concert parties visiting the Front during the First World War to entertain the troops. This was a precursor of E.N.S.A. in the 1939–1945 war, but was run on a shoe-string with little or no help from Government sources. Lena maintained, against strong opposition from the high-ups in the Services, that the Tommies would

. Clere, a drawing by Studiati-Beini

The Norman clan plus Simon and Peregrine

oor Place, a drawing y P. Studiati-Beini

Cruising in Jamaica (L. to R.) Lord Reith Mont, Lena Ashwell (Lady Simson) and myself

Plodge garden in summer

St. Clere: Personalities There and Elsewhere

respond to Shakespeare, good plays and classical music and she was amply vindicated by full houses and enthusiastic applause from audiences. Thus, Nope's varied experience amongst many different people and in many parts of the world made her a delightful companion. At times she was more than a little critical of the B.B.C., so the sparks flew!

Walsham was teetotal, and very standoffish at first. Gradually he was thawed by our unconventionality, and took a little whisky before dinner and even a glass of wine. He also learned to mix with some of the passengers, at which times a smile would transform his granite face. I became very fond of him and even to love him when, after some silly quarrel when he had been intolerable, he slipped into my cabin, unseen except by Mont, and laid a huge bunch of Parma violets on my pillow. He had been on shore at Lisbon especially to buy them.

We visited Jamaica, had a fascinating trip through the Panama Canal, and I saw the Pacific for the first time. After our return from the cruise Walsham often came to dinner, full of complaints and asking for advice which he never took. He seemed to relax at Plodge and always invited himself when things had gone especially wrong for him, such as when he retired from the B.B.C., was unhappy as head of B.O.A.C. and was finally dismissed without notice by Churchill.

After his death I attended, with Mary Stocks, his friend and mine, the Memorial Service arranged by the B.B.C. in Westminster Abbey. The choice of music was imaginative and beautiful. The Prelude to *The Dream of Gerontius* interpreted the agony of mind Reith so often imposed upon himself, and his spirit might have been moved by the Lament played by a Scottish piper in full highland dress, from the East end of the Abbey, down through the choir and nave and out of the West door. It was truly dramatic and as Mary whispered to me: "How he would have enjoyed the Service"! Perhaps he did; anyway the theme on the service paper—"Nation shall speak peace unto Nation" was appropriate to the first Director General of the B.B.C. who sowed the seeds of integrity and commitment to public service which, in part at any rate, survives to this day.

On returning from our cruise the social round started again

In the Way of Understanding

and I remember one occasion when we were invited to the German Embassy and met the Ambassador, von Ribbentrop. Sir Josiah Stamp[1] joined us (he was later killed by a bomb) and as we chatted to von Ribbentrop I had a most curious sensation which shook me and made me feel sick and faint. It was as if someone were tapping me on the shoulder and saying: "Never forget this moment—you are in the presence of Evil". When we were driving home I told Mont of this horrible experience and he laughed rather sardonically, saying that I must really not let my imagination run away with me. The memory of this experience came back vividly during the Nuremberg trials.

Perhaps this is where I should mention Hjalmar Schacht, called Horace by Mont and many colleagues at the Bank. In contrast to Ribbentrop this man was not, I think, a sinister figure. He was President of the Reichsbank and Mont admired him and in turn he was devoted to Mont. They met monthly in Basle for meetings of the Bank for International Settlements, when world finance was discussed by the Governors of national banks. Mont considered them to be one of his most important commitments and he never missed a meeting. They took place at weekends when, often very tired, he travelled by boat and train as I did not like him flying. Horace was an extraordinary man, tall, broad-shouldered and very ugly, with a tremendous streak of egocentricity. I met him soon after my marriage. He had asked us both to Berlin because Mont had accepted an invitation to be godfather to his grandson. The child was the son of his only daughter, who was married to a man on the staff of the German Embassy in London. This was in 1933 when Hitler had recently come to power. Schacht was definitely against the Nazi regime and all that it stood for, especially its diabolical anti-Jewish campaign. The small christening ceremony took place in the Governor's parlour in the Reichsbank. It was a simple service, with just the relatives and a very few friends and colleagues of the Schacht family. I was told that the pastor had given a moving address about the

---

[1] 1st Baron Stamp (1880–1941), leading statistician and Director of Bank of England.

St. Clere: Personalities There and Elsewhere

Christian virtues of brotherly love, stressing peace and tolerance amongst the nations. At the luncheon party afterwards in a hotel Dr. Schacht talked politics to me in a loud voice, despite the presence of the waiters who might so easily have denounced him. If the politicians and the dictator had been prepared to leave this undoubtedly able man (perhaps too clever by half) to work out a solution, who knows whether the tragic war that ensued might have been averted?

I believe that Dr. Schacht was sincere. When he came to stay at Plodge after Munich he shocked and angered me by saying that we should have gone to war at that time, and not postponed the decision, since things would now be far worse. Remembering the 1914–1918 war only too clearly I was horrified, but there are many people today who believe that Chamberlain's policy was a disaster. Maybe Schacht remained in the Nazi circle because he believed he could check some of the worst excesses and rally the few saner people in its ranks. He failed dismally and was one of those who stood trial at Nuremberg, although he escaped the death penalty. He came to see me after Mont's death when he must have been over 80. He was still upstanding, still egocentric, still arrogant despite his years of imprisonment. I only caught a glimpse of his inner soul when in sympathising over Mont's death he almost broke down. I was left deeply moved and shattered, and was haunted by the thought of the futility and tragedy of war.

Clouds were forming over Europe, and Mont realised that St. Clere would be a house likely to be requisitioned for hospital purposes in case of war. Because of my close association with the Rachel McMillan Nursery School, we considered lending it to the School should it be evacuated. This was especially apposite as part of the School was already housed at Wrotham, only a few miles away. The Committee and staff welcomed the idea, so when the time came we had delightful tenants. We kept just a few rooms for ourselves, so that we could stay there when necessary in order to cope with estate matters.

Stark Reality

10
Clouds Gathering and War in 1939

In peace there's nothing so becomes a man
As modest stillness and humility:
But when the blast of war blows in our ears,
Then imitate the action of the tiger;
Stiffen the sinews, summon up the blood
William Shakespeare, *Henry V*, Act II, Sc. 1.

By 1937 the international situation was looking increasingly stormy and there was concern about civil defence. Stella Reading, widow of the first Marquis of Reading, Viceroy of India, was invited to the Home Office to discuss the formation of a Women's Voluntary Service for Civil Defence. (It was later called simply the Women's Voluntary Service and after the war the Women's Royal Voluntary Service). Sir Samuel Hoare, the then Home Secretary (later Lord Templewood), and other members of the Government were seriously worried about the situation. After protracted discussions the outcome was a bold, imaginative scheme to recruit women volunteers from all over the British Isles to help with civil defence and air raid protection in the likely event of war. Lady Reading was made Chairman and in 1938 I was invited to be Vice-Chairman. Because of my experience on the L.C.C. I was given special responsibility for London and the Home Counties.

There were six of us who, I think, could be said to be the original founder-members of this great national movement, together with the unforgettable Miss Blampied, Lady Reading's invaluable secretary, without whom we should never have got going so quickly or so efficiently. I remember Miss Blampied typing endless reports, sitting at old tables in odd corners and taking dictation in taxis and trains. She once said to me in despair: "That woman (Lady Reading) can recruit *thousands* of women in the twinkling of an eye, yet I want only

In the Way of Understanding

one man and can't find him!" With her wit and attractiveness I hope she found the lucky man.

Miss Smieton, later Dame Mary Smieton, came to the W.V.S. from the Ministry of Labour as our permanent secretary and civil service administrator. She was a remarkable, calm and unflappable lady, an Oxford graduate, who later became Permanent Secretary to the Ministry of Education. She dealt most efficiently and diplomatically with a stream of enthusiastic amateurs and I have always had a great admiration and affection for her. Her job was a difficult one and she carried it out to perfection.

In my responsibilities for London I had the support of the late Mrs. Creswick Atkinson who at that time was busy training volunteers in civil defence for the Red Cross. Her knowledge of local government in London was invaluable and she advised me to visit all the Boroughs, and especially their civil defence advisers. This was a big undertaking and involved a good deal of diplomacy, for in 1938 there were still officials and their Councils who could not see the writing on the wall. Lady Reading with her unrivalled flair for picking the right person persuaded Miss Kathleen Halpin, who had a full time job organising the Woman's Gas Council[1] and was a keen member of the Girl Guide movement, to come to join me as Head of the Metropolitan Division and she became my right hand.

Our first important job was to appoint regional administrators, regional organisers and borough and county organisers, corresponding to the Civil Defence organisations all over the country. The local authorities were empowered to give accommodation in their offices to W.V.S. personnel and the government provided for the franking of letters and for telephone expenses. No salaries were paid except to the regional organisers, but later reasonable expenses were allowed.

The evacuation of children from London at the outbreak of war was the first operation assigned to the W.V.S. It was carried out with military precision. Children wearing identity

---

[1] Now Women's Gas Federation and Young Homemakers, 29 Gt. Peter St., London W.1.

Clouds Gathering and War in 1939

labels reported to their teachers on the platforms of London stations and were carried off to safety in the country by trains leaving according to well-planned timetables. The mission was accomplished successfully, with great support from the Women's Institutes. But although no alternative action seemed possible at the time, I could not feel entirely happy about it. My experience in the world of child guidance made me question the wisdom of this separation of many of the children from their families. Two years later I was to discover that my fears were not unfounded.

I made some life-long friends while working in the W.V.S. Besides dear Kathleen Halpin there was the late Lindsey Huxley, the able first wife of Gervas Huxley, but my closest friend of all was the late Lady Iris Capell, then head of the Transport Service. She succeeded me as Vice-Chairman in 1941. Her sense of the comic, her truthfulness and her wisdom endeared her to everyone but, like me, she was never one hundred per cent in sympathy with the W.V.S. and she only wore uniform when this was de rigueur.

It is easy with hindsight to be conscious of mistakes. In my opinion a critical mistake was made by the government during the early negotiations, in not realising the depth of hostility which would be felt by the many already existing voluntary organisations and associations in the U.K. at the formation of yet another voluntary body—a body moreover which was to receive considerable financial backing such as they themselves had never received. They deeply resented this upstart which appeared to be cashing in on the war with premises and telephone expenses paid for by the government. The Red Cross and St. John Ambulance Brigade were particularly vulnerable, as were the Women's Institutes, but in the event all co-operated most loyally, especially with the evacuation scheme. Lady Reading's dynamic personality and her determination never to take 'No' for an answer; the friendship she cultivated with members of the Cabinet, and her hospitality, enabled her to achieve her objectives. She was a remarkably able woman, never missing a trick and the country in war-time owed her a tremendous debt of gratitude. I, for one, salute her memory in sincere admiration.

In the Way of Understanding

The experience I gained in the W.V.S. gave me a valuable insight into the work of local authorities, not only in London but also through my travels about the country urging people to take civil defence seriously. The magnificent administrative structure conceived by the Home Office and copied by Lady Reading was useful to me later in my work with Miss Fox and the Emergency Committee for Mental Health.

During my time as Vice-Chairman of the W.V.S. I was their representative in the National Council of Social Service (N.C.S.S.). It was a difficult and at times delicate situation for me as the hostility towards the W.V.S. which was shown by the representatives of voluntary organisations, and especially the women's organisations, was obvious. At that time the N.C.S.S was under the remarkable and able chairmanship of the Warden of All Souls, Dr. Adams, C. H. These were also the days of Sir Wyndham Deedes, Sir Ernest Barker, Lord Lindsay of Birker and my brother-in-law, R. C. Norman. Sir George Haynes was the able Secretary who, until his retirement, was to play such an important part in making it possible for all the voluntary organisations and associations to voice their opinions through the Council to government departments and to the public in general. On the Executive Committee debate and discussions were of a high academic quality. This was only natural, given such great minds, and to me it was one of the most exciting and worth-while committees on which I have ever been privileged to sit.

As the W.V.S. representative my task was to try to explain that the W.V.S. was supposed to co-operate closely with all the organisations, and to work with anyone and everyone willing to help in the war effort—for our whole title was Women's Voluntary Service for Civil Defence and was thus all-embracing. Unfortunately the emotional reaction of the long-standing voluntary organisations and especially the women's organisations—just emerging as a force for emancipation—was overtly hostile to the W.V.S. and its chairman. To me however, they were always courteous and even kind. I was forced to admit to myself that our critics had a point, Lady Reading, like Churchill as war-time leader, had no time for democracy. She made swift decisions without consulting her

Clouds Gathering and War in 1939

committee, and this influenced my eventual resignation. It was a great relief when capable Kathleen Halpin took over from me when I left the service.

During the difficulties the N.C.S.S. tried to pour oil on troubled waters and to reduce the heat of controversy. In the end, after discussion with government departments, and with Lady Reading's agreement, they decided to set up a committee, to be called the Women's Group on Public Welfare, to deal with problems arising from evacuation. That remarkable and wise little lady, the Rt. Hon. Margaret Bondfield, J. P., LL.D., Minister of Labour in the first Labour Government, was to take the chair, and to my astonishment I was made Vice-Chairman. Letty Harford, the Chief Woman Officer of the N.C.S.S., was made Secretary.

Maggie, as we came to call her, started the first meeting by calling for a "silence and a few minutes of reflection to gather strength to find and make wise decisions". This certainly set the stage for this miscellaneous gathering of women, and we were an extraordinarily harmonious group. The silence was subsequently always the first item on our agenda and this precedent was followed by successive chairmen and is still I hope the practice today. It was quite a moving experience, and I am sure it contributed to peaceful discussion and an almost universal agreement in formulating resolutions.

The first task of the Women's Group on Public Welfare was to set up a Committee which was to take evidence and to hear grievances arising from the evacuation of children from cities to the country. This committee worked diligently and produced its findings in a report which became famous, entitled *Our Towns: A Close-up, A Study Made During 1939–42* (O.U.P. 1943). It described the first exodus which took place hurriedly in 1939. Town and city children were bundled, with scant preparation and with no medical examination, into the country. They fled from the various parts of London, from the docks and from their homes near railway lines and gas works—as it seemed for dear life. The reception areas in the country and the nation as a whole saw the people of the towns, some the 'lowest of the low', as never before. It was a sad and depressing sight which filled the country hostesses with a

In the Way of Understanding

burning zeal to improve their conditions, exposed as they were for the first time to the gaze of the general public. It all came as a great shock, although much of it was not unknown to social workers. What was seen was perhaps only a submerged tenth of the total situation of children in the towns, many of whom had been living in dirt and vermin, ill clad and ill shod. The hostesses were alarmed and their visitors were not always quick to settle, so complaints emanated from both sides. In the report's Introduction it said "This book has no pretension to literary merit, it is addressed to readers with stout stomachs who appreciate facts, including the unpleasant". And certainly many unpleasant facts were revealed.

Looking back now I am amazed that the eight women on this Committee—all doing a full-time professional job—found time and energy to work often late into the night during heavy periods of bombing to produce the report. An able civil servant, Miss D. Ibberson, was the inspiration. I know that at the time her department frowned on her interest, and her part in the report was hushed up and only became known after the war. The Russell Sage Foundation of New York financed the publication and Mrs. St. Loe Strachey gave invaluable help in its preparation. It is now out of print. This is unfortunate because much of what it revealed would be of tremendous value to students of social history and child psychiatry.

By this time St. Clere had been handed over to the Margaret McMillan Nursery School and was fully occupied by about 100 children under five, who had been evacuated from Deptford. Mont and I kept only a few rooms for an occasional weekend in order to keep contact with estate and farm matters. It was a curious and at times comical experience to see the Governor of the Bank of England emerging from his bedroom to weave his way amongst these little ones charging about the polished landing floor on their potties!

In October 1940 Plodge was bombed. It was a horrid experience, and came on a night when we and our devoted staff were all sleeping in the parts of the house considered most suitable to resist blast. So, although we were shocked, no one was injured. During the repairs to the damaged building Mont and I moved to the garden cottage at Moor Place, taking with

Clouds Gathering and War in 1939

us Nellie and Edith, a housemaid, christened "The Mouse" by Mont because she was always on her knees cleaning and polishing. Dear old Mrs. B. had retired to a flat in the country. Mont slept in the Bank during the week with hundreds of other employees for at that period the bombing was heavy. I commuted from Hadham station and on one winter evening, while walking home through a field I fell over a cow, losing my precious committee papers and provisions in the mud. I don't know which was the more indignant, me or the poor cow!

Moor Place was choc-a-bloc with the Normans and their children—quite a nursery school. Ronnie's daughters-in-law, Margaret and Toby, whose husbands, Hugh and Mark, were soldiers, were living there. My two sons were also in the army, and Simon later became a prisoner of war. Dear Ronnie Norman, now known as the Patriarch, presided lovingly over his children, grand-children, flocks and herds. Florrie, alas, had died before the war, mourned by all, including the whole of Hadham village.

During the time that I was associated with the N.C.S.S., the Citizen's Advice Bureaux were born. I was a member of a small select committee under the chairmanship of R. C. Norman, with Miss Dorothy Keeling as its Secretary. The C.A.B. gave invaluable service during the war and are still rendering useful service today. Miss Keeling was a splendid, hard working Secretary but she had strong political views of Socialist persuasion. She viewed me with grave suspicion and was heard to say how sorry she was to think of my being married to "that dreadful man, Montagu Norman". She had of course been fed on political socialist slogans, "bankers' ramp", and so on. One day I took my husband up to see her unexpectedly. He entered into the fun of it and afterwards they became firm friends. He teased her unmercifully and she thoroughly enjoyed it.

The W.V.S. and the N.C.S.S. occupied most of my time, but what little was spare was seized by Miss Fox. She made me take the chair of the Mental Health Emergency Committee, which was anticipating the implementation of the recommendations of the Feversham Report. Miss Fox's strong personality and remarkable influence overcame the inhibitions and fears of the other mental health organisations, and we were united in our common war effort. She and I worked together in a rather scrappy little office in Buckingham Palace Road, Miss Fox being the undoubted boss. Here I learned the facts about mental ill-health, the difference between mental illness and mental deficiency, and of the jealousies between professionals trained in different schools of thought—Freudian, Jungian, Adlerian, and so on. I met the leading professionals in the movement at that time, including some who were very young and were just going into the Forces. I listened to discussions and heard reports from the twelve Regional representatives. These were all psychiatric social workers, appointed at the request of the government departments concerned, and financed by them. Their work included the care of evacuated children, either in institutions or billeted on local inhabitants, many of whom faced emotional problems of separation from their families. The Regional Representatives also dealt with patients discharged from the Services or from psychiatric hospitals after mental breakdown. These patients had to be encouraged, whenever possible, to get back to work to help with the war effort. Employers and management needed to understand the difficulties of such people. This was a difficult task, and these psychiatric social workers were helped by other social workers and by many volunteers who, under expert guidance, proved invaluable. Perhaps this was one of the first instances of professional workers using volunteers: it was certainly so in the mental health service.

11

My Husband's Illness, Retirement and Convalescence in Isle of Man and Later in South Africa

There is a great change coming, bound to come. The whole money arrangement will undergo a change: what, I don't know. The whole industrial system will undergo a change. Work will be different and pay will be different. The owning of property will be different. Class will be different, and human relations will be modified and perhaps simplified.

If we are intelligent, alert and undaunted, then life will be much better, more generous, more spontaneous, more vital, less basely materialistic. If we fall into a state of funk, impotence and persecution, then things may be very much worse than they are now. It is up to us. It is up to men to be men. While men are courageous and willing to change, nothing terribly bad can happen.

D. H. Lawrence (1885–1930), *Assorted Articles*.

In January 1944 my husband became critically ill with meningitis. He was one of the three "guinea pig" patients to receive the new pioneer penicillin treatment—one being a baby, one a young airman and the third, an elderly man, my husband. During this traumatic experience I met Alexander Fleming, the discoverer of penicillin; Sir Hugh Cairns who performed the brain operation; Dr. George Riddoch, the neurologist, and Lord Moran, all exceptionally gifted men whose understanding and sympathy during this terrible crisis in my life I shall never forget. I was also much encouraged and sustained by our tireless G.P., Dr. Zoe Leitner—a refugee from Hungary—and by Miss Fraser-Gamble, now Chief Nursing Officer at Hammersmith Post-graduate Hospital, and at that time a student nurse at St. Mary's, Paddington.

It all arose one nightmare weekend at Moor Place when Mont was alone. I was struggling back from staying with my

In the Way of Understanding

mother in Lancashire during a bad fog in early January. He had apparently opened a gate in the drive for the car that had been sent to Much Hadham station to fetch him back to the cottage. He had fallen over a large granite stone, grazing his leg badly, and had neglected to clean it properly. Later, he walked to the station, which was about a mile away, to meet me. I was very late because of the fog. I found him distressed and more weary than usual. I cleaned his wound and he made light of it, but I could see he was not his usual self. As far as I can remember we motored up to London on the Monday. He insisted on going to the Bank and then to dine with his mother that evening, even though hardly able to stand.

He had a very bad night and had a high temperature by the morning. On the Tuesday our G.P., Dr. Leitner, diagnosed something serious and asked Lord Moran to see Mont at once. Lord Moran had him admitted immediately to the Lindo wing at St. Mary's hospital, which was where the experiments with penicillin were taking place. A delightful young nurse came with the ambulance and took as much care of me as of her patient. This extraordinary exhibition of the perfect nurse struck me forcibly at the time and I was not surprised at her rise to fame later.

In a tiny room the consultants were gathered together. Mont was by now unconscious. Sir Alexander Fleming and I stood huddled miserably in a corner and I whispered to him, "Will there be enough penicillin?" for at that time I knew it was an extremely rare commodity. He smiled a sweet, gentle smile and assured me that treatment was never started unless they were sure of enough serum. The "high-ups" around the bed were talking in low tones and one of them was explaining that Mont was now incontinent. At that, the young nurse cried out, "Excuse me, Sir, he is not. I always know when he wants a bottle as he raises his hand and squeezes mine, and then afterwards relaxes, having relieved himself." I was always thankful to this nurse. In those days children and nurses spoke only when spoken to, so her interjection must have required real courage in the presence of all those pundits.

A day or two later there had been little improvement, despite the horror of a lumbar puncture, so it was decided to put

My Husband's Illness, Retirement and Convalescence

penicillin into the brain and Sir Hugh Cairns was asked to operate. In his turn he asked his assistant to make up the necessary dose of penicillin. By pure chance this happened to be Dr. The Hon. Honor Smith, Mont's god-daughter. Dr. Moran and Dr. Riddoch[1] explained the situation to me as kindly as possible. It was a tremendous decision for them to have to make. I am thankful to say that at that moment I didn't fully realise the possible consequences. All I wanted was that Mont should live. Had I known more of the dangers of a brain operation of this nature, and its possible after-effects, I should have hesitated. Knowing as much about mental illness as I do now I shudder at my quick decision, but Mont lived, although his health was sadly impaired and the doctors decided that he must retire from the Bank.

This decision was a brutal one for the patient but, looking back, I believe it was right even though at the time I thought otherwise. Many people now believe that Lord Moran[2] should have taken a similar decision for another famous patient. Those responsible for national and international affairs need to be always in full control of their faculties in order to cope with the awesome problems in war, and to have a clear, fresh vision so that they can plan for peace. It is often said that the patient must be a doctor's first consideration. However, I now believe that in war and perhaps at other critical times in history there may be more serious and far-reaching considerations to be made for the good of the whole world.

This was a terrible time for me, for the Bank and for Mont himself. I think that in his heart of hearts he would rather have been left to die. He was heartbroken at having to desert his Old Lady at such a time in her history.

Convalescence took place at Balkmanaugh, Ramsey, Isle of Man, the new home of Mark and Violet Collet—a modern house built for them by Henry Fletcher[3]. It certainly was the best constructed house that I have ever lived in, with good proportions and constructed of first-rate materials, with a

---

[1] George Riddoch, M.D., F.R.C.P.
[2] Lord Moran, M.D., F.R.C.P.
[3] Henry Martineau Fletcher, F.R.I.B.A., (1870–1953).

perfect staircase running all along one side of the house and huge windows looking into the hills.

We spent nine miserable months there, though our hosts were kindness itself. Mont and I hated being idle and being away from the war effort. The plentiful food made us realise that nourishment for the body does not also feed the soul. It is a lovely little island and the garden in which Mark and Violet worked unceasingly was very beautiful. It had a stream running through it, and terraced walls of local stone, with plants of all kinds that were worthy of Kew. But nothing cheered us, the wind blew endlessly and the war news, which we listened to three times a day, was depressing.

Once a month I flew back to my mother in Burnley because she had suffered a stroke. I travelled in a blacked-out plane to Liverpool where I entrained for Burnley, exchanging one set of trouble for another. Nurses had to be found for her but our butler, James Burton, was like a rock to me when the nurses and domestics quarrelled. James was now in the Home Guard and took his duties seriously, going out onto the hills at night but never neglecting his care of my mother by day. He was a wonderful nurse and when in Africa before the war with my mother he had nursed her single-handed for three days and nights until nurses arrived from Johannesburg, hundreds of miles away.

Also at this time my elder son Simon was missing for some weeks but was eventually found to be a prisoner-of-war. Peregrine was preparing to go out on D day, so my life was grim and became more so when Mark Collet had an operation in Liverpool for cancer and died soon after. This left all the legal problems to be faced by Mont and a widow very broken in spirit who had to be coped with by me.

D day came at last and Mont and I felt we must go back to London. We camped partly in Plodge and partly in the garden cottage which was now free again—my mother-in-law had been living there since her house in Kensington was badly bombed but she had now vacated it.

I remember vividly the last of the doodle-bugs that fell near Tottenham Court Road at nine o'clock one morning. I had just finished cleaning the sitting room fireplace and was about to

My Husband's Illness, Retirement and Convalescence

light a match when the sickening thud of the explosion shook me and fine dust enveloped me. Somehow this seems much clearer in my memory than the bombing of Plodge in 1940 which was far worse.

After the war Mont and I moved back into St. Clere. The doodle-bugs had come down thick and fast over Kent and the Rachel MacMillan nursery school which had been evacuated there had moved to a safer area in the North. We still had Plodge but now Mont hated London, having no longer any work or commitment in the City. However, I continued to go to London during the week for various committees. I tried to keep in touch with my child guidance work and with the Mental Health Emergency Committee. I had many domestic and family problems, because we tried to make St. Clere a focus once again for family and friends at weekends. This meant getting domestic staff and this was not easy after the war. My mother too needed visiting at Dyneley. She was now in a wheel chair and depended on me to help her with the property and the farm. Mr. T. A. Miller, who later succeeded Mr. Fraser, was now our invaluable agent and farm manager and was the mainstay of the Worsthorne estate. He taught me much, especially about farming with Ayrshire cattle, and I am grateful to him for his loyalty and hard work over many years. Miss Fox also needed as much of my time as I could spare. Much work was needing to be done in the change-over from war to peace and the full amalgamation of the voluntary mental health services as recommended in the Feversham Report.

During the winter of 1948–1949 Mont and I decided to visit South Africa so that he could continue his convalescence in that glorious country with its lovely climate. While Mont stayed resting in Johannesburg in the house of our hosts, John[1] and Nora Martin, I had time on my hands and welcomed the opportunity to see something of the social services, especially the mental health services, in that great city. This included hospitals, schools and the nursing service, which was just

---

[1] John Martin (1894–1949) Chairman, Argus South Africa Newspaper Group, Director, Bank of England 1937–46.

emerging from the war. All was made easy for me by the South African authorities. I saw the work of the voluntary organisations and the statutory services, for both Black and White communities, and also the welfare services for gold-miners. This included going down one of the biggest gold-mines.

I now felt on the active list again and all that I saw gave me much food for thought.

Looking back at the reports I made at that time for the Provisional National Council for Mental Health and the National Council of Social Service I see that I took every opportunity to visit European and non-European institutions. I made detailed reports on hospitals, native townships, homes for the blind and the deaf and the now-famous Tara Psychiatric Hospital. Iris Marwick, its first matron, became my dear friend, and later joined me on the Executive Board on the World Federation for Mental Health. I also went up to the Northern Transvaal to pack up the Kraal, Lala Panzi, that my mother had built for herself near Tzaneen and where she had spent her winters before the 1939/45 war. Nora Martin took James Burton and me in her car, as we had brought James out with us to valet Mont and to help care for him. James had of course been at Lala Panzi with my mother when she first went out so he knew her Kraal, as she called it, and all the natives were thrilled to see him. He told me amongst many other things of how mother had put him into shorts and an open-necked shirt and red cummerband, despite his hairy legs! But there was nothing he would not do to please Her Ladyship and he now proudly introduced me as her daughter.

The Northern Transvaal scenery was glorious, the Drakensburg mountains were magnificent, and to sit talking on his stoep to an old Boer farmer, Mr. Coetze, was a fascinating experience. He had fought in the Boer War, which he called "the last gentlemen's war" and the tales he told made me feel that this was probably true. The 1914/18 war and the 1939/45 seemed unreal to me and to him, as we sat in the dark on a windless, starlit night, with the old man smoking his clay pipe and endlessly reminiscing. He was a passionate admirer of the British and of their way of life.

From the stoep and garden of Lala Panzi I watched the

My Husband's Illness, Retirement and Convalescence

incredible beauty of the High Veldt. To look down upon the uninterrupted view of hundreds of miles of the Low Veldt made a vivid impression on me. I was reminded of the temptation of Jesus so realistically recounted in the Bible (*Matthew* 4, v. 8). "The devil took Jesus to a very high mountain and showed him all the kingdoms of the earth in their glory. 'All this will I give you', the devil said, 'if you will kneel down and worship me'." This theme kept recurring in my mind while looking at the long distances and endless vistas of that Beloved Country[1]. In the words of John Buchan in *Memory Hold the Door*:

> *Scents, sights and sounds blended into a harmony so perfect that it transcended human expression, even human thought. It was like a glimpse of the peace of eternity.*
>
> *There may be peace without joy and joy without peace but the two combined make Happiness. It was happiness that I knew in those rare moments. The world was a place of inexhaustible beauty but still more it was the husk of something infinite, ineffable and immortal, in very truth, the garment of God.*[1]

The "native question," as it was then called, was uppermost in many people's minds. I see that in 1948 I made certain comments in my reports which are applicable today, so I quote: "It is impossible for those people who have not actually lived in those countries where there is a colour question to understand the finer points involved. First of all, the question is an enormous one and it must be realised that there were two million Europeans in the Union in 1948 and about ten million non-Europeans. These two million have to support the ten million and without a great increase in taxation and social services for the non-Europeans, standards for the non-Europeans cannot begin to compare with those for Europeans. There is the size of the country and the transport difficulties, the divisions in local government betweeen the cities and the

---

[1] Alan Paton, *Cry The Beloved Country*, Chas. Scribner & Son, 1948.
[2] John Buchan, *Memory Hold the Door*, Hodder & Stoughton Ltd., 1940.

In the Way of Understanding

provinces, and the Union Government. It would take too long to go into the native question: it is not merely a question of black and white: there are the Natives, the Coloured, the Malays. There are English and Boers who fought each other in the Boer War which is still very real in South Africa, for the 1914–18 and 1939–45 wars seem of little consequence to them in comparison.

There are the Boers who fought with the British and helped them and they too are looked at askance by the real Boers or Afrikanders, as they now call themselves. In these days, such people would be called 'Quislings'."

In no country is mental health more needed and by 1976, when I returned again, I found that the situation was horrific and that the goodwill and good intentions I had sensed under the Smuts regime were no more. There had been a tragic waste of precious time, and a misunderstanding of the urgency of the racial problem by all political parties. The myopic vision of the governments that succeeded the Smuts regime made me despair of any just or peaceful solution.

Thanks to my husband and our host, John Martin, I was able to meet the then Prime Minister, the Rt. Hon. Field Marshal Jan Smuts. We stayed with him at Groote Schuur, the P.M.'s official residence in Cape Town. My husband and Jan Smuts had fought on opposite sides in the Boer War but here they were, chuckling together, their philosophies being very much the same. Had I been able to see him earlier in our visit he would have arranged various contacts for me, as his word was law at that time and his ideas carried great weight. His quick mind immediately seized on what I wanted to do in the field of mental health and in the social services generally. He picked up the thread of what I told him and was away with it like a kitten with a ball of wool. It was a fascinating experience to watch and one that gave me enormous encouragement. He wanted me to meet the principals of the various universities and was anxious to build up professional standards of social work. Alas, we were leaving the next day but as he bade me "Goodbye" he said in his Afrikaans accent, seriously and almost affectionately: "Come again, my dear child and I will arrange your programme". Unhappily, except for his brief visit to my

My Husband's Illness, Retirement and Convalescence

husband's bedside in 1949, I never saw him again. To meet him was a dramatic experience; he was the greatest mind I have ever been privileged to talk to, except one . . . His quiet understanding and his listening capacity were remarkable. To quote from his *Holism and Evolution*:

> *To be whole is to be real, to be valuable, to be good. This centres in the idea of being whole.*[1]

Not a bad definition of positive mental health! Smuts believed in creative evolution, in the evolution of wholes and in the whole as being something more than the combination of the parts. He saw the universe as "a great community of wholes". He thought those who felt as he did would find that

> *instead of the hostility which is felt in life, this is a friendly universe. We are all interrelated. The one helps the other. It is an idea which gives strength and peace, and is bound to give a more wholesome view of life and nature than we have had so far.*[2]

Later, this very same theme was to be enlarged on by Teilhard de Chardin, the great Jesuit palaeontologist, in his book *The Phenomenon of Man*[3]. These two men had much in common and were known to each other. In 1951 Smuts invited Père Teilhard to visit him, but through illness he was unable to accept the invitation and Smuts had died, I think, before Tielhard eventually went to South Africa.

---

[1] Macmillan & Co., 1926.
[2] *Ibid.*
[3] Wm. Collins, 1959.

Some Post War Activities

12
Justice of the Peace

The psychiatric aspects of crime and juvenile delinquency, dependence on alcohol and other drugs, marital incompatibility, and difficulties at school and at work form part of the mental health problems of any community.
   To Dispel the Myths, World Health Organisation, Geneva, 1977.

Understanding comes more slowly, trailing behind knowledge.
                Cardinal Basil Hume O.S.B., *Searching for God*,
                                Hodder & Stoughton, 1977.

In 1944 I had been made a magistrate and took my fair share of the petty sessional work in my area. In those days magistrates were required under the Mental Treatment Act of 1930 to undertake duties in the locked wards of hospitals for the certification of mental patients. This came as a great shock to me as I had to take the chair at my first such Court without any briefing or proper explanation. The Clerk to the Court and I, plus the hospital psychiatrist, sat in a little room off the ward. A patient would come in with a nurse and sometimes a relative. Details of the case, which I had not seen before, were on the table in front of me. I read rather slowly in those days and the long silence while I acquainted myself with the problem must have seemed interminable. The doctor gave his view, as did the patient if he were able to do so, and so did the relative. It was all farcical and must have seemed strange to all those concerned. I did the best that I could in the circumstances and tried to take the steam out of what often became a heated argument. But I had to administer the law as best I could—happily it was altered by the new Mental Health Act of 1959.

It was not always easy to calm the very real fears of the patient and relative. Most likely the patient would have been brought in by the police or the mental welfare officer, having been found wandering or drunk or he could have been just old or lost or perhaps had had a blazing row at home and been turned out into the street. The simpler cases were dealt with by

In the Way of Understanding

the psychiatrist and the social worker. Those who needed psychiatric treatment and refused it were the hard core. The magistrate had either to persuade them to accept treatment or to enforce a compulsory order. Many cases were straightforward and with a sensible talk to the patient and the relative it was possible to persuade them to accept treatment in a mental hospital in their catchment area. For those who refused it was more painful, as force sometimes had to be used.

On one occasion I had to visit a patient in a padded cell. She was a very old lady who refused to put on any clothes and she was sitting quietly in the very warm atmosphere of the padded cell with its soft flooring like foam. I asked to be left alone with her as I felt I must talk to her before taking the final decision. I told her who I was and she asked me to sit down with her on the floor. She told me that the world was a wicked place and that I was much safer in the cell with her. We had quite a long talk but the nurses kept on opening the door. This infuriated the old lady as it let in the cold air. I forget the details of her case but, of course, she qas quite insane. We prayed together and I was told later that she went peacefully to the appropriate hospital to sit, I fear, like a vegetable until called to a happier place.

While I was a visiting magistrate in Holloway Prison, concerned with matters which came under a section of the same Mental Treatment Act, 1930, I had similar duties to perform, sometimes late at night. One especially horrific episode which I shall never forget concerned a Greek Cypriot woman. It was a case full of tragedy for she had murdered her daughter-in-law, a British girl. There was a difference of opinion between the hospital psychiatrist and the panel of psychiatrists called in to decide on the woman's sanity. My feeling was that she was insane but the panel of eminent psychiatrists thought otherwise and she was one of the last women to be hanged. My visit to her in the death cell, the day before the execution, was painful for all concerned and for many nights I was haunted by the unfortunate woman's pleas for mercy.

I am thankful that the death penalty has been abolished. Not only was it barbarous but during the last days before the execution the whole atmosphere in the prison was electric. The tension and the effect on the staff and inmates, not to mention the visiting magistrate, was traumatic.

To me, most of the petty sessional work was dull but my work on the licensing committee was rather fun. We visited pubs to see whether they were well run and the hygiene satisfactory. The domestic court was also interesting but there was not much chance of saving a marriage from going on the rocks unless the probation officer was an exceptionally far-seeing human being, prepared to do much home work with the warring parties. However, one learned the facts of life, often painful and without dignity.

The Children & Young Persons Act, 1933, (sect. 44) said:

Every court in dealing with a child or young person who is brought before it, either as being in need of care or protection or as an offender or otherwise shall have regard to the welfare of the child or young person . . .

This was to be the first consideration, and I was often privileged to sit with some of the finest chairmen on the juvenile bench at that time. However there was sometimes the disadvantage of sitting with those magistrates who, in their remarks to children and parents, made one squirm. The late Eileen Younghusband, Baroness Wootton of Abinger, the late Madeleine Robinson (née Symonds), together with the late John Watson were, in their different ways of handling children and young adolescents—some of them very tough and very difficult—quite remarkable. Another chairman, well known for his social work, Sir Basil Henriques, was unpredictable but fun to sit with. He and John Watson were known to us as the Heavenly Twins.

In their varied ways these colleagues, with their wisdom and their tender, loving care, and a strict adherence to the law, all taught me to think and not to let my emotions run away with me. The lucidity of the Clerk's exposition of the facts helped me to become, I hope, a useful member of the team, for I am not blessed with a judicial mind.

In the Way of Understanding

Team work in these courts was good. Magistrate, probation officer, clerk, school enquiry officer, all had the interest of the child at heart. We also had the special help in conference of the late Dr. Peter Scott and of Professor Gibbens. They would discuss many problems with us and give us their valuable advice. These two wise psychiatrists had a wonderful psychological understanding and insight into the adult as well as the adolescent mind and Dr. Peter Scott's untimely death in 1978 was a great loss to the mental health movement both nationally and internationally. He taught me a great deal, and I rarely missed any of his brilliant lectures at the Institute for the Study and Treatment of Delinquency.

In the juvenile court one hears some hard truths and learns never to be shocked. The more truculent the client the more one has to remember the miserable, frightened youngster inside, unable to understand the mumbo-jumbo of the court's language. In my old age, as I watch the violence on T.V. and in films, and read of the hideous crimes in which the media wallow, I think of my time on the juvenile bench. Nothing seems sacred any more. What was once for the private eye of the judge, the magistrate and the probation officer is often on the front page of many newspapers and is elaborated in horrible detail in documentary television programmes.

The Court of Appeal for cases sent up from the juvenile courts was quite an experience in those early days. The adjudication was often given without receiving the probation officer's report which had been presented to the lower courts. I once had the temerity to ask to see the probation officer's report because I was puzzled at the verdict arrived at by my colleagues on the juvenile bench. The Judge looked at me in amazement and asked what I was referring to. When I explained, he had the report produced and I believe he continued this practice ever afterwards.

Later improvements have been good, notably the training of magistrates and the requirement that they should visit some of the institutions in which their clients might have to reside for long or short periods. My work as a magistrate would have been far more useful had I had the benefit of such a training. But I did visit, off my own bat, approved schools, borstal institutions and juvenile prisons to try to educate myself, both in the U.K. and abroad.

It would not be right if on this pilgrimage I did not mention the late Mr. C. A. Lyward, the most outstanding and extraordinary head master of a remarkable school, Finchden Manor, immortalised in Michael Burn's excellent and charming book, *Mr. Lyward's Answer* (Hamish Hamilton, 1956). Lyward was a genius and with his unkempt clothes he made me think of John the Baptist. When I first met him I knew I was in the presence of a great man and a great healer of boys' souls. He was doing something which few others have ever achieved. There was a peace in this old Jacobean house, full of tempestuous youths, mostly psychopaths, allergic to rules, untidy and even dirty. Mr Lyward's answer was love and never-ending tolerance.

The boys, toughest of the tough, the sick and the mentally ill, some out of the top drawer and from public schools, needed psychiatric treatment. However, Lyward was shy of psychiatry, only using it discreetly with background advice from the late Dr. Peter Scott, one of the few psychiatrists he accepted as a friend. Yet Lyward tamed these problem boys and they even called him "Sir". His love was stern but just. "Stern love" was his answer but the phrase became so bandied about at Finchden that he may have regretted having coined it. One boy is reported to have said "He has brought me up against barriers and helped me over them—or not so much helped me over them but helped me to help myself over them". Perhaps a Finchden boy always knew he was forgiven before he committed a crime. As I watched these boys and talked to some of them I realised that they enjoyed what they called having their minds stretched. The school demanded something of them because it believed that they had something to give. Besides the high academic work in the classroom, the boys were rebuilding part of the old house, decorating, mending furniture, putting in new floors, under the expert guidance of a craftsman, himself a genius. He whipped up enthusiasm in these young men who might be feeling their way to home-making themselves in the future. Perhaps the whole atmosphere engendered by Lyward's personality had something to do with their gradual growth to a more stable way of living and an acceptance of tolerance as the means of learning to live with a problem. I accept that many are not cured, but they became more livable and even lovable after they left.

There was culture and much beauty in the flat at the top of Finchden Manor where Mrs. Lyward, a sculptress and a lovely person, made a home for her husband. Sometimes the boys, as they became more stable, would steal up and sit on the floor quietly listening to Bach or Mozart while basking in the warmth of this happy home, something they might never have experienced before and might never experience again.

Years later, just before Mr. Lyward died in 1973 at the age of 79, he came to my flat with his son John in order to discuss the future of the school with the late Dr. Peter Scott, Dr. Pamela Mason and Dame Eileen Younghusband. Mr. Lyward was deeply discouraged and kept on repeating "They are frozen and I can no longer get through to them". It became clear, alas, that without him Finchden could not carry on nor expand to meet the needs of a growing population of violent and destructive boys, bent on destroying themselves as well as others. It was heart-breaking for those of us present that night to realise we were saying farewell for ever to this forbearing, courteous, and beloved teacher, "one of the life-givers" to quote from *Mr. Lyward's Answer* (p. 288).

His son drove him to hospital that night for an operation from which he never recovered.

During my work as a Magistrate I always felt there was inadequate training for Prison Officers, and especially for those dealing with young offenders. At the end of the 1939/45 war many excellent young girls left the services and joined the prison service and many had learned much from their experiences in this country and abroad. But the all-important problem facing them in punitive establishments (and it is no good balking the word) is that they receive little, if any, training in psychology, in human relations and in the difficulty of dealing with the hard core of their prisoners other than by strict discipline. Only just lately I asked a friend who is Prison Governor what training is given to prison officers, and was told cynically that training given in locking and unlocking doors is still very efficient. Those of us who have tried to learn from Prison Governors and have heard evidence given in lectures by the Institute for the Study and Treatment of Delinquency know that the so-called "short, sharp shock treatment" has failed. What kind of staff is a punitive establishment likely to recruit if the staff are only to be warders? The most enlightened among Prison Officers would gladly be more involved with training programmes for custodial care. Prison duties on their own are soul-destroying, and supervising scrub-outs and square-bashing is hardly sufficient for anyone who is interested in attempting the reform of prisoners and in helping them to prepare to live a normal life in the community. However, much has been done by some brave hearts in the prison service, and I take off my hat to those who are pressing for reform despite set-backs and with little support from others outside. May their "still small voice" of enlightenment eventually reach the end of the long dark tunnel of despair. Perhaps the violence that tends to control the world today is a symptom of that universal mental sickness or malaise that I have been trying to bring to the attention of the powers that be throughout my pilgrimage. To face this fact globally and to act upon it in unison is perhaps the only hope of prevention and possible cure.

As a magistrate dealing with adults and juveniles, I can only endorse what was so clearly stated by Professor Kathleen Jones in her address to MIND at one of their Conferences in 1979, from which I now quote freely:

> *Law cannot cure the mentally ill. Law cannot fully protect the mentally ill. It can only provide the enabling framework, the "open-textured" system, within which good policies can develop. Beyond that, it is counter-productive, creating fear, secrecy and deception*[1]

Indeed, legal formalism such as the short, sharp shock treatment meted out to youngsters in juvenile detention centres

---

[1] Professor Kathleen Jones, 'The Limitations of the Legal Approach to Mental Health', Paper presented at the International Conference of Law and Psychiatry, Oxford, 1979.

failed twenty years ago during my time on the Bench, and yet I notice that our present government intend to try it again. (Written in 1979). This must be despite the warnings which they must surely have received from those who administer the law and from experts in criminology. To quote Professor Kathleen Jones again:

> *Good community care has never been tried, because we have never had the money, the plant or the training facilities.*[2]

In my experience this is also true of the hospital service as well as in the treatment of delinquents. I look back on the needs of the members of the community needing treatment and care. According to the White Paper[3], every year some 200,000 receive treatment in a mental hospital, some 600,000 are referred to psychiatrists, and about five million (more than ten percent of the population) consult their G.P.s about mental health problems. Barbara Castle once called this "a major health problem, perhaps the major health problem of our time". I would say this is as much the concern of the Home Office as the D.H.S.S.

---

[2] *Ibid.*
[3] *Better Services for the Mentally Ill*, H.M.S.O., 1971.

13
National Association for Mental Health: Scottish Association for Mental Health

The N.A.M.H. has shown that mental health is part of the better understanding between one human being and another.
　　　　　　　　　The Baroness Elliot of Harwood, in a speech in
　　　　　　　　　　the House of Lords on Community Care.

The mental health movement had shown that it was not merely a wartime concomitant of the evacuation scheme of the 1939/45 war, but an indispensable part of the new National Health Service which was the result of the Beveridge Report[1]. However, the movement could not succeed without a strong central body to co-ordinate the work and to secure and maintain high standards of training.

The reader may remember Mont's interest in the mental health movement (see p. 86) and the part Plodge played as the setting of discussions amongst the important associations—especially the famous dinner party in 1933 when I suggested the idea of the Feversham Committee. The report of that committee saw the light of day at the very beginning of the war. It recommended the amalgamation of the three existing associations and it was unanimously agreed that we should work together as closely as possible during hostilities under the title of "The Emergency Committee for Mental Health" I became its chairman, over and above my work for the W.V.S. When hostilities came to an end it was realised that full amalgamation had now to be faced, and so the Provisional National Council for Mental Health started to look into the possibilities. My husband persuaded his friend and colleague,

---

[1] *Social Insurance and Allied Services*, H.M.S.O., 1942.

In the Way of Understanding

Sir Otto Neimeyer, C.B.E., K.C.B., a Director of the Bank of England, to be its chairman. He was a very good one, and managed a mixed team with delicacy. He kept their noses to the grindstone with the ultimate aim of the complete amalgamation of the four previously separate bodies, in order to create a National Council with one Executive Committee. This would involve the acquisition of a new building—our poor old shabby premises in Buckingham Palace Road were proving quite inadequate.

Sir Otto was an intolerant man, unable to suffer fools gladly, but he was warm-hearted and a considerable scholar, able to converse and write in Greek. Once, as a gentle hint, Mont put on Sir Otto's desk at the Bank a wooden carving of one bear and four little bears with the inscription "Bear and forbear" in his inimitable script.

Otto became a great friend of mine and a keen supporter of the mental health movement, even though he *would* refer to patients as "loonies". His niece, Mary Applebey, C.B.E., was appointed General Secretary to the N.A.M.H. in 1951 after a remarkable career in the civil service, graduating via the War Office, and the Control Commission for Germany in Berlin, to Principal in the Foreign Office after the war. Thus she had considerable experience of administration and of dealing with men and women of all shades of opinion. She certainly inherited her uncle's clear thinking and his expertise with figures. She had no experience of the wide canvas covered by the N.A.M.H., but her intelligence and background soon enabled her to familiarise herself with the problems. She coped ably with the heavy responsibility for running the Association for the next 20 years. Miss Fox (by now Dame Evelyn) and Sir Otto worked perfectly together. He appreciated her intelligence and when she died he wrote of her "Evelyn Fox feared neither God nor experto credo—neither man nor Whitehall."

No wonder that out of such a team was born the National Association for Mental Health (renamed MIND in 1973). It was a great achievement, and much is owed to these pioneers by workers in the movement today. They faced far greater difficulties than the mental health workers of today, for the ground was then completely uncultivated. The Rt. Hon. R. A.

National Association for Mental Health

Butler, M.P. became President of the N.A.M.H. and the Earl of Feversham became Chairman of the Council. I became Chairman of the Executive Committee. This landed me well and truly in work for the mentally ill and the mentally handicapped, while not forgetting my first love, child guidance. Although most of the child guidance clinics now came under the new National Health Service or the local education authorities, there was still much to be done during the takeover period. Even after the appointed day in 1948 when the National Health Service came into being I believe that most child guidance clinics still kept close to the N.A.M.H., as they felt that in that body they had a mother figure. The 1959 Mental Health Act made the service compulsory. The general aims and objects of the N.A.M.H. were to foster an understanding in the community of the importance of mental health in the relationships of everyday life, and to establish the firm principle that its foundation must be laid in early childhood if any semblance of mental and emotional development was to be achieved.

We wished to encourage research and to establish training courses, lectures, conferences and generally to combat the fear of mental disorder so prevalent at that time. Through information we hoped to make known the many existing facilities available, and to provide advice for schools and those many disturbed persons who were perhaps too nervous to seek help in a mental hospital or from their G.P.

In 1950 I steeped myself in the post-war voluntary mental health movement in the U.K. and also learned about the work of the statutory services. Local associations for mental health were springing up in various parts of the country. As chairman of the Executive Committee of the N.A.M.H., and under the tuition of Mary Applebey and the other heads of departments, I attended expert committee meetings at the new office in Queen Anne St.

In addition to the monthly Executive Committee there was the Education Sub-Committee. Besides its courses for teachers, social workers, nurses, and clergy, and its close contact with various government departments, the Sub-Committee organised an Annual Conference at Church House, Westminster.

In the Way of Understanding

This was usually attended by the Secretary of State of whichever government department was most concerned with the theme or topic to be discussed. The Hall was always filled to capacity for the two days' deliberations, and although set speeches from the platform were delivered by eminent men and women, the audience, made up of representatives from local authorities and Regional Boards and other bodies, had an opportunity to air their views by questions and impromptu addresses. This brought out the problems and difficulties facing the mental health movement in the country as a whole. These interventions were most valuable not only to N.A.M.H. but to the many from government departments and local authorities and Regional Boards who were present.

I recall the 1961 Conference which came just after the implementation of the new Mental Health Act. Enoch Powell—then Minister of Health—gave his now famous speech which is still remembered with some cynicism. It was delivered most dramatically with his penetrating eyes gazing into the future over the heads of a spell-bound and hypnotised audience:

> *They [the mentally sick] for the most part ought to be in wards or wings of general hospitals. Few ought to be in great isolated institutions or clumps of institutions, though I neither forget nor underestimate the continuing requirements of security for a small minority of patients. Now look and see what are the implications of these bold words—they imply nothing less than the elimination of by far the greater part of this country's mental hospitals as they exist today. This is a colossal undertaking . . . there they stand, isolated, majestic, imperious, brooded over by gigantic water tower and chimney combined, rising unmistakable and daunting out of the countryside—the asylums our forefathers built with such immense solidity to express the notions of their day.*

This was 20 years ago and most of them are still standing, although one tower at Bexley was brought down lately, I believe. I now confess, with some shame, to have been taken in by such eloquence, and even moved to see a light at the end of the dark tunnel of mental ill health—nor was I dashed by the Chairman of the Board of Control, Dr. Walter McClay, who (amused by my naivety) said "I hope you will live to see it"! Today's T.V. programmes and newspaper articles reveal that the same problems face us today, so I had indeed underestimated the power of resistance to change and the inertia of the public.

To return to the N.A.M.H. the Education Sub-Committee had also a specialist department dealing with mental subnormality. For a time it ran the only diploma course for teachers until this was taken over by the statutory services. The Medical Officers course was famous in those days for the training of school medical officers, whose task was to make an assessment of the children to be admitted to special schools. These were all invaluable pioneering efforts, and in due course they were taken over by the D.H.S.S. and the Department of Education. Until then they had given their approval for this work, but had no official responsibility for it.

There was a Social Services Sub-Committee and a Public Information Sub-Committee. But perhaps the most active sub-committee of all was the Local Associations Sub-Committee, whose brief was to set up local associations all over the U.K. These local associations were all-important in spreading interest in mental health in the provinces. I call them our eyes and ears, for without them the N.A.M.H. could not have had any influence in government circles nor been able to give reliable evidence to government commissions. Our local associations informed us of what was being done locally, and, more often, of what, alas, was being left undone. Each local association had its own particular character and interest and one could see how they varied. For instance, early in the 1950s the "open door" policy was introduced by Dr. T. P. Rees who was later to be Medical Adviser to the N.A.M.H. He stressed that patients should have their own clothes, and especially underclothes, for, as he once said to me, "How can any doctor who is trying to treat his patients as individuals be expected to help them if the matron and the nurses look upon them as numbers and issue communal pants?" This communal clothing was one of the old institutional methods which local associations had to fight against, using much diplomacy to overcome staff prejudices.

Sir Otto Niemeyer chaired the Finance Sub-Committee, and although I attended meetings regularly in order to keep in touch with current problems (mostly caused by lack of cash), I could only listen and try to understand what the experts talked about. He had an amusing habit, (perhaps it was a slip of the tongue), of referring to millions instead of thousands.

All the sub-committee members were experts in their various fields and the staff were professionals. All sub-committees had government observers who often had to listen to adverse reports on the work of the mental health services in their departments. No holds were barred, and in consequence the N.A.M.H. was invited to send representatives to the various government commissions and committees.

I found the work enthralling. With expert briefing by Mary Applebey, who achieved so much in those early days, and with the expertise of her heads of departments I was able to keep abreast of what was going on, despite my lack of training. Perhaps my gift of intuition and my innate ability to see a jump ahead of some people, and my deep interest in my fellow-beings, gave me an advantage. My mind worked on a very wide canvas and I seemed to sense the psychological implications of a problem almost before it was discussed. However, I had great difficulty in expressing myself clearly, and preferred to support those members of committee whose opinions were lucid and practical. I found this difficulty frustrating, because I would have liked to have taken part in the cut and thrust of an argument. But I felt that my mind was untrained and that I was therefore unfit to put into words what was in my mind. Thus I often kept silent, and trusted to my intuition to guide the discussion as wisely as possible. My experience in chairing committees gave me the wit to pull out the arguments from the wisest brains round the table, and to call forth the expertise of able professional staff, and thus reach a conclusion. One friend likened the role which I played as chairman to that of being the conductor of an orchestra. I was unable to play any instrument myself but I brought them together in the hope of achieving harmony. Should discord erupt I would coax the players back with tolerance and patience, to a harmonious ending. However, I was never happy if it were decided to take no action on any particular matter, as this would have been negative and I was a positive person.

It was difficult to act from the position of primus inter pares. Each member of the Executive Committee took the lead at some time or another in performing some particular task—such as chairing sub-committees. The professional head of the department concerned would draft reports, summarise material, explore conference venues, find speakers, and so on. My task was simply to facilitate and support the others in their various activities and to chair their meetings. All the same, this was no easy task. I always tried to keep in mind something which I had written in a Paper called "The Lay Committee and the Professional Worker":

> *It is the duty of the committee member of the statutory or voluntary organisation to pay due regard to the report or the advice of the professional worker, but at the same time it is the duty of the committee member to take some trouble to ascertain the facts and figures and to have made himself or herself conversant with the problem under discussion.*[1]

As the years went by I visited, and in many cases set up, local associations. This was a fascinating experience, and since these associations grew in time to number over a hundred, I had the opportunity of watching interest in mental health spread gradually all over the country. Each local association had its own identity and worked in different ways. Many of them tried to alleviate the problem of mental deficiency by setting up hostels or centres.

Besides the massive work of voluntary mental health services throughout the country, the N.A.M.H. administered some residential services, ran holiday homes for mentally-handicapped boys and girls who came from mental hospitals, and also ran homes for mentally-handicapped boys and girls

---

[1] Not published.

who went out daily to work but had no homes willing or able to care for them. This was all pioneering work.

Immediately after the second World War and the disruption in family life which it had entailed, many girls who came before the courts were found to be suffering from severe emotional disturbance. In view of this, the N.A.M.H., with its considerable expertise in running residential establishments, was asked by the Home Office to manage its first approved school for girls and to provide psychiatric treatment and long-term therapeutic care. This school, Duncroft, Staines, was opened in 1949 for 26 girls of high I.Q. between the ages of 14 and 17.

Not all were before the court for having committed an offence. Some were there because they needed care or protection, or because they were beyond control. The N.A.M.H. with its considerable knowledge of child guidance and its contacts with experts in child psychiatry was considered the right voluntary society to administer a school whose aim was to give treatment and not to punish. It was to be undenominational, and was open to girls from all parts of the country. I became chairman of the school from 1955 until 1966. After some initial growing pains had been overcome, I worked with an excellent team of managers. Some were local but others represented the probation service, the social services, the psychological and psychiatric professions and the magistrates. The first headmistress of the school was Miss Brown, a diplomat, a woman with a cultured background, a collector of antiques, and "a woman of the world". She had high standards, and her girls and managers responded to this iron hand in a velvet glove and so much of her spirit remains. She was a gentle woman, yet when one of the girls absconded and was known to the police as a frequenter of West End night clubs, Miss Brown never hesitated to go up to Soho to search until the girl was found. This head was well known to and helped by many night club proprietors and their staffs.

Alas, she died of cancer some time after I became chairman, but not before she had set a pattern for a planned environment where social, recreational, education and psychiatric resources were available to give a total understanding of each girl and her family. A comprehensive approach was thus provided by the staff, including the psychiatric team, and Duncroft became a therapeutic community.

After the death of this remarkable woman it was no easy matter to replace her, especially as her deputy was a very recent appointment. So the Home Office—always helpful to me in a crisis—agreed to second to Duncroft one of their senior woman inspectors, Miss Francis, for a limited period. Her task was to continue a policy that had worked so successfully, and to support the staff and the girls, who not unnaturally were anxious about their future. Miss Francis, a very wise lady, was supportive yet firm in her attitudes. She was a great comfort to all concerned, and especially to the Committee and to me. We had the real responsibility for the future of these girls, not to mention the running of a school which was looked upon as an important pilot scheme, in a new effort to deal with serious delinquency and emotionally disturbed adolescents. When Miss Francis returned to the Home Office Inspectorate she was succeeded by her deputy, Miss Margaret Jones. She was a young woman of exceptional vitality who, together with Dr. Pamela Mason, a remarkable child psychiatrist, shepherded the school along progressive lines and evolved a special psychiatric technique which was second to none. The school was enlarged in 1959 to include better dormitories and leisure rooms for the girls, three flats for the staff, and a house for the headmistress who could therefore be a married woman. This concession was not achieved without a battle with the Home Office, who at that time failed to see the importance of married women in their establishments, although their headmasters were invariably married men! In 1963 a purpose-built hostel was opened called Norman House. I was delighted that they gave my name to this house where girls could stay and go out to work before facing what might be a hostile world.

Duncroft attracted people of intelligence and vision, people representing different walks of life, different backgrounds and different professions. This expanding and successful venture owed much to the wholehearted co-operation between the Home Office and the N.A.M.H., and to the support of local personalities, societies and churches—not least to Dr. Wilfrid

In the Way of Understanding

Warren, Consultant to the Children's Department of Maudsley Hospital, who joined the Committee and succeeded me as chairman.

As a result, the N.A.M.H. was invited by the Home Office in 1965 to run a similar school in the North, Springhead Park, near Leeds, which was opened by H.R.H. Princess Marina in 1967. I was appointed the chairman. It was a delightful task but hard work. A suitable house had to be found and, when found, difficult alterations were necessary. Interested local people had to be vetted as possible managers, and finally the all-important headmistress had to be chosen. Again we were fortunate to find an excellent person in Miss Shelagh Sunner, who had worked at Duncroft and had had considerable experience in social work with the L.C.C. She was entirely different from Miss Brown and Miss Jones in her approach to the girls, but had a breezy, jovial manner, and a strength of character which appealed to these northern youngsters and gave confidence to her committee and staff—not forgetting the parents.

My work on Springhead Park lasted for nearly four years, and I had the help of Cordelia James, the wife of Lord James who was then the first Vice-Chancellor of York University. This was great fun for me, as the Jameses were delightful hosts on my monthly visits to Leeds. Besides the teething problems of starting the school I had the excitement and pleasure of watching the building of this splendid University, the arrival of the ducks on the artificial lake, the planting of already half grown trees and the building of the modern house for the Vice-Chancellor.

I believe that Duncroft and Springhead Park were valuable experiments in the management of emotionally disturbed but clever youngsters, who needed the kind of care and treatment so well understood by the N.A.M.H., with its roots in child guidance. Under the Children and Young Persons Act 1969 the N.A.M.H. could have continued to administer these thriving establishments when they became community homes, but MIND (the new incarnation of the N.A.M.H.), decided otherwise. The new Director considered these schools to be punitive establishments—something which to those who worked in them seemed as ridiculous as it was erroneous. This was a tragic break with the past work of the C.G.C., and a great loss to the emotionally disturbed, maladjusted and often sick girls so well known to the courts, to the probation service and to social workers generally.

When I retired from the chairmanship of N.A.M.H. in 1971 I was succeeded by Hester Adrian, wife of Lord Adrian, O.M., F.R.S., M.D., F.R.C.P., a truly great man who gave the N.A.M.H. the full weight of his understanding and support. Hester was the daughter of Dame Ellen Pinsent, a tireless worker in the field of mental deficiency and a colleague of mine on the Feversham Committee. Hester followed in her mother's footsteps; this was perhaps rather unusual considering the subject, but Cambridge possessed one of the very first Associations for mental welfare. It was supported by many famous members in the academic world, and Mrs. Keynes, mother of Lord Keynes, became its President. Hester gave me her loyal support, and she had been a tower of strength even earlier, in the battle for the amalgamation of the various agencies for mental health. Through her, I always felt I had the wise guidance of her husband, who was no less devoted to the cause of mental health. While he was Master of Trinity, the N.A.M.H. held several small conferences in Trinity and even one big residential one, when Lord Adrian and Hester gave all the Executive Committee and the speakers a dinner in their lovely Lodge. In such a glorious setting it was easy to relax, and just such an occasion was kindly repeated in Lord Butler's day. Adrian, as his friends called him, was a perfect host, suffering fools, or shall I say the tongue-tied and shy, in a gracious manner. When one sat next to him at dinner he seemed the most easy of conversationalists and, like Mont, was interested in people and drew them out. He went to immense pains to explain to me the making of the atom bomb, a conversation I shall always remember for its clarity and simplicity. Alas, the technical points floated in one ear and out of the other, but I was left in a pleasurable daze, remembering the delight of the whole evening and my host's beguiling voice and his fascinating conversation on a variety of subjects.

Hester was a member of the Royal Commission on the Law

In the Way of Understanding

Relating to Mental Illness and Mental Deficiency (1957). She also became Chairman of her Regional Hospital Board. She died in 1966, leaving Adrian bereft but courageous, his gay wisdom standing him in good stead, and surrounded by a lovely and brilliant family. I last saw him on a visit to Cambridge after his retirement as Master of Trinity. I found him gallant and brave, entertaining some undergraduates in his delightful rooms in College, with lovely silver, a perfect butler to serve us, simple food, excellent wine—a civilised lunch which I am sure the young men and this old lady will long remember. He was as keen as ever to talk about changes in the world and the new outlook in the mental health movement. His sparse body might be frail, but his mind and memory seemed as clear as ever.

Since giving up my work with the N.A.M.H. at the Bethlem and Maudsley hospitals, and with the statutory authorities where I was a volunteer, I have given more thought to the great movement towards giving voluntary help to the statutory services. The realisation of such a movement has now begun to penetrate the minds of the professionals, because leisure-time activity is a new way of life. With the outcome of the Welfare State and the fact that hours of employment have been reduced, many are finding that watching T.V., doing a little gardening, or just keeping their home fires burning, is not satisfying enough for health of mind or body. Thus, the majority of thinking people are concerned about the best way of finding leisure-time satisfaction. This is something which neither I nor my peers ever had to bother about. We had a tradition of service to the community instilled into us at a very early stage. We were fortunate, but now numbers of men and women in this country and overseas are trying to find a solution to this major problem in their lives. Professional social workers, too, realise that they can no longer cope with a soaring number of customers, anxious for their help. They are therefore prepared to accept the services of volunteers who would assist them part-time. I think that both the professional and the volunteer could benefit immensely by this partnership in team work. I believe that professional social workers have come to realise that people trained in other skills, retired people, and people with no specific training could under their guidance assist and even enhance their work, and bring a breath of fresh air to what can become an overwhelming and thankless task.

As I listened to reports from professionals on the statutory committees on which I have served, be they doctors, nurses, social workers or administrators, I used to feel I had a useful role to play—if only by listening and trying to understand, and then, with my colleagues, taking decisions. The same could be said of the N.A.M.H or of any other voluntary organisation. Co-operation between professional workers and volunteers is becoming closer; much closer than in my early days. I started by being an amateur, working towards a partnership in caring where we, the part-timers, hoped to be an asset to the professionals. I have come to realise once again how much I missed out in my early days in social work, for there was no Volunteer Centre as there is now which could have helped to support or train me. I had once again been thrown in at the deep end, and had to learn to make my way amongst many who, I knew, considered me just a "do-gooder". There were, however, the majority, who gave me unqualified support and encouragement and made my life worth living, and to them I am truly grateful. We both needed to be secure, and only then did we work cosily together.

The Scottish Association for Mental Health was a quite separate organisation from the N.A.M.H. and, when visiting them by invitation, I naturally brought greetings from the sister organisation south of the border. They had their own chairman and officers in a Council of Management, and in some ways worked more closely with their statutory authorities than we did at that time. I attended many conferences, usually held at the University of Edinburgh in the new halls of residence called Pollock Hall, which were built for the 1960 Olympic Games. I once had a room overlooking Arthur's Seat, and the beauty and charm of Edinburgh were always very attractive. The Scots are excellent hosts, and the strain and stress of meetings were much relieved by visits to hospitals in the lovely countryside, and by the warmest of welcomes. They seemed to understand the art of caring for the physical needs of those dedicated to the service of mental health. It was here that I acquired a taste for 'Grouse Whiskey', for after driving long distances in my car I would be very tired. To be brought back to life by psychiatrists ordering me a strong drink was more than pleasant! They were solicitous of my health and we all enjoyed ourselves, combining business with pleasure in the Scottish countryside. Our hosts gave us a full life, and one Edinburgh conference coincided with the Festival which turned our work into great pleasure. For me it was always a joy to be in Scotland, as I had Mont's Balfour relatives at Dawyck and there I always felt at home.

At one of the early Festivals I was invited to lunch by the late Mr. and Mrs. Alexander Maitland. Rosalind Maitland was a founder member of the Festival and a doctor of music. She worked hard on the Organising Committee. Sir Alexander (knighted after her death) left his very fine collection of pictures to the Scottish National Gallery in Edinburgh. This is known as the Maitland Collection. Another guest at this lunch was the famous contralto singer Kathleen Ferrier, a lovely woman. We sat next to each other, and the warmth of her personality enveloped me. She was humble, as are all truly great persons, completely without the prima donna's temperament, and her voice and manner were gentle. Lunch was rather late, and I was becoming a little anxious at not being on time for a special film I wanted to see. I had enquired of Miss Ferrier if it would be difficult to pick up a taxi afterwards: her reply had been vague but later, over coffee in the drawing room, she came up to me quite quietly and said: "I have got you a taxi, Lady Norman"—typical of her loving and caring personality. This meeting was a prelude to her interest in mental health, and her willingness to come to Plodge on two occasions with Gerald Moore to sing in the Music Room to large audiences in aid of charity—which I have described earlier.

14
First Congress of World Federation for Mental Health (1948)

*So friend, let it be our endeavour
To make each by each understood.*
Elizabeth Wordsworth, "Good and Clever."

Those of us who had been concerned with the future of the mental health movement in Britain, and had worked for the amalgamation of the voluntary mental health associations before the war, became aware after the war of the growing mental health problems of the world. After the end of the war we were alerted to these by the growing concern shown in reports from devastated Europe—notably by reports from doctors and social workers who attended the international meeting of the Society for the Study of Child Victims of the War (SEPEG)[1] held in Zurich in 1945. Robina Addis, a senior psychiatric social worker, who had worked with me at the Canonbury Clinic, was one of those who attended the SEPEG meeting. On her return she convinced me that the newly formed N.A.M.H. should set its sights on the international field as well as the national. On hearing this, my mind leapt immediately into the future, realising that this country was peculiarly fitted to be one of the leaders of this movement. Great experience had been gained from our war experiences, so with the N.A.M.H. and with the U.S.A., our great ally, there was a real chance for us to influence governments in war-weary Europe. Young psychiatrists from the services had seen war-devastated Europe at first hand, and were also aware of the mental health problems of India, Asia and Africa. They

[1] Semaine d'Etude pour l'Enfrance Victimes de la Guerre.

In the Way of Understanding

were naturally keen to take part in a great drive to make known to the governments of the world the unhappy state of the mentally sick and the mentally handicapped, as well as the needs of displaced persons, evacuees, refugees and returning P.O.W.s. This applied also to their more mature colleagues whose names were already famous in psychological medicine.

Robina Addis, a close friend as well as a colleague, was also a friend of Mont's because her father, Sir Charles Addis, was on the Court of the Bank of England. He was a specialist in Chinese affairs and a man of vision and integrity for whom my husband had a high regard. Both Sir Charles and Lady Addis were citizens of the world, and inspired in their thirteen children a devotion to a life of service to mankind. All of them served their country in times of war and peace. During the war Robina played no small part in service to her country as Regional Representative for Mental Health in Kent, Surrey and Sussex. These were badly bombed areas, where she coped with the evacuation of children and the admission to hospital of the mentally ill who had been discharged from the services, as described in Ch. 10. When we heard of the tragic condition of the children who had been physically and mentally damaged as a result of the wars and of the large numbers of child refugees who had lost their parents or been abandoned by them, it seemed to us both that the N.A.M.H., which now included the C.G.C., had a duty to act.

Robina possessed a penetrating mental vision, and her psychological training had enhanced her understanding of people and their problems. Born in Edinburgh of Scottish puritan stock, her slight fragile body encased a tough spirit. She faced her sometimes difficult life with extraordinary calm and physical endurance. To look at she was a mixture of both parents, having her father's fine bone structure, smiling grey eyes and wiry body, with her mother's lovely serene face and gentle speech. Robina came in the middle of a large family. There were six younger and five older children, and thus she learnt from her early years to understand babyhood and adolescence. In fact she was her mother's right hand, for Lady Addis was the ideal wife upon whom her husband relied, and he came first in her life. They were away together for long

The de Laszlo portrait of
Montagu Collet Norman,
1919

Myself at W.V.S.
Headquarters, 1939

Robina Addis, 1980

First Congress of World Federation for Mental Health (1948)

periods on her husband's business, and as in those days air travel was uncommon, Robina was left to cope with domesticity at home—a role she still plays. I cannot remember the date when we first met, but from that time we have been close friends in work and in private life. She is a stimulating person, full of energy, artistic, fond of music and the theatre, but also a wonderful listener who keeps her advice until requested. She has a host of friends. The young flock around her, while at the same time her contemporaries and seniors sense her humanity and enjoy her conversation and wit. Her feet have always been firmly on the ground, and unlike some of her profession she acknowledges the art of the possible. With her enthusiasm she galvanised me into action for world mental health. Gone were the days of the Canonbury Child Guidance Clinic, the war work and all we had done together. A new chapter was beginning for us both, and I found the ideal travelling companion at my side.

In Europe the organisations with which we were most concerned were the International Conference of Child Psychologists, the International Committee for Mental Hygiene and the Federation of Medical Psycho-therapy. There was an urgent need to examine in depth not only children's needs, but the problems facing the mentally ill, the mentally handicapped and those who were battered and hurt, mentally as well as physically.

After much to-ing and fro-ing, and endless correspondence and meetings, these organisations agreed to ask the N.A.M.H. in London to organise a conference for all the organisations, associations and individuals who were willing to discuss the ways and means of improving the services for the mental health of the world. This was surely a task to daunt anyone, but it did not daunt Dr. J. R. Rees C.B.E. of the Tavistock Clinic. His military experience during the 1939–45 war had given him an international perspective, and a grasp not only of individual psychological differences but of differences that reached far beyond national cultures. He had already done excellent work in helping to amalgamate our own voluntary mental health services, and his psychiatric training of the doctors working in the Services made him the obvious link

In the Way of Understanding

between the national and international organisations concerned, while at the same time his drive and vision gave these the courage to tackle what seemed to some an impossible task.

In true British fashion a committee was formed in London in 1947 with Dr. J. R. Rees as Chairman, and it was decided to get the work done by means of preparatory Commissions in each country. These Commissions did much effective work by bringing together, in some twenty countries, about 4,000 people, drawn from many different professions, who were involved in preparing the papers for discussion and the main Congress agenda. The objectives of the Congress were the following:

a) to get people concerned with the problems of mental health to meet each other;
b) to work together to try to understand each other's point of view and develop greater toleration;
c) to evolve certain new concepts in human relationships.

"Since war begins in the minds of men, it is in the minds of men that the defences of peace must be constructed."[1] "Health is a state of complete physical, mental and social wellbeing, not merely the absence of disease or infirmity."[2] Both these concepts were uppermost in the minds of those working for the World Federation for Mental Health Congress which was to be held in August 1948.

The United Nations had been established in 1945, together with its specialised agencies, W.H.O., I.L.O. and U.N.E.S.C.O., but it was clear that these were international, governmental organisations, who had to interpret their governments' points of view. Unless the people (themselves) could in some way voice their opinions, many creative ideas springing from voluntary groups and from psychiatry and psychology would be lost in the clutter of politics and bureaucracy. For those concerned with mental health it was important to advance its concepts in the corridors of power, in W.H.O., U.N.E.S.C.O., I.L.O. and U.N.I.C.E.F.; agencies who at that

[1] U.N.E.S.C.O. Constitution.
[2] W.H.O. Constitution.

First Congress of World Federation for Mental Health (1948)

time were woefully ignorant of the meaning of positive mental health, even if they recognised it at all. The aim of the World Federation of Mental Health was to do just that. It held its first conference in 1948 in Westminster School, which had been just evacuated by the Army, and it used Central Hall, Westminster, for its plenary sessions. The theme was "Mental Health and World Citizenship" and the N.A.M.H. acted as host. The Chairman was the Rt. Hon. R. A. Butler, M.P., later Lord Butler of Saffron Walden, President of the N.A.M.H.

I would have welcomed the challenge to take an active part in the organisation of the Congress but Mont was not well and was living in retirement at St. Clere. I was rarely in London, so under these difficult circumstances I only managed to take on the chairmanship of the Hospitality Committee and of the Ladies' Committee. I was ably supported by the wife of the then American Ambassador, Mrs. Lewis Douglas. All the embassies agreed to entertain their nationals, as we were still in a period of austerity. Visits of observation were organised to our psychiatric hospitals, schools, etc., as well as excursions to Windsor and other places of interest, with visits to theatres, concerts and films for the spouses who accompanied their wives or husbands. There were about two thousand delegates, all of whom paid their own expenses, but financial support was given by H.M. Government, who also gave a large garden party in Regent's Park. The British Council gave a grant, as did U.N.E.S.C.O. The languages used were English, French and German.

One sad note, I remember, was that only a handful of brave souls came from Germany. They had no one to sponsor them, and I felt this to be both cruel and uncharitable and surely lacking in a true understanding of mental health. These difficulties were however overcome within the circle of Robina and our friends. Years afterwards an old German lady came up to me and said that she had been a delegate at the 1948 Congress, and had realised the difficulties of those early days. She said she remembered the kindness of her English hosts and had nothing but happy memories. A happy ending, if a sad beginning!

The Congress opened with a galaxy of V.I.P.s from all over

In the Way of Understanding

the world on the platform. Among them were representatives of government departments; famous doctors like the late Lord Moran, President of the Royal College of Physicians, and Anna Freud, daughter of Sigmund Freud, who gave a superb paper on "Modern Trends in Child Psychology". The late Margaret Mead[1] from the U.S.A. welcomed the Congress and urged the formation of a World Federation. Eventually she became a founder member, and kept in close touch until her death in 1978.

There were many Ambassadors and High Commissioners and the Chairman in his opening remarks said:

> *During these weeks we have been welcoming people of many nations to the Olympic Games, where we have seen the Flame lighted, and now here, at Westminster, we are gathered to see the lighting of the torch of the mind ... In some ways this may well form a model for international gatherings ... What agencies are more important than those which contribute to the expansion of the social sciences and, in particular, attempt to explore and to chart the puzzling wilderness of the mind? ... the minds of men are thrown out of balance by ... upheavals of war and economic distress ... Mental health is essentially a matter for team-work—the pooling of ideas and experience in tackling problems, whether they be practical or theoretical. I have, therefore, high hopes for the results of this gathering, because here you have represented every profession concerned with mental health. Thus may your conclusions be a spur and a stimulus to your colleagues all over the world, and through them to our associates, the administrators, the diplomats and the politicians.*[2]

I quote at some length because R. A. Butler always turned up trumps whenever the N.A.M.H. needed support. He was for

---

[1] Margaret Mead, Ph.D., Associate Curator of Ethnology, American Museum of Natural History, New York City.

[2] Ed. Prof. J. C. Flugel, *International Congress on Mental Health, London, 1948*, Vol. IV, Proceedings of the International Congress on Mental Hygiene 16–21 Aug, 1948, H. K. Lewis & Co. Ltd., London, 1948.

First Congress of World Federation for Mental Health (1948)

many years a President whom I could always rely on in a crisis and one who, I believe, understood mental health in its widest sense, although he was much too reticent in speaking about it, and even failed to mention his interest in his splendid book *The Art of the Possible*.[1]

From the platform, Brock Chisholm, M.D., first Director General of W.H.O., begged W.F.M.H. not to be afraid of being called visionaries. He said:

Visionary is only a term of reproach if the vision is not followed by action . . . What has been done at this Congress and in the work that preceded it and in its Report is an earnest, consistent and persistent work that will go on. It is in effect an attempt to face reality and to help other people to do so.[2]

Julian Huxley, F.R.S., the first Director General of U.N.E.S.C.O. gave a warning on the last day of the congress. He said:

I am extremely glad to hear that you have decided to set up a permanent world organisation in the domain of mental health, representative of professional interests . . . Do not expect quick results to appear overnight . . . the problems are too difficult, and . . . any international organisation can only work slowly . . . It has to be in contact with its supporters all over the world.[3]

So the World Federation for Mental Health was born on August 19th, 1948. Its membership comes from countries with national associations and societies who are working for mental health, and also from individuals and associations with a like concern for the problems.

I had made many life-long friends from many parts of the world, and my vision has broadened from that of work for

---

[1] Lord Butler, K. G., C. H., *Art of the Possible*, Hamish Hamilton, 1971.
[2] Ed. Prof. J. C. Flugel, *International Congress on Mental Health, London*, 1948.
[3] *Ibid.*

In the Way of Understanding

mental health in this country to encompass a fascinating glimpse into the mental health services of other countries, and it was here in London in 1948 that the international bug entered my blood stream. I hoped one day to be able to give some service to the world community, and I was proud that my close association with the N.A.M.H. had led me into a much wider field, but little did I visualise then the extent of the journey, or the pleasure that it would give me.

In Widowhood

15

Widowed (1950), Loneliness and the Solace of Work

> *It is only in the desert that you can learn to turn loneliness into solitude, and it is only when we have learnt solitude and freedom—the capacity to be alone—that we can safely be involved with others.*
> Cardinal Basil Hume, O.S.B., *Searching for God*,
> Hodder & Stoughton, 1977

Mont died in 1950 after a long illness and much depression. For him work was what mattered, and being struck down at a period in history when he could have been giving service to his country and the Old Lady gave him great agony of spirit, especially when he knew that his powers were failing.

We had returned to London from St. Clere, and during the last months of his illness he was moved down to sleep in what was then the dining room at Plodge, which had a French window leading out to the garden. He was thus able to be pushed about in a wheel chair, but this lack of independence was more than irksome to him, and he needed nursing day and night. During this time one of his visitors was Field Marshal Smuts. On entering his room he electrified a little young Irish nurse when, with a twinkle in his eye, he took her hand and said, in his strong Afrikaans accent, rolling his Rs with great emphasis, "Do you know why your patient is ill? Well, it is because he fought on the wrong side in the Boer War and I fought on the right side, so you see, my dear, I am strong and healthy and he is sick!"

Mont and I had often talked about what would happen when he died, for he had always been anxious about what would become of me as I was so many years his junior. At that time I laughed it off, because I didn't want to think about it and believed that my many interests and my mission for mental

In the Way of Understanding

health, which we called my work, would keep me occupied and act as an anodyne.

I was young with many years before me: my friends and especially Mont's friends and colleagues and the Norman family, who had welcomed me into their fold, were all close to me. My sons did all they could to comfort me, but I knew I had always been something of an enigma to them.

The moment came when I was alone, and it was all very different from what I had expected. A wonderful letter from a very dear friend, which I found on my return from the crematorium, included the words "don't indulge in self pity". This gave me a necessary injection of courage. Family and friends rallied round, business had to be attended to, and there seemed little time to mope. Another dear friend gave me the practical present of an electric blanket to keep me warm in my single bed. (This was rather daring in 1950 but I have used it ever since with comfort and joy).

The late Sir Edward Peacock, G.C.V.O., one of my husband's intimate friends and a close colleague at the Bank of England, was particularly anxious that I should return to work. He took pains to get me into action again with the National Council of Social Service in which I had served during the war and of which he was the Treasurer. It happened that just at that time the N.C.C.S., together with the King Edward Hospital Fund for London, had decided to undertake a study of voluntary service in hospitals, where striking and far reaching changes were taking place as a result of the new National Health Service Act. I was asked to chair a small committee of experts, and Mr. John Trevelyan O.B.E., (later to become Censor of plays and films), was made Director of the Enquiry. I enjoyed working with him, and he was a colourful and controversial personality.

Attention was addressed to two main questions: (1) the role of the volunteer on boards and management committees, and (2) the part played by individuals and societies in rendering voluntary service to hospitals. The Director travelled widely, visiting Regional Hospital Boards throughout the country, and bringing back the views of the many hospitals he visited. Almost unanimously they expressed the opinion that voluntary service was now needed more than ever. In view of what happened, and is still happening, as a result of the emergence of volunteers in statutory services, local government and hospitals, the report[1] when it appeared was of considerable value and is now of historical interest. It was acclaimed by the press, and especially the medical press, when it was published in 1952, and it seemed to be looked upon as a blueprint for future voluntary effort.

Another job which I found most stimulating at this time was one that I was asked to undertake by U.N.E.S.C.O., which had convened a small conference in Hamburg on Education and the Mental Health of Children in Europe. Among the many topics raised, but not fully dealt with, at this conference was the large and important question of how the modern sciences of child study and educational psychology could be brought into more efficient relationship with the work of European schools. The experts were all from the psychological services for schools in Belgium, France, Germany, Sweden and the U.K. I was representing the World Federation for Mental Health, but I found myself elected unanimously as the Chairman of this high-powered group of educators, psychologists, psychiatrists and members of U.N.E.S.C.O., with Dr. W. D. Wall as my Secretary. No lectures were given nor any papers read: meetings proceeded by the quick give-and-take of discussion, and we did not rest until a reasonable working agreement had been reached. Each evening Dr. Wall would brief me on the next day's work, and I also had discussions with various individuals in order to reach some kind of agreement or compromise between the representatives of so many countries and so many different schools of thought. Language was a problem as we had no interpreter, but we got by thanks to Dr. Wall's knowledge of German and his and my knowledge of French. My training and experience in child guidance and mental health helped me to take an intelligent view of the discussions, and the courteous way in which the members treated their Chairman made the meetings some of the most

---

[1] *Voluntary Service and the State: A Study of the Needs of the Hospital Service*, Published by Geo. Barber & Son Ltd., for The National Council of Social Service and King Edward's Hospital Fund for London, 1952.

In the Way of Understanding

stimulating of my life. I never worked harder or with more concentration, and, as a vote of thanks, the Committee gave a dinner for me and took me to one of the notorious Hamburg night clubs. This was not really my idea of fun, but after some good German wine I enjoyed the remarks and witticisms made by these experts in psychological medicine regarding the various naked ladies who paraded before us. These remarks were extremely funny and by the end of the evening I had laughed a lot. The conference was a success, and in Dr. Wall I had an excellent taskmaster who took immense trouble to teach me my lines, and I was most grateful to him.

So in widowhood I was finding work a solace, and very shortly I was provided with an unexpected opportunity to take a calculated look at what loneliness really means. This was when a London University student who was engaged in research on patterns of human loneliness, wrote to ask if I would be willing to tell her what loneliness meant to me personally, so that I could help in her research. I answered her as follows:

> *Your letter is not an easy one to answer because, as you say yourself, loneliness has a different meaning for different individuals. It also varies with one's upbringing, temperament and inner resources. Age is another factor, and likewise the question whether one has been married or not, or whether one has had the sympathetic background which is provided by a large family. Loneliness can also be acutely felt by a child, even an only child such as I was, who had to invent a large family of children in order to help me live in a world of my own.*
>
> *I was happily married and shared my life completely with my husband, so that when the break came I was absolutely alone. We had both faced the possibility of his death squarely, but when it came I was numbed for a considerable time—like someone who has had a limb severed and, although still conscious, feels no pain for a considerable time. Then gradually feeling returns (I hope in the case of a limb the anaesthetic takes over) and the mind squares up to the fact that life is no longer as one had lived it, and the process of living, thinking and acting now takes on a new*

Loneliness and the Solace of Work

shape. In my case the awareness came as no shock, but daily the meaning became clearer and the adjustment more difficult. With a still active mind and body, and with my work and domestic and family problems needing attention and concentration, the pattern changed; but there was no more sharing of pleasure and sorrow, no more dependence on advice—just the stark fact that I had to depend on myself alone and that many people depended on me. I had never really considered such a state of affairs, and panic could easily have taken over had not some inner resource made itself felt, so that outwardly there was no groaning and moaning in order to ease the pain by seeking comfort from others. Loneliness is to me the absence of any opportunity to share happiness, laughter, jokes, gossip or gaiety, as well as the sharing of grief, unhappiness, unkindness and deep sorrow: the realisation that being alone is a preview of death, an adjustment to facing reality at its starkest. It can be exhilarating and even stimulating as well as awful.

Again, I have felt most lonely while watching those I love deeply die slowly over a long period, because at such times one feels so helpless. There is also the loneliness of knowing mental illness and being unable to alleviate the suffering of delusion and depression. These two examples make for acute and horrible loneliness. There is happily the reverse side, but perhaps equally tragic, of going to a gay party, with lots of people, beautiful women, charming men, much gaiety, but facing the crowd alone and then going home alone to one's lonely bedroom.

But it is never as bad as it seems, for there are always compensations, and if there is a real sense of humour, as apart from a sense of fun, loneliness can never be a killer and is sometimes a comfort. But if you as a researcher want the truth, then go into a mental hospital, especially in the old people's ward, where you will find real loneliness, in a life that is miserable, inactive, dull and hopeless. Alas again loneliness is not killing, since many inmates live to be nearly near 100. Look also at the young depressives and talk to a wise Chief Nursing Officer, and you will get valuable information for your research . . .

In the Way of Understanding

... in answering your letter I have taken more than a skin off the wound of loneliness which is still raw.

1950 was for me a year of death and loss. My mother-in-law, who was very frail and aged 99, died two weeks after her son. This was sad in itself, as I was deeply attached to her, but now I had the added sorrow, as Mont's widow, of taking my share of responsibility, along with Ronnie and Gertrude, my brother-in-law and sister-in-law, for the disposal of her many possessions, clothes, etc. and the other petty problems which inevitably have to be faced.

A few months later my own mother died, and this was the loss of someone who had been very close to me despite our many disagreements. Often she did not approve of my actions, but she never failed me as a mother and her love was always there. I grieved that she had never understood why I gave up the religion she was steeped in, and I wonder whether it would have made any difference if the great changes that have now overwhelmed the Roman Catholic church had come sooner. For the third time I was faced with the disposal of material belongings, and this time there was the problem of the future of Dyneley. Both my sons, as usual, were most supporting, but Simon was not yet married and therefore was in no position to take responsibility for the house, and I myself had no wish to dig up my London roots. Also, the advent of open-cast mining close to the house would inevitably cause disruption, and time had to be left for the ground to settle afterwards. I therefore decided to close Dyneley, at least temporarily.

James Burton was perhaps my greatest comfort at this time, for he was very intuitive and knew much more than I ever told him. He felt mother's death deeply, and the thought of closing Dyneley came hard, for he had nursed her there and had managed a difficult household of domestics and nurses throughout the war, interspersed with his Home Guard duties. He left Dyneley only for a brief spell during mother's illness, when accompanying Mont and me in South Africa.

So we packed up Dyneley, and James came to Plodge as butler. I think he enjoyed this period, but in any case it was bliss for me because he ran the house, and Nellie—Mont's parlourmaid—became cook. While I worked very hard by day there were evenings when I would entertain friends and colleagues and gave them pleasure by meeting together in a relaxed and civilised way.

After Mont died I knew I would have to leave Plodge, even if the lease had not come to an end, for the expense of upkeep made it impossible for me to live in the way I felt such a house deserved. I looked at many flats and small houses, but all were unsuitable or too expensive. I went to consult my dear neighbours, the Misses Alexander of Aubrey House on Campden Hill. Rachel and Jean, two lovely old ladies, lived in their beautiful mid-18th century house rather like the ladies in Cranford. Their father, William Alexander, went to live there in 1870 and one of his daughters was painted by Whistler. The portrait called "Harmony in Grey" now hangs in the Tate Gallery, and I have one of the few original reproductions. The house was full of exquisite furniture and pictures. Miss Rachel, the elder sister, received me most courteously and told me about Aubrey Lodge, a Victorian house, which she had had converted into flats. A tenant was leaving so, on her suggestion, I was lucky enough to acquire a home so near to Plodge which enabled me to keep in touch with old haunts, shops in Notting Hill Gate, and so on. The flat overlooks Holland Park, and there is a small garden which became James' delight. The flat had some drawbacks, but dear Ronnie said it had 90% of what I was looking for and one should never ask for more. How wise he was.

Thus it was in 1954 that the dramatic experience of leaving Plodge took place. The lease was up, and the L.C.C. had acquired the house and garden under a compulsory purchase order for a comprehensive school. Ironically, as it turned out, I was delighted that it had not been acquired by a property developer for a middle class housing estate! I had considerable trust in the L.C.C. and its Education Committee, and entertained Mr. Hayward, the then Leader of the Council, and some of the chief officers. They were courteous and obviously interested, and anxious to preserve as much of the house as possible. They agreed to my leaving some of the furniture which had been specially built for the Peacock room, the hand

In the Way of Understanding

embroidered pictures of peacocks on silk which Mont had bought in Hiroshima, some experimental seven-sided arm chairs made of wood, and two chairs of wood and slatted brown and gold leather. The garden shoe-scrapers of polished steel with Mont's initials M. N. which stood on both sides of the front door, and some lovely William Morris plates over the doors of the various sitting rooms, were also left. There were, also curious electric light fittings made from ostrich eggs, and one particular lamp of silver and coloured glass "cloisonné" in the music room (the room so exquisitely described by Janet Ashbee, Chapter 8, p. 90). The little iron garden gates, also encrusted with Mont's initials, I left as it seemed that so much belonged to the house and would not fit in elsewhere. They were all the brain children of a gifted man making his shell or nest. Little of all this, alas, has been preserved. Local authority members come and go, as do chief officers, and one house—however beautiful—gets lost amongst the vast number bought, sold and destroyed by succeeding generations. I am sure that in 1954 the L.C.C. meant well, and intended to keep the house as near a dwelling place as possible when they built their large comprehensive school for 2,000 children on the garden site. The music room was to be a library, and the many other rooms were to be studies for sixth formers. I had small labels specially made for each room, giving the names of the woods in Latin and their places of origin and the names of the craftsmen and dates. But the beauty and peace that existed has died. Plodge is no more. I will not enlarge on what has happened except to say, with hindsight and a heavy heart, that I now realise that a clean sweep—a housing estate, or even the destruction of the old house, would have been preferable. I should have given much of the interior to the Leighton House Museum, who would have welcomed it and preserved most of it. I feel ashamed of myself now for my naive faith in local authorities who, of course, are not real people but administrative bodies. I should have remembered Psalm 49, verse VII "And yet they think that their houses shall continue for ever: and that their dwelling places shall endure from one generation to the other, and call the lands after their own names".

The last night I spent alone in Plodge (though dear James

Statue of Mont by Sir Charles Wheeler R.A. in Garden Court,
Bank of England

James Burton and Lilian Whitchurch

Dominique, Peregrine's daughter

Simon's seven children
Front Row: Peregrine, Cosima, Victoria
Back row: Charlotte, Alice, Baby Frances, Katharine

and other staff were in the background, preparing for the removers to come next day). At about midnight, with a full moon streaming in the window, I said farewell. I willed myself to remember the music room, with its beauty and peace, the panelled walls of cedar wood, the floor of huge wide-cut English elm, the tables and chairs which had been especially made for it, so loved and cherished and looking so beautifully shiny and happy. I impressed the whole picture on my memory, willing myself never to forget; then gently closing the double doors I had one last look at the other rooms, finally moving up the staircase made of solid blocks of Scottish elm and stopping for a few minutes more to look down on the music room from the gallery. I then went to bed after bathing in the sunken bathwell, with its dark Morris blue tiles on the floor and the pale green ones on the walls. And so I left Plodge forever.

James and I now moved into Aubrey Lodge with Nellie, but flat life did not suit her and she decided to retire. James and I were therefore alone, but he too decided this new life-style of mine was not really to his liking and we were too much on top of each other. He sometimes saw me pottering about in my dressing gown before breakfast, and this was not what he was accustomed to, so he went to his widowed sister in Blackburn and worked daily as a luncheon butler to a bank in Manchester.

So now it was that I persuaded Lilian Whitchurch to come to be my housekeeper in place of James. I had first come across Lilian when I first visited St. Clere in about 1930, before marrying Mont. She was the head housemaid, a sweet gentle young girl and very pretty, with lovely hair in a neat bun and a tiny waist which I much admired as she knelt to make up my bedroom fire. She was always carefully dressed in pretty coloured print dresses, and was a professional to her finger tips, caring for the furniture, curtains, carpets and the general upkeep of that old house to perfection. Her peaceful temperament and smile endeared her to all, and she kept harmony in the establishment—something that is not always easy amongst domestics. I believe she had grown up the hard way, her mother having abandoned her at a tender age to an unkind aunt, and her father—a sea captain in the Merchant Navy—rarely saw her. Her two brothers were in Barnardo homes. At 13 she had taken herself off to domestic service, proceeding slowly up the domestic ladder until becoming a fully trained head housemaid. She was also the perfect personal maid, unpacking and packing for guests and seeing to their comfort. She went with the Collets in the winter to Costabelle in the South of France. Later she married a Welshman called Whitchurch and left St. Clere for Wales, but I think her husband's family never really appreciated her and treated her as a foreigner. Her husband died and she had no children.

Lilian and I were living happily together in the flat when James, after having been with his sister in Blackburn for two or three months, noticed that I was billed to speak at some mental health meeting in that city. He wrote and asked if he could talk to me. He came to the station about lunch time, having obtained time off, and we sat on a long hard bench, like two birds on a telegraph wire. He said, diffidently: "Do you remember what you said to me, Milady, when you said 'Goodbye'?". I had completely forgotten, but hoped it had been something appropriate. James went on to explain, and repeated the words I had used: "Remember, James, my home is your home". "Did you mean it?" he asked. My heart missed a beat, as I was now completely happy with another old friend, Lilian. Recovering myself quickly, I said: "Of course, James" and then he told me the following story.

The directors of the bank where he worked had given a big luncheon for V.I.P.s and had asked James to prepare salad with French dressing. He told me he had made it exactly as her Ladyship (meaning my mother) had taught him, but the Chairman had seized the bowl and poured bottled salad cream into it. After that, he said, he could no longer work for such people, and he would like to come back to my flat if I agreed. Indeed I did, for he was my friend, and my initial misgiving vanished. After he came back to the flat the happy association of the three of us worked well. Lilian proved an ideal nannie to my grandchildren, whom she loved, and they were devoted to her. She was a Cordon Bleu cook and served delicious dinners, or dainty little meals when I was alone, and was an ideal nurse when I was sick or tired. James was his usual invaluable self, and the three of us lived in harmony, though in close quarters. Lilian rigged up a lovely yellow velvet curtain between my room, the bathroom and the rest of the flat so that I was carefully screened from James' view.

Without Lilian and James I could not have given so much time to my mental health work, nor gone away on the long journeys I undertook. They both took an active part on the annual Mental Health flag days, rattling tins and calling on neighbours in house-to-house collections. Both these devoted friends did much to alleviate loneliness, for when I returned from a world journey or from a hard day's work they were always there, ready to administer to my needs and ready to take an active interest in what I had been doing. In my absences they answered the telephone and kept my friends and colleagues informed of my whereabouts, appointments, etc,— acting in fact as my secretaries. I was able to entertain my friends, and thanks to their devoted service I was able to keep open house, thus bringing colleagues together, which is often a pleasant way of transacting business and solving problems. No wonder I was referred to as the "Best kept woman in London"!

One of the delightful advantages of Aubrey Lodge in those days was that we were all tenants with more or less the same interests, and therefore the atmosphere was cosy and harmonious. Lady Lister, another Alexander sister, lived on the second floor when I came to Aubrey Lodge. She was an invalid with two nurses and two devoted maids. She was a good-looking old lady and her flat was always in perfect order and her dear sisters visited her daily. I believe Aubrey Lodge was bought in order to house this sister who was a widow and, like the other sisters, full of interest in life. Perhaps Lady Lister was the senior citizen amongst us, and I certainly treated her with respect.

Mary Stocks (Baroness Stocks) lived in the basement and was a great personality, an educationalist in the true sense of that word, and an economist. She was gallant and extremely witty, though a serious academic, a writer and the famous broadcaster in the programme "Any Questions". We became very great friends and had many discussions—though perhaps

In the Way of Understanding

I should say I listened with great pleasure to her views on almost every subject under the sun, on all of which she expressed herself decisively. Politics came first—she had been a Socialist and we shared many opinions on this subject, but she left the Party in 1966 in disgust, being unhappy and angry at Mr. Wilson's leadership and with nationalisation. One topic we often talked about in depth was sex, and the fact that it seemed to be such an all-important subject for the young, with their craze to bring it into the open and discuss it ad nauseam in books, plays and so on. She found the subject boring, and I found her description of her own very happy marriage with three children fascinating. The young couple, who were both of great intelligence and had high academic qualifications, had to learn emotion the hard way by trial and error. It was a curious conversation for two old ladies, but though our experiences had been different—mine I think at a deeper level—we both ruled out the word "sex" and called it "the act of love". It was an act of faith too, splendid in surrender, creative and communicative. We agreed that the moment of love is a moment of union of body, mind and spirit and the act of faith is mutual and implicit.

Mary had many friends and in her flat I met politicians, theatre folk, writers and dons. The talk was swift and amusing, with Mary dominating, yet bringing us all together. Sometimes we had drinks in her flat and then came up to mine for an exquisite dinner cooked by Lilian and served by James—they were Mary's devoted slaves and admirers. She admired them too and, they were also her friends. Mary was no cook and refused to try. Had it not been for the devotion of her daughters and son-in-law she would surely have starved to death, since tins of baked beans and a can-opener were all that she asked for.

Another remarkable character on the top floor was Mrs. Tozer, a very old and frail lady, a friend of William Morris and May Morris. Mrs. Tozer had original Morris furniture and wall-papers. It was like turning back the pages of history to pay her a visit. She sat in an old black satin frock in winter and in grey cotton in summer, with a little lace cap on her grey hair. There was peace in her flat, and beauty too, and the view

Loneliness and the Solace of Work

overlooking Holland Park above the tree tops was breathtaking. It was said that sometimes Windsor Castle was visible on a clear day.

These friends have died, other tenants have moved in, and the Lodge has lost something rather special. Mary wrote an inscription in my copy of her book *My Commonplace Book*.[1] It reads: "Greetings from Mary Stocks in the basement to Priscilla Norman on the first floor; may she long continue to share the same front gate, the same dustbins, the same Western sunsets and the same taste for convivial drinking on one another's premises."

Peter Davies, 1970.

16

The Bethlem Royal and Maudsley Hospitals

An island of sanity in a world of madness
Professor Sir Denis Hill, Founders
Day Speech, Bethlem Royal Hospital,
October, 1979.

Presumably because of my connection with the N.A.M.H. and my close association with the W.F.M.H., in 1951 the then Minister of Health invited me to serve as a member of the Board of Governors of the Bethlem Royal and Maudsley Hospitals. In his letter he told me, "The Board of Governors acts as the agent of the Minister for the administration of the hospitals for which it is responsible. Membership is normally for three years with the possibility of re-appointment". I was re-appointed every three years by successive Ministers, regardless of their political allegiance, until 1975, when in accordance with the age limit I retired. Governors are unpaid, but are allowed out-of-pocket expenses for travel, etc.

This was just the work I was looking for, although I felt shy in the presence of so much psychiatric expertise—especially Sir Aubrey Lewis, the formidable Professor of Psychiatry, who was supposed to have reduced some of his doctors as well as his social-worker students to tears! Governors and staff were welcoming, and I decided to start by listening to discussions in committees, and by learning from all those who were willing to explain the work and answer my questions. This was time-consuming for busy nurses and administrators and I am not too sure in those early days how much new Governors, especially laymen, were considered to be useful.

At that time there was very little written about these two hospitals for amateurs like myself, unless one had access to learned tomes on the history of psychiatry. My ignorance was

The Bethlem Royal and Maudsley Hospitals

very real, and in the rarified atmosphere of the "Gilded Cage" (as the Bethlem Royal and Maudsley were called by other mental hospitals), I wondered if I should ever be of much use.

Patricia Allderidge, the archivist of Bethlem Royal and Maudsley, has since written historical notes—published in the *Bulletin of the New York Academy of Medicine*, December 1971—and I am much indebted to her for the information below.

The Bethlem Royal Hospital was one of the five Royal Hospital Foundations of the 16th century, but, before that date, Simon Fitzmary, an alderman and twice Sheriff of the City of London, granted all his lands in the parish of St. Botolph without Bishopsgate in 1247 to the Church of St. Mary of Bethlehem. The object was to establish a priory, but the land is now covered by part of Liverpool Street station! The name Bethlem has many variants; the best known is Bedlem, a corruption of Bethlehem. Development over the centuries is well described by Miss Allderidge in her excellent pamphlet, but for my purpose it is enough to say that by the 14th century a hospital or hospice was provided for the care of men deprived of their reason as well as a refuge for the infirm. The priory seems to have had many moves, and one resting place was Moorfields where sightseers thronged the galleries to see the lunatics in chains—as seen in some Hogarth prints. Another resting place was what we now know as the Imperial War Museum, which had accommodated criminal lunatics until the building of Broadmoor in 1864. A period of enlightenment and reform took place about this time, with kindness and understanding replacing the former policy of coercion. Clinical instruction and lectures were introduced, leading to the hospital's reputation as a teaching centre. A final move was made to a purpose-built hospital on the beautiful Monks Orchard Estate near Beckenham, Kent in 1924.

In 1948 the National Health Service Act, with the consent of the then Board of Governors, linked Bethlem Royal Hospital with the famous Maudsley Hospital on Denmark Hill, London, which was then administered by the L.C.C. and was renowned for its post-graduate teaching of psychiatry.

The two hospitals, though seven miles apart, are now

administered jointly by one Board of Governors as one postgraduate teaching hospital, together with their medical school, the Institute of Psychiatry.

The Maudsley Hospital owes its foundation to the initiative and persistence of one man, Henry Maudsley (1835–1918), who, after matriculating at London University, decided on a medical career. He had ambitions to be a surgeon, but turned to psychiatry and eventually became Superintendent to the Cheadle Royal Lunatic Asylum Manchester at the age of 24. Later he returned to London in order to get more experience in the treatment of lunacy, and to write books on the subject. He became one of the most eminent psychiatrists of his day.

In 1907 Maudsley offered £30,000 to the L.C.C. towards establishing a hospital for early and acute cases, and an out-patients' department for some 75–100 cases, some paupers and some fee-paying. Due provision was to be made for clinical and pathological research, for a laboratory, and for a teaching unit. This was to be part of a teaching unit which was to be recognised as a School of the University of London for the study of mental disease and neuropathology.

Work only started in 1913, and when war broke out in 1914 the buildings were handed over, with Maudsley's consent, and fully equipped, for use as a military hospital. This was used for the treatment of nervous disorders arising from war service. This hospital was demobilised in 1919, and in 1920 Dr. Edward Mapother, my friend in the early days of child guidance, became the first Medical Superintendent of the Maudsley Hospital.

With the Bethlem Royal and the Maudsley jointly administered, the medical school became the Institute of Psychiatry, in a new building opened in 1967 on an adjacent site. This is now the Medical School of the joint hospital. The importance of this link was vividly illustrated by Mr. Paine, the House Governor, when in a lecture he used the metaphor of a marriage ceremony. He described the union as a match between Maudsley, the impecunious student, and Bethlem, the wealthy bride with her dowry, which could now be spent on research and the treatment of mental illness.

Looking back, it is curious to remember my reluctance to

Bethlem Royal, 1746

My portrait by David Poole, R.A. 1973

Princess Alexandra, Eileen Skellern C.N.O. and L. H. W. Paine, House Governor at Bethlem Royal

St. Dymphna, Patron Saint of mental health

Myself with Deirdre O'Connor, Head Mistress, Bethlem Royal & Maudsley Hospital School

The Bethlem Royal and Maudsley Hospitals

join the Mental Hospitals Committee of the L.C.C. when I think of my later involvement in the child guidance movement and the first W.F.M.H. Congress. Now I had been appointed as a Governor of the best-known post-graduate psychiatric hospital in the world, and because of its considerable endowments and the trust of its Governors I was able to travel and to help promote voluntary mental health associations in many countries. Writing these memoirs has made me notice some events that propelled me along a road I had not knowingly intended to take: for instance, at Bethlem Royal the connections of the Founder, Simon Fitzmary, with the City of London were a reminder of my own not inconsiderable connections in the past with the City. It was here in Bethlem and Maudsley that I found a niche for myself, where all concerned, and especially the doctors, nurses and administrators gave me over many years an insight into what I once heard a French psychiatrist describe as "psychiatrie sérieuse", and I was reminded of the Niebuhr prayer (see beginning of chapter 18).

Earlier in my mental health work at the N.A.M.H. money had always been very tight, but now it was different. The joint hospitals had many beneficiaries, and wise husbandry of investments, together with their connection with the City, made them sound financially. The Finance and General Purposes Committee attracted some of the best financial and administrative brains, who took immense pains to discuss and to sift the items on the agenda at meetings—which were usually long! In the early days they met at Guildhall, which made it easy for City members to attend. The Hospital Committee met monthly at each hospital in turn. The big acreage of the Bethlem estate necessitated a Farm and Gardens Committee, but eventually the farm was discontinued. It was felt to be unsuitable as occupational therapy for patients to work on the farm. The old idea of working on the land, caring for animals and working in the lovely gardens and greenhouse, seemed to me much more therapeutic than basket and rug making and improvised carpentry, but more on this later. At this particular time it was deemed better for patients to do these things under the guidance of expert occupational therapists, thus enabling

In the Way of Understanding

the professional farmers and gardeners to get on with their job unhampered by having to teach or supervise patients. The trees and grounds are beautiful, thanks to the care bestowed on the property by those early Governors, and I shall never forget my many visits of inspection to Bethlem, especially at night during a full moon.

Prior to my joining the Board of Governors I had mixed with followers of various theories of psychiatry, and sometimes had found the more analytical amongst them extremely puzzling. I was in no way rigid, but always willing to learn and to try to understand, but I wondered then, and wonder still, whether the general public are yet ready to accept the theories expounded by the followers of Freud, Jung, Adler and others, and whether their theories do not occasionally do ill service to the mental health movement. This may be a harsh comment, but I prefer what Dr. Wilfrid Warren said in his Sarah Stolz lecture in 1970: "Some pronouncements by psychologists and psychiatrists have not always helped the public to clear their minds." Also in the Spring 1979 number of the *Bethlem and Maudsley Gazette* I was amused to I read an article by Dr. Anthony Clare who quoted Carl Rogers of California as saying he "rejected psychoanalysis because it had become a petrified religious orthodoxy, because it was elitist and incorporated a body of inchoate and opaque ideas impenetrable to the average man, and because it was superfluous. Love, otherwise known as empathy, caring and genuineness, is all you need." (p. 15).

However, there was rapid growth in those early days, not only in new buildings but in upgrading the Maudsley wards—grim in 1951. There was the new Alcoholic Unit and a Neurosurgical Unit at the Maudsley. At Bethlem there was a purpose-built adolescent school unit, new wards for drug takers, and the Hilda Lewis Unit for research into mental handicap in children. Perhaps I was more at ease in the children's ward at the Maudsley and in the adolescent unit at Bethlem, where I could fit into the multidisciplinary team of psychiatrists, psychologists, social workers and teachers who were doing a remarkable job. One consultant once told me that the teachers gave an invaluable service to all concerned and were a most important part of the treatment, with the headmistress often playing a leading role. Yet another consultant, treating an adolescent on an adult ward, and confronted with the fact that he could only have one hour a week of a teacher's time, expressed frustration. He said he wished he could prescribe education as he could pills or occupational therapy.

History has it that when the adolescent unit was first mooted, the then Governors expressed alarm at the idea of disruptive youngsters being housed in the grounds of Bethlem. They feared the damage these youngsters could do in the grounds, besides annoying other patients. This did happen when the unit opened, as some boys extracted bits of wire from their bedsteads and made a key to enable them to start the hospital coach, which they then proceeded to drive round the grounds. This escapade was in due course reported at a meeting of Governors who expressed their displeasure, some of them suggesting the closure of the unit. A wise voice was raised by one of the older Governors who obviously understood frustrated youth because he told his fellow Governors that in *his* youth he had stolen a steam roller and driven it on the open road. He expressed the opinion that the boys had only shown healthy high spirits in what amounted to a prank. Thus the heat was taken out of the argument, and the Governors merely expressed the hope that the staff would deal with the incident in an appropriate manner. The possible closure of what was a highly successful experiment was therefore averted. This shows how a wise and open-minded layman on the Board of Governors influenced an important decision by common sense, and it proves my point that a lay man or woman can play an important part amongst professionals.

Staggering changes in the joint hospitals took place during my 24 years, not only in the up-grading of the buildings but in personal relationships. There was a gradual but steady build-up of confidence between Governors and senior staff. This was, I am sure, due to much constructive work behind the scenes between the House Governor, the Chief Nursing Officer and the Chairman of the Medical Committee. The Chairman changed every three years, thus giving all consul-

In the Way of Understanding

tants a taste of the difficulties of administrative and financial affairs. When I first joined the Board of Governors the Chief Nursing Officer was known as the Matron, but later the Royal College of Nursing belatedly recognised that male nurses could reach the highest nursing post. Thus the title Matron would be incongruous, and the term Chief Nursing Officer was used instead.

I had the greatest admiration and respect for our team, whose task was to re-shape the administration after the retirement of the House Governor and Matron—both of whom had been at the Maudsley in the days of the L.C.C. The Chairman of the Board in those early days of 1948 was also a member of the L.C.C., and gave devoted service during the very difficult period of the take-over, as did the then House Governor and Matron. Changes there had to be, and I personally felt more and more drawn into the process. It was for the benefit of patients and staff, and certainly it gave each Governor a more imtimate knowledge of the work of both hospitals.

Future policy discussions at Board level were always stimulating. Sometimes we had to plan for periods of up to five to ten years ahead, and the final planning report I saw just before my retirement in 1975 was a formidable document, whose recommendations I hope to live to see implemented. The report embraced international, national and community commitments, especially the need for a close relationship with the local community. This neighbourly commitment had only partially existed in the old days, but these changes meant far more work for the administrators and the nursing and medical teams. These senior officers were constantly discussing with their counterparts from other hospitals the enormous growth of the psychiatric hospitals, and the many changes which were being made in the hospitals for the mentally handicapped. The Board of Governors were indeed making psychiatric history alongside the Institute of Psychiatry.

One of the important changes to be made while I was a Governor was the abolition of nurses' uniforms, except in the neurosurgical unit. This issue took over two years to resolve. One difficulty had been that the male members of the Board of Governors, and especially our then Chairman, held the view that the gentle female with her fair hand soothing the brow or taking the pulse could be far more effective in uniform. The nurses, when consulted by means of a secret ballot, were not all agreed, but eventually the then daring decision was taken to allow nurses to wear their own clothes, but such clothes as were approved by the Chief Nursing Officer. The decision was a difficult one, for while my head told me that psychiatric nursing did not need aprons and caps, my heart listened to those who explained that an emotionally disturbed, mentally sick person might find it easier to cry on the shoulder of a nurse in uniform whom the patient recognised as such, than of someone not in uniform who did not satisfy the image of a caring profession. Nurses, too, were divided at the thought of the possible variety of clothes and colour schemes, ideas of women wearing trousers, and so on, and these were difficult details to adjudicate on. But all such dilemmas find their solution in time.

The nurses also benefited by the building of a Nurses' Hostel which was named after H.R.H. Princess Marina, who had agreed to be Patron of the joint hospital in 1955. There was much discussion in the hospital service at that time about the merits and demerits of Nurses' Homes. At one time it was considered wise for every hospital to have its own residential home so that especially young nursing students and probationer nurses could be accommodated at work and avoid the need to travel long distances. These homes were under the management of an administrator, usually a nursing sister, and were run under strict rules. Nurses had to be back at 10 p.m.; they had to apply for late passes and be tidy, and there were difficulties about bringing in boy friends, etc. These restrictions outweighed the advantages of living in and became resented. More and more senior and junior staff lived out, but accommodation was hard to find in both Camberwell and Beckenham. After much discussion in the hospital world, hostels or hotels under a Warden—who is not a member of the nursing staff—were provided, and these have proved very successful, solving the problems of travel and of rigid rules. Princess Marina House was well planned by the Hospital architects (Architects Co. Partnership, with Paul Gell as De-

In the Way of Understanding

sign Consultant), and included flatlets for sisters, bed-sitters for nurses, spacious lounges and a T.V. room as well as bathrooms, hot and cold water in basins in bedrooms and a well equipped kitchen and a space for washing and drying.

The Warden is trained in domestic science, and has to deal with a complex set of inmates—not only nurses, because when space is available doctors and other professionals are also given accommodation. This measure has proved highly successful, and watching its evolvement has given me much satisfaction. The complex benefited by the generosity of the Board of Governors, who devoted a large sum of money to improve the amenities. The D.H.S.S. were, as usual, under a financial crisis and our mandate was to build as cheaply as possible!

An important new appointment to the joint hospitals was that of an archivist. It had seemed to the Governors that the huge quantity of material accumulated over the years would be of historical value and I more than agreed with them. Miss Allderidge took on this task and worked in the small ground floor room first ascribed to her at Bethlem. It soon became apparent as the material came to light that not only did we need a dry store room for papers and even a museum but certainly a better room in which the archivist could work. As I have said earlier, I am indebted to Miss Allderidge[1] for my historical account of the hospitals and her work will prove invaluable to students of psychiatric history and to historians interested in social history. I think she will agree she now has a good building and suitable museum for her important work, and well worth a visit by anyone interested in psychiatry.

Just before I left the Board of Governors, a full-time Church of England chaplain was appointed to serve the joint hospitals, and this was something for which I had argued for a long time. At Bethlem, where there was a lovely chapel or small church in the grounds, we had always had a chaplain part-time, and there was also a chaplain half-time at the Maudsley, but over the years I had been very unhappy about this arrangement. It

[1] Patricia H. Allderidge, "Historical Notes on the Bethlem Royal Hospital and The Maudsley Hospital", *Bulletin of The New York Academy of Medicine*, Second Series, vol. 17, No. 12, pp. 1537–1546, Dec. 1971.

was true that services had been taken and the wards visited, but somehow the real work of a parish priest as guide, philosopher and friend seemed wanting. I felt that it was essential to convince the Medical Committee of the wisdom of having a full-time chaplain, and it proved to be no easy task. They were, not unnaturally, apprehensive at the thought of a man whose task was to be the daily pastoral care at both hospitals, someone whose duty it would be to make himself aware of the treatment carried out by doctors, the intricate work of psychiatric nursing and the delicate handling of patients by social workers, and who yet had to retain the role of a parson. He would have to walk a tight rope and not confuse his role with that of others. He had to be someone with a deep understanding of psychology, who would not interfere yet would be readily available to all concerned and gain their confidence. The D.H.S.S. only allowed money for a half-time salary, so the Governors had to be persuaded to pay for the balance from endowments. I pursued a long battle for a full-time appointment, and sometimes felt defeated and very depressed. However, our always helpful House Governor devised a scheme by which the two half-time chaplaincies—which also involved relief holiday duties at King's College Hospital, our near neighbour—were deemed to equal one whole-time appointment, and this was ultimately agreed to the satisfaction of all concerned. Both senior and junior medical staff interviewed the candidates, and eventually the Board of Governors made an excellent appointment. This was someone who through study came to understand psychiatry and psychology and was prepared to give time to the needs of patients and staff. He gained the confidence of the medical and nursing professions, was willing to think ecumenically and to work with his Roman Catholic and Methodist counterparts, was interested in the children and adolescents and made services come alive. Earlier sermons on Founder's Day at Bethlem with many sceptical scientists in the audience had left much to be desired, and at times they had made me squirm. But now in this new appointment we seemed to have found everything we needed, and this made my long and frustrating battle with the Medical Committee worth-while.

In the Way of Understanding

The last appointment which was made when I chaired the interviewing panel was that of the head occupational therapist. Earlier on I had been very critical of basket and rug making, but as I listened to the successful candidate's account of how the whole theory of this profession had come full circle, and of how occupational therapy was developing on the lines of useful work of the type we all have to do in our own homes, and in which patients found security, I became much happier. Supervised occupational therapy with modern aids was explained, and it was good to see psychotherapy and occupational therapy being joined together, with the patients not working just for occupation's sake as in the old days.

A small, useful legacy I left to the joint hospital on my retirement was the idea of having three dinner lectures each year. I am happy to say that these are still carried on, two at the Maudsley and one at Bethlem. The idea came into my head when I found how little the lay members of the Board of Governors understood about the work of the medicos in the different units, about the role of the consultants, the problems of the nurses, the schools or the social work and occupational therapy departments. It seemed to me important that, if lay Governors were to take an intelligent interest in the treatment given to the patients in their care, they should hear at first hand from those in charge, and be able to ask questions and thus to educate themselves. Such social occasions also gave the professionals a chance of talking to the Governors and of getting to know each other under easy conditions. The idea proved a success and was, I think, useful and pleasant for all concerned. While the lay Governors were good attenders, the professional Governors, though invited, tended to keep away. Perhaps this was helpful, as it was an educational and social occasion which enabled lay Governors to ask questions, uninhibited by their professional colleagues. It was quite amusing and interesting during the first lectures to see from the questions which were asked how little the laymen understood the problems of treatment, therapy, psychiatric nursing and the part played by the School of Nursing and the Hospital School—not to mention the difference between mental illness and mental subnormality.

The Bethlem Royal and Maudsley Hospitals

Subjects for the lectures are now very varied, and cover a much wider canvas. The dinners are less formal, and sometimes take the form of a buffet supper. This enables a relaxed atmosphere to develop so that Governors and staff alike have time to appreciate each other's personalities. I wish all psychiatric hospitals could indulge in this kind of get-together between professionals and laymen, so that a system of communication between them can be established. Alas, neither the D.H.S.S., nor the Regional or Area Health Authorities have the money for this. It could be described as a luxury, but to me it would be money well spent to secure a management team that is equipped with a basic knowledge of their functions—the kind of in-service training which is now compulsory for all magistrates. For Governors and members of regional and area health authorities this is surely equally important from the patients' point of view, and would perhaps make for more understanding and better human relations in our very sick health service.

The joint hospital and the Institute of Psychiatry are intertwined. The latter was opened by Her Majesty Queen Elizabeth in 1972; a Neurological Building was completed in 1974 and later a Child Psychiatry building was completed making in all a very large but not unpleasing complex adjacent to the Maudsley Hospital. At first I was always very much in awe of the Institute and its many professors, whose names always escaped my careless memory, and whose "ologies" I was never able to distinguish, however much I tried. As the years went by they seemed to take me for granted, and I began to relax. I even enjoyed telling Sir Aubrey Lewis, when in old age he mellowed so beautifully, of my travels and of my meetings with so many of his former students, often by then professors themselves, in many parts of the world. Both the joint hospital and the Institute with their community commitment are now much more open to the public and they even have an annual open day and fête, thanks to the Dean, Dr. Jim Birley.

Animal research is part of the work of the Institute, and it was in this field that I had to keep a balance between my head and my heart. My deep love for animals should not be

In the Way of Understanding

confused with sentimentality and the kind of love that wants to possess animals big or small simply for one's own pleasure, and not the animal's. I have never enjoyed the circus because animals are on show there for amusement and gain, and I am not naive enough to believe there is more carrot than stick in their training. The animal house at Maudsley is carefully administered and the animals groomed and given every possible attention. Experiments are conducted under scrupulous adherence to the law. It is also worth remembering that once an operation is over the recovery is also part of the research, and here it is that the dumb animal can expect comfort and sympathy. The devoted attendants do all they can to alleviate suffering. The psychological research at Bethlem in the cattery and the monkey house was also well administered, with inmates kindly cared for. Some time ago, after much pressure from the Governors, ground was made available in an orchard for larger enclosures for the monkeys, who had seemed previously to be in such small cages compared with the free life they had been born to. Princess Marina, after seeing the Bethlem premises, had been concerned by the lack of space, and had talked to me of her anxiety. This royal interest in animals as well as that shown by staff and patients was a stimulus to the Board of Governors to take action, and I know that it pleased both the Royal Mother and her daughter. Since that time the monkey house has fulfilled its function and is no more.

Much remarkable progress in research, both in the treatment of disease and in the relief of pain in the physical and mental fields is due to research on animals, and whether it is right or wrong—always a debatable point—is not for me to say. It has always been at the back of my mind in my years at Bethlem and Maudsley and on the Regional Board. But such research is being carried out under less favourable conditions all over the world, and if it could be co-ordinated and not duplicated it would be a step in the right direction. Man's inhumanity to man is only excelled by man's inhumanity to animals—and maybe plants.

17
Two Royal Ladies

The Bethlem Royal Hospital, as its name implies, has been connected with the throne since it was given its charter in the reign of Henry VIII. James I took a personal interest in its welfare when he ordered an investigation into the conduct of its keeper and reminded the Commissioners that "those who suffer from mental affliction ought to be treated with all the care necessary to their state by the rules of medicine". Surely this was a remarkable statement in a non-enlightened age. Charles II placed Bethlem, together with the other Royal Hospitals, under the care of the King's Commissioners, and from that time the monarchs were less personally involved in hospital affairs.

The royal family had been carefully sheltered from any contact with mental illness since the time of George III until this century, when Queen Mary opened Bethlem on its present site in 1930. She was at that time a Governor of the Hospital and later became Patron of the joint hospitals from 1940–1953. When the Institute of Psychiatry was transferred from the Maudsley Hospital to its new home in de Crespigne Park, the buildings were officially opened by Elizabeth the Queen Mother, as Chancellor of the University of London in July 1960.

When the final arrangements for the amalgamation of the voluntary mental health associations were complete as recommended by the Feversham Report, one of the bodies to be incorporated was the National Association for Mental Hygiene. Their chairman suggested that the widow of their late patron H.R.H. the Duke of Kent, tragically killed in 1942, might like to be associated with the newly formed N.A.M.H. Princess Marina was a remarkably clever and intuitive lady who would surely grasp the importance of this amalgamation. The President Elect, R. A. Butler, undertook the task of talking

In the Way of Understanding

to the Princess, who indeed happily agreed to be the first patron.

It became a great pleasure for me to work with Princess Marina all through the years I was at the N.A.M.H., and also when she became patron of Bethlem Royal and Maudsley in 1955. She was never just a figurehead, for she steeped herself in the aims of the N.A.M.H. and took pains to educate herself in the different problems of the mentally ill and the mentally handicapped. When planning her programme at the beginning of each year she tried to ensure that she would be able to attend any ceremony we might have in mind, e.g. our annual conference or the opening of one of our schools or hostels. There were many informal occasions too when the Princess would come along and talk to those concerned, whether committee members, doctors, nurses or teachers. She showed her intelligence and real interest in the work on these occasions, and before any formal introductions she always told me not to worry too much about the names, but to be sure to tell her what each person was doing so that she could have an intelligent conversation. Names never came easily to me, and the addition of professions and special interests or work made my task of introductions a responsible as well as an intimidating one. There was one occasion I shall never forget, at a home for very low-grade mentally-handicapped children where parents deposited their children for a short stay while they took a much-needed break. The children were all under five, very disturbed and all too obviously subnormal—a sight not easy for anyone to look at. But this lady, with a cheerful smile, went into every room, talked to each nurse or attendant and asked about each case. Many of us were moved as she showed her admiration of staff and parents, and her real sympathy and understanding.

Her visits to our two approved schools, later known as community homes, were great events because our patron, always elegantly dressed, gave much pleasure to staff and pupils. They were inclined to mob her, but she seemed to take these delinquent girls in her stride and by the time she left we were all laughing and joking together.

Later, after Princess Marina became patron of the Bethlem

Two Royal Ladies

Royal and Maudsley, her visits became a little more formal, with the chairman of the Governors and the Chief Nursing Officer guiding her round the wards and different departments, and introducing her to the consultants and nurses. Even under these circumstances of protocol she would appear relaxed, and was always questioning and anxious to learn. The relationship between patron and chief nursing officer became close as the new approach to psychiatric nursing was explained.

In August 1968 the W.F.M.H. was due to hold its meeting in London, and the opening ceremony took place in the Albert Hall. I was then President of the W.F.M.H. and the Princess agreed to open the proceedings. However, just 24 hours before the event, it became known that she was seriously ill and that her daughter was to officiate in her place. This was a great shock to us all, and perhaps especially to me as I had grown to love and admire her great qualities. I was a little apprehensive about young Princess Alexandra who was to deputise for so remarkable a mother, but I need not have worried. When she arrived she was just as gracious, and seemed quite relaxed in what must have been for her very strange surroundings among representatives of the mental health movement from all over the world. As she walked slowly down the long aisle of the Albert Hall she paused to speak to the workers who were seated on the edge of the stalls and her manner conquered everybody. I had only to mention a name of the country and she would grasp its importance. She had herself visited many of the countries represented, especially those of the Third World. Everyone soon felt at ease, and this was all the more incredible because she had only stepped into her mother's shoes at very short notice, and had the terrible anxiety of her mother's illness in her mind.

Princess Marina had made a study of the various factors in mental health and it was to her that the Department of Health had often turned for opening new hospitals and extensions of buildings. She had made mental health her speciality and had covered the vast ground of mental illness and mental handicap. Her death left a void, and we all wondered if her daughter could be brave enough to fill it. Princess Alexandra did in fact

In the Way of Understanding

agree to succeed her mother as patron of the N.A.M.H. and of the Bethlem and Maudsley, much to my personal delight. She carried on her mother's roll beautifully but differently. She was not only gracious and concerned but brought also a sense of fun. There was always informality in her visits. She would never be hurried, and at one party I remember her stopping to talk with a Hospital gardener to seek advice on plants. Her humanity and deep concern for the mentally sick was obvious, and her training as a nurse was often apparent when she visited the wards which contained disturbed and very depressed patients. On one occasion a young woman patient was in tears and huddled in an armchair. Our young Princess went over and sat on the arm of the chair, put her arms round the patient and said "Yes, I know how unhappy you are, but this is a good hospital and you will soon be better". I could hardly restrain my tears to see such understanding in such a young girl. Eileen Skillern, the Chief Nursing Officer, was also much moved by so spontaneous and intuitive an action. On the same visit she sat amongst the doctors and was full of questions, some of them quite searching, and though her knowledge was not yet as deep as her mother's, her heart was in the right place. Her visits to the adolescent unit and her talks with the emotionally disturbed and even angry boys and girls will never be forgotten by those who witnessed them.

One delightful occasion for me was when Princess Marina met my dear butler James and after shaking him warmly by the hand cautioned him to look after me carefully. Years later, when Princess Alexandra was moving about unaccompanied, she met Lilian Whitchurch and on learning that she was my housekeeper she told her that she was one of the most important people at the reception, for without her care and attention at home I could never accomplish the important work I was doing. How right both mother and daughter were.

In 1963 my name appeared in the Birthday Honours list for a C.B.E. This award was for services to the mentally ill and the mentally handicapped. At last the voluntary mental health movement was being recognised, and I was more than happy and proud to receive my decoration which I felt to be for all concerned. It was a very happy occasion for me, for my son

Two Royal Ladies

Peregrine and his little daughter Dominique came with me. Her Majesty the Queen Mother told me she had watched with pleasure the progress of the mental health movement and how important it was for the whole world. This care and interest must surely have been fostered by her sister-in-law and later by her niece. I sincerely hope that the royal link with mental health in this country and overseas will continue, for such brave leadership is invaluable in the uphill work of a task which grows no less as the years go by.

18

South East Metropolitan Regional Hospital Board

God grant me the serenity to accept the things I cannot alter—the courage to alter the things I can—and the wisdom to know the difference.
A prayer by Reinhold Niebuhr.

My appointment to the S.E. Metropolitan Regional Hospital Board came about by chance, a method sometimes rather characteristic of the British way of life. At one of the Bethlem Royal and Maudsley Founder's Day lunches Sir Ivor Julian, then Chairman of the S.E. Metropolitan R.H.B., was the guest of honour and I was placed next to a senior civil servant from the D.H.S.S. who in course of conversation asked me why I was not a member of a Regional Board. My answer was simple: I have never been asked, nor did I know much about the working of Regional Boards. As a result of this casual conversation there came an invitation from the then Minister of Health, Derek Walker Smith, to serve on the S.E. Metropolitan Regional Hospital Board, the region which included Bethlem Royal and Maudsley in its area. The invitation read as follows:

> *As you will know, Regional Hospital Boards are set up by the Minister of Health under the National Health Service Act to act as his agents for providing a complete hospital and specialist service for every citizen. The day to day operation of the hospitals is in the hands of local Hospital Management Committees, but it is the Regional Board's duty— subject to the Minister's general advice and guidance—to plan, develop and guide the hospital service for their area. They carry a big and important responsibility in building up the scope and quality of that service. Membership of the Boards is normally for a period of three years, with the*

South East Metropolitan Regional Hospital Board

possibility of re-appointment, and if you accept this invitation your term of office will start on 1st April, 1958 and consequently will expire on 31st March, 1961.

I should mention that the general position is that members are unpaid, but that reasonable out-of-pocket expenses incurred on travel, meals, etc. are met, together with a limited reimbursement of financial loss shown to have been suffered through absence from work on the business of the Board.

I hope that you will feel able to accept this invitation, since it is on the voluntary work of the members of Boards and Committees that the effective conduct of the hospital service largely depends.

Here was another challenge I was glad to accept, a different one from Bethlem and Maudsley because it administered the large geographical area of Kent and East Sussex, including the County Boroughs of Brighton, Canterbury, Eastbourne and Hastings. In Greater London the Board's area included Bexley, Bromley, Greenwich, Lewisham, Southwark and Lambeth, with a population of three to five hundred thousand, 45,000 staff and an expenditure of £77 million a year. I tremble to think of the size of the budget of this area today, which has become the South East Thames Regional Health Authority under its new name.

The first administrative offices were in Portland Place and later alongside those of the other four London hospital regions in Eastbourne Terrace near Paddington, but these soon proved too small and a move was made to better accommodation in Croydon, Surrey. The Board of 22 members met monthly at Guy's Hospital, one of the three teaching hospitals in the region (the others being King's College and the Maudsley). The members shared committee work, which was heavy: a General Purposes and Finance Committee; a Mental Health Committee and a Nursing Committee and I was a member of all three. It seemed to me important – just as it had been for me on joining the Board of Governors of Bethlem and Maudsley – to learn something of what was expected of me, but I always got the same answer to all my questions: "It is up to you to

In the Way of Understanding

make what you like of the job". I felt this to be unsatisfactory, but there was no guide-lines. Some members were conscientious, others were very busy as M.P.s or with commitments to salaried professions and did as much as they could under these circumstances. The burden was carried by the Chairman and the willing horses, perhaps a majority being women members. Members of Parliament with a constituency in the region can be very useful, but I am doubtful if a full time executive running a business can be expected to do more than attend a monthly meeting of the Regional Board. Yet at the very least an acquaintance with the workings of the various hospitals and their staff and committees should be a high priority and this should be made clear before an appointment is made.

I decided to tour the region, first to visit each mental hospital, five in Kent and two in East Sussex with roughly 2,000 beds in each. The visits meant a whole day at each hospital with my long-suffering Norman family in Kent giving me generous hospitality for the night when I returned, pretty exhausted. I usually wrote a report and made notes of problems to talk over with the always patient Chief Officers at headquarters. I was not however 100% in harmony with the Board or with its Chief Officers. I felt, and on looking back believe, that the region in those early days was run by the Chairman, the officers and a few vocal members who lived in certain areas and were influential in getting a larger slice of the financial cake for their particular home patch. Politics, alas, came into the situation and the less extrovert though perhaps more experienced came off second best. I never felt the Chief Officers during my first three years quite knew what to make of me, wondering if I might be out to make trouble (which I was not). Twice I threatened to resign when I discovered on visiting a hospital that plans for reconstruction or reorganisation had been made, known to hospital staff but unknown to me as a Board member; it seemed to make a mockery of the work of Board members and thus was a complete waste of their time. However, my proposed resignation caused such a fuss that I was persuaded to refrain from this action, and was promised there would be briefing sessions for members so that we could all know what was planned. This promise was not kept, but a

South East Metropolitan Regional Hospital Board

big tour of all the mental hospitals in order to meet the Chief Medical Officers in each County and County Borough was organised. I was made chairman of the touring committee and it was nicknamed the "Norman Circus". It was a very big exercise, lasting three months or more, and entailed a whole day in each hospital, with discussions with the staff on the spot about their problems and attempts at dialogue with the Medical Officers of Health concerned in an effort to get the co-operation of their departments—a preview of the later reorganised health service. The senior administrative medical officer was always with me and was most helpful in his guidance at what were difficult and at times acrimonious meetings. One Medical Officer of Health told us he had no wish for his department to work with us, and that he was not interested in co-ordination of services unless he was the chief co-ordinator. This was not said so openly by other Medical Officers of Health but was indicative of the feeling we were up against in those early days. Those of us in my Circus certainly learned much from members of the hospital committees and staff face to face, meeting the more vocal and influential on their home ground. It was a useful exercise and if it did nothing much to change matters at that time, it paved the way for a new regional health service, the one we know today and which some of us still criticise, for perfect co-ordination and communication are alas still far away.

I tried to attend as many psychiatric hospital management committee meetings as I could, and I was a member of two Kent psychiatric hospital committees which happened to meet on Fridays and Mondays, thus making it possible for me to spend peaceful weekends in lovely surroundings with my Norman family in Kent, reading agendas, writing reports and trying not to be too outwardly concerned with mental health. Inwardly I was of course wrapped up in my concern for the appalling conditions I found in the hospitals. The lack of finance meant the buildings were grim, but all that could be done was done by devoted, overworked staff. They worked in huge, long wards with sixty or more beds and in the day rooms with the mentally sick and the mentally subnormal all mixed together, sitting round with vacant faces, some more hopeless

In the Way of Understanding

than others. At night after these visits, safe and cosy in my bed, I would think of what I had seen and feel despair because of the enormity of the problem—not only in my region but possibly magnified by the other fifteen regions into a huge nightmare. I only survived because luckily I have some sense of humour, and my family, although not interested and not wanting to hear about my adventures with disordered lives and the underprivileged, made me look upon a lighter side of life. I would chuckle to myself at the double life I lived in two different worlds, and never the twain must meet.

I remember with amusement an occasion when I visited a hospital near East Grinstead. The medical superintendent, who had progressive views and was not always in sympathy with the ways of the Board and its officers wanted, I think, to see what stuff I was made of. Taking me round his hospital he opened the door of a side room in which an old lady was packing; took me in, shut the door and left me. The dear old soul was quite sprightly and very talkative. She had two large trunks, one on her bed and the other on the floor. She was packing all her belongings, of which there were many, china, photos, clothes, etc., each in tissue paper. She explained she was going on a journey and had to get all her belongings in order. She gave me news of her family and her background, spoke well of the hospital which she in some way thought was a hotel, and of the staff, saying that in her opinion hotel staffs varied. We had a nice chat and I was helping her to wrap up a few bits and pieces when the doctor came back laughing heartily. We jokingly said good bye to the old girl and I was then told that she packed and unpacked daily. Later I saw her walking to the town where everyone knew her. She had been a patient for many years, and perhaps today she would be living in the community. By the end of my visit I felt the hospital to be an enlightened and caring environment and its Superintendent and staff were to be congratulated, and after the above incident we were all friends together.

This hospital had two most remarkable music therapists; one an older woman who dealt with the mentally sick and the mentally handicapped. She used her radiogram and classical records with percussion instruments and tambourines for the mentally handicapped and I saw her bring laughter and gaiety into the lives of some toothless old ladies. The second therapist was a young man dealing with patients of various ages who might have been in hospital for years. To the music from his radiogram he got them on their feet to move around and to dance. He went over to one middle-aged woman who was withdrawn, silent and looked half dead to me, and I saw this woman literally come alive while dancing with the young man; her eyes had been lifeless but they now shone. When he took her back to her chair she relapsed into nothingness. In both cases I was moved to tears, and the nice nurses came to comfort me and asked if I was feeling ill, but my feeling was one of humility and an awareness of the power of music for these patients. I was left wondering whether more such work could be done with such therapy.

Some years ago a splendid organisation calling itself "Sesame" did much to open the door for music therapy with the aim of giving a fuller life to the sick and handicapped through applied drama and movement. Jonathan Miller is their President. It is now the British Institute for the Study of the arts in Therapy and is the first association in Great Britain to represent Arts therapists in all of the major fields (visual arts, music, drama, movement/dance, and writing). Its work has gained support both in this country and abroad. In 1978, at my suggestion, the founder of Sesame worked with urbanised black schizophrenic patients in sanatoria in South Africa with remarkable success.[1,2] I now have great hopes that this Institute will be able to convince any sceptics who are left of the psychological benefit its techniques can have for the sick, disturbed and handicapped.

A few years after my appointment a dynamic surgeon joined the S.E. Regional Hospital Board. One day, sitting next to him at lunch, I asked him if he had recently seen a psychiatric hospital and he said No, not since his student days. We were meeting in a psychiatric hospital of which I was a manager so I suggested that I should show him round. To the dismay of the

[1] The British Institute for the Study of the Arts in Therapy, *Report of Seminar July 1978*, (27 Blackfriars Road, London SE1 8NY).
[2] See South Africa, p. 301.

In the Way of Understanding

Chief Nursing Officer I asked to see some of the worst wards, and we watched poor old, senile and toothless ladies being shepherded into bed in shapeless night-dresses. The beds were so close together that the first lady was gently pushed and pressured to crawl along about six beds to reach her own. This was at 3 o'clock in the afternoon, and the other old ladies all obediently followed the lead with the help of kind staff. We saw the antiquated washing facilities for the weekly baths, horse-box lavatories (open top and bottom), and endless long, cheerless wards. I also showed the surgeon some happy signs of upgrading, nice pale shades of paint, flowers, etc. but the overall picture struck my new friend with horror. He had seen such conditions in his training days twenty years earlier but believed things had changed. He assured me, in his distress, of his support in any application I might make to the Board for money. I thanked him for his understanding, but when I said that he might have to take the awful decision between voting for vast sums of money to upgrade wards for some burnt-out old schizophrenics or some low-grade mentally handicapped patients versus some new piece of electronic equipment or the latest surgical instruments to operate on some young patients—in short money to alleviate suffering amongst patients able to start new lives—his enthusiasm was sobered. This was the awful dilemma for all those holding the purse strings, whether to make bearable the lives of the mentally sick and mentally handicapped, or to cure by surgery and the latest medical techniques young and old patients able to face new lives after treatment. The mentally sick might possibly qualify for the latter category, but the mentally handicapped could only have their lives, and the lives of their families, made more bearable. Which has priority? Which of us can or ought to judge?

There were large numbers of children, from babies to adolescents, in each psychiatric hospital, the majority mentally handicapped, and the size of the problem made one sad. In most cases everything possible was done by the devoted staffs, according to their lights and their sometimes inadequate training. The buildings were old and grim. Some hospitals had schools, and adolescent units were beginning to spring up. I

South East Metropolitan Regional Hospital Board

was on the Committee of St. Augustine's Hospital in Kent which pressed for the first purpose-built hospital unit and school in the region to cater for adolescents. It was only officially opened after I had retired, having taken ten years to get off the ground because of cuts in expenditure and endless discussions between the Regional Hospital Board, the Management Committee and Kent County Council. It is now a fine achievement, modelled on the lines of the Maudsley Adolescent Unit, and a credit to all concerned, but perhaps mostly to Kent County Council who were persistent and patient.

These units for adolescents remind me of child guidance clinics in the early days. They are run in an educational atmosphere, are multidisciplinary, and help to redeem the emotionally disturbed lives of their young patients, hopefully returning them to their families and to a normal life—perhaps the most important work of any hospital, health or education authority.

We were a mixed bag on the Regional Hospital Board: lay members, representatives of local authorities, hospital consultants, people from teaching hospitals, dentists, university staff, nurses, etc. I was re-appointed by successive Ministers of Health from 1958 until 1974 when I had reached retirement age, just before the advent of the reorganised Health Service. My comments therefore concern the past, but I wonder how much things have really changed and if there is fundamental improvement on the old hospital service? Problems have grown, and perhaps too much discussion, with no one able to take decisions, even wrong ones, creates greater difficulties. Another look at the mental health service is under way as I write, and one can only hope and pray there will be some improvement.

In the middle '60s my Regional Board in a moment of enthusiasm accepted an invitation to take part in a conference concerning problems of how to deal with difficult adolescents. The conference was held in Southampton University, and together with a representative of the medical staff I went to listen to the views of about 60 specially-selected people from various adolescent units and schools throughout the U.K. This small and cosy get-together was under the able chairmanship

In the Way of Understanding

of Dr. Mary Capes[1], and as it was a residential conference there was plenty of time to talk to interesting individuals who were trying to cope with the growing problems, each hoping they had found a useful solution. It was very informal, and when on the Sunday evening we were saying farewell and patting each other on the back at the end of the final session I asked "Where do we go from here?"—to the consternation of the chairman who threw the question back squarely into my court. I suggested that all present might like another meeting the following year, which would include a wider selection of delegates; perhaps those working in what were then known as approved schools, in borstals, etc. Those present were keen to continue this association of like minded workers, all of whom had obviously been stimulated by this small conference, and this was the small beginning of the Association for the Psychiatric Study of Adolescents which became a flourishing multidisciplinary organisation, and has recently taken on an international look. Dr. John Evans when he organised the conference in Edinburgh in July 1976 invited American and Israeli colleagues to participate, and Brian Molloy did the same for European colleagues when he organised his conference at Canterbury in July 1980. The annual conferences are held in various universities, and there is no doubt that A.P.S.A. is looked upon by workers in the field of adolescent psychiatry and social psychiatry as a valuable platform to evaluate new ideas and discuss techniques. Membership is now roughly 500, and this large number is indicative of the need felt by workers in this field for such an Association. The organisation of the now large gatherings at annual conferences is efficiently handled, and the plenary sessions are stimulating and often controversial. One conference held in London, superbly organised by Dr. Mary Ellis from Feltham Borstal as a psycho-drama and entitled "Catch a Thief" was of especial interests: its participants included magistrates, police and some delinquents themselves who gave us their opinions with no uncertainty.

[1] Dr. Mary Capes, formerly Consultant in Child and Adolescent Psychiatry, Wessex Region.

South East Metropolitan Regional Hospital Board

A.P.S.A. produces a useful quarterly journal, *Journal of Adolescence*, and is an Association of which I am proud to be a member. I am happy to have been in at its birth pangs, thanks to the S.E. Metropolitan Regional Board.

Having touched on hospital treatment and the care of illness and incapacity, I end this chapter with my concern for the dying. The Board had contractual arrangements with St. Christopher's Hospice, Syndeham, for a certain number of beds. St. Christopher's is a medical foundation, seeking to offer the best professional standards of care to patients with chronic and terminal pain, both in its wards and in patients' own homes, especially—though not exclusively—to those with advanced malignant disease. I remember that on one occasion the Regional Medical Officer, in giving us his report, was not unnaturally anxious for some members see for themselves the quite remarkable work being done by Dr. Cicely Saunders, D.B.E., F.R.C.P. and her team for terminal cancer cases. This suggestion was not received with much enthusiasm, but out of curiosity and because I felt I was capable of seeing and bearing most things after my mental hospital experiences, I offered to spend a day in the Hospice. I went with some trepidation because I believed I might be prying into private grief and might therefore be an object to be rejected by staff and patients alike. However, with stiff uper lip I took my car into this charming spot in South East London. Syndenham stands upon a hill upon which are built large detached houses with gardens and long avenues with trees. An occasional bus goes down the road, but otherwise there is little but domestic traffic. The administrative building was in one large house, but well-planned and architectually-designed additions covered the large garden. The receptionist was an elderly lady, sitting behind a desk in a delightful, large entrance hall with beautiful bowls of fresh flowers, comfortable arm chairs covered in soft colours and with carpeted floors. There were some good reprints of landscapes on the walls, and the whole atmosphere was as if one were entering a private house with a hostess willing and able to help you as her guest. After a few happy moments in this hall, my fears vanished and I knew I was welcomed into a team and a society dedicated to loving care.

In the Way of Understanding

Cecily Saunders received me with friendship, and not as a possibly nosey Regional Hospital Board member. I was at my ease and knew at once I was in the presence of a great woman. She had the quality of George Lyward and was a genius in her field, as he had been in education. She gave me details of the work, a history of the Hospice and then took me round in a practical but unhurried way, saying, "I shall leave you to go on by yourself later. Don't be frightened, talk to everybody, they know you know they are dying so you need not be embarrassed". So until lunch time I wandered round the wards, talking to bed patients and staff with an extraordinary feeling of happiness, completely relaxed and at my ease. The rooms and the wards were gay with flowers, there was no hospital atmosphere nor smell, only peace. Nobody rushed about, staff were numerous and were mostly young and very pretty with gentle ways of smiling. Of course there were screens around some beds, and relations and friends were around looking grave, but all, including me, were facing death calmly and squarely. It was a wonderful experience and relief not to have to pretend, but just to face the fact of death and to know that all concerned were either facing the last breath of life in themselves or were watching others do so harmoniously. Treatment and drugs are not my field, but I know that in the Hospice physical and mental pain are kept at bay, and that the highly trained staff and their numbers make it possible that no-one dies alone. Along with a full commitment to the needs of each patient, the staff are studying the relief of pain and other terminal distress. Such individual care is impossible in our busy national health hospitals, however devoted the nurses. Despite the best intentions in the world, they are compelled to deal with life, and they have the responsibility for many patients. They therefore have to leave relatives or friends to take on the last tragic service to a dear one.

Here at St. Christopher's the whole patient is under care. This means care for body, mind and soul, plus the responsibility for relations and friends. Talking to men and women either in bed or in day rooms, or to those who had just been home for a spell, I sensed the trust they had in Cicely Saunders. The atmosphere she engendered in her staff, whether doctors,

South East Metropolitan Regional Hospital Board

surgeons, nurses, ancilliaries or domestics, was permeated with truth and integrity. Nothing was hushed up or brushed under the carpet, everything was faced squarely, and happiness broke through the last barrier.

I talked with doctors and nurses during and after lunch, and visited a building for ageing patients which was beautifully decorated, each room having a basin and hot and cold water. I found a friend of mine serving teas. She had apparently done this for some years, unknown to me and her many other friends. Perhaps in those days working in a Hospice for the dying was even more unmentionable than my efforts in the field of mental health, but maybe she was simply too modest to mention her work.

Returning home and reporting back to the Board, I could only say that I had lived through one of the happiest days of my life, the memory of which will remain in my mind for as long as I live. In saying farewell to Cicely Saunders I told her laughingly how I wished I could book a bed and she answered "Give me the date and it shall be done"!

After my retirement I worked for a few weeks in the library of the hospice, but alas, on giving up my car, I found that I could no longer do so, as the hourly bus was too uncertain and the underground station was too far in wet weather. However, during my short time in the team I became more and more aware of a Christian way of life at St. Christopher's, the completely undenominational service given by the chaplain, the co-operation of all religions and of those who came as unbelievers and were sometimes as rebellious of death as they had been of religion. I am happy to know that the new S.E. Thames Regional Health Authority has increased its contractual arrangements with the Hospice, thus ensuring a little cash-flow to this remarkable pilot scheme which lies outside the National Health Service. I fear that no service such as I saw at St. Christopher's can ever be within a national health service, not only because of lack of money and shortage of staff and but also because of the sheer size of the problem. However, more hospices are springing up, and Cicely Saunders' work is now known throughout the world. Here at St. Christopher's is demonstrated the true meaning of service, whether voluntary or salaried; here is a Christian foundation, ecumenical and practical, searching for God's plan for its work and development. Truly in dying we learn to live.

Fresh Fields and Pastures New

19
World Travels

And finally don't take yourself too seriously—take life seriously, take God seriously—But please don't take yourself too seriously.
Cardinal Basil Hume, O.S.B., *Searching for God*[1]

Introduction

It will be remembered that the World Federation for Mental Health was founded at a historic Congress in London in 1948. It was then planned that world representatives of the major caring professions of different disciplines should meet annually and hold a five-yearly Congress, having a Council and an Executive Board. It was a grand vision of a voluntary mental health movement that was to embrace psychiatry, psychology and interested caring professionals, mostly from Europe and North America. They would give of their time on a purely voluntary basis, paying their own expenses.

The Council and Executive Board were elected with all the necessary democratic paraphenalia and some evolving process of natural selection. It was the coming together of great minds in the medical profession who were determined to act together to secure recognition by governments and the public of the grave consequences of mental ill health throughout the world.

The moving spirit was undoubtedly the late Dr. J. R. Rees, C.B.E., a Welshman from the Tavistock Clinic in London, whose experiences in the army and his wide friendships in the medical profession all over the world made him a good choice as leader. He devoted his time to the promotion of mental health, travelling the globe to meet with Heads of State as well as leading lights in psychiatry and psychology. He visited hospitals and started National Associations of Mental Health on the lines of such Associations already functioning in the

[1] Hodder & Stoughton, 1977.

U.S.A. and the U.K. These latter were tender plants in those days, and as such needed more support than the W.F.M.H. and its small staff were ever able to offer in finance or administration.

I have admiration and respect for those brave men and women who gave so much of themselves. Many of the early pioneers are now dead, but their spirit lives on, and I pray that recognition will one day be made in their various countries to mark this spontaneous convergence of brave souls.

In the early years I was one of the very few non-professionals who were involved, and with my experience, and possessing enough time to devote myself to what was quite an arduous task, I was able to keep in touch with the Cinderella of the health services throughout the world. My correspondence was vast, and therefore having a desk at the N.A.M.H. London office, to which I went most days, was useful. In addition, I visited psychiatric hospitals and local mental health associations throughout the British Isles, thus keeping in touch with the latest developments.

As the journeys progress and the years roll by, my readers will glimpse a few of the highlights of the gradual progress of the mental health movement in many parts of the world, and my part in it under the sponsorship of N.A.M.H. and later of the Bethlem Royal and Maudsley Hospitals. My motivation for these visits abroad was to dispel fear of mental illness, through the education of the public about mental health in whichever country I visited, and to attempt to make non-professionals like myself realise the size of the problem and its wider implications. It was necessary to find alternative remedies to hospitalisation and to prevent institutionalisation. This work gave me an opportunity of seeing much of countries I would not otherwise have visited, and the opportunity of personally getting to know various people abroad in their own homes. Many of these stimulating people have become real friends. I moved out of the national field and entered the complicated international field in which the W.F.M.H. worked alongside the W.H.O., U.N.E.S.C.O., and other international bodies.

At first my journeys were by sea, and these long, restful

periods gave me time to adjust to my husband's death and to realise that there was now a niche for me in a world mental health movement. Later I travelled by air, and again this symbolised the bird-like quality of my life as I alighted in fresh fields and pastures new.

Switzerland

My first hesitant steps were to take me in 1951 to Vevey in Switzerland with Robina Addis who, like many friends, encouraged me to set my sights on the European mental health situation before venturing into the world-wide mental health work. Europe had had its European Mental Health League long before 1948, when the World Federation for Mental Health was formed, and was conscious of its own identity. In many ways the League was jealous of the new world organisation which was monopolised by the English-speaking countries and had its headquarters in London.

This was my first appearance at a European gathering, and my first taste of the political differences which bedevilled even the mental health field. I was treading on dangerous ground in this professionally-dominated psychiatric world, and a British woman psychiatrist made it plain to her colleagues that I was only an amateur and therefore should have no say in their deliberations. Later this lady was to be a close ally, even though she was not always playing in tune with the mental health orchestra which I tried to conduct. Perhaps this demonstrates the closed-shop attitude of the professionals who feared the intrusion of a layman into their psychiatric secrets. It was a decade before this attitude changed even in the U.K. Voluntary service as we know it in the U.K. was unknown in European countries and is still little understood. My arrival on the scene was intriguing to the foreign professionals, but as I could speak French fluently I was able to express myself and thus capture the imagination of the volatile South Europeans and even the more staid Germans. The Scandinavians and the Dutch seemed to understand that this new breed of bird had its uses and had a flair for administration and organisation which the European League sadly lacked.

In the Way of Understanding

On our way to the Vevey Conference Robina and I stopped over to stay with Dr. Oscar Forel at St. Prex, his lovely old house overlooking the Lake of Geneva. Dr. Forel was an old friend and admirer of Robina Addis. Their friendship had begun just after the war when they were both working in S.E.P.E.G. He was a fascinating extrovert, a brilliant psychiatrist and the director and owner of the famous Rives des Prangins, a psychiatric clinic which housed many of the aristocratic and royal personages in Europe who needed treatment. The Clinic when I visited it looked like a luxury hotel. It had an entrance hall with attractively dressed nurses at a reception desk, a salon with gorgeous flowers, a dining room with small tables, and a perfectly organised kitchen with a shining copper "batterie de cuisine", coloured tiled walls and white-capped chefs. Individual bedrooms were provided to suit varying tastes and, I presume, pockets. The linen room was a perfectionist's dream with different coloured sheets and towels with exquisitely embroidered monograms. The patients worked in the linen room because for them, as for other sufferers, work itself is a therapy. Bowls and vases of flowers were to be seen on all sides, artistically arranged by the patients in the manner and style later made fashionable by Constance Spry. The Clinic was under no financial stress and the patients came from backgrounds of constant gaiety and movement, so there music, dancing and painting were employed as occupational therapy. Thus in Prangin I encountered the early stages of the co-ordination of the arts in alternative medicine.

Other hospitals I visited in Switzerland were also spotlessly clean, women were strictly segregated from men even in the gardens, and in the wards gentle nuns did the nursing in homely conditions. Many pot plants hung on the walls and this indoor gardening made the wards and rest rooms attractive. The men's wards were much more austere and clinical, needing a woman's touch and understanding in the care of senile old men and young defectives. The difference between mental illness and mental deficiency was defined more clearly in Europe than in the U.K., their legislation being different from ours both in medical and legal terms.

One day we visited the Swiss Rudolf Steiner school and

World Travels

farm, where we were impressed by the care given to the mentally handicapped patients of all ages. We saw the happy lives they were leading through working at toy making, carpentry, dressmaking and on the land among vegetables, flowers and livestock, all of which were well cared for. This was my first visit to a Rudolf Steiner community and as the years have gone by I have been much impressed by their excellent work in many countries, including our own, and with the philosophy behind the work.

I am afraid a spirit of nationalism rises up within me at these international conferences and, however hard I try to hide my feelings, I become very British. This showed itself in an amusing way at Malevoz, a huge psychiatric hospital run by Dr. Répond, our host at this Conference. He prided himself on the excellent food he gave his patients and this was certainly true, judging by what he produced for over two hundred guests on a lovely lawn in summer weather. The feast ended with 'Raclette'—a kind of Welsh Rabbit—toasted cheese cooked in front of the guests on charcoal fires. Someone started a contest to see how many raclettes could be eaten one after the other and foolishly I took part. My British colleagues urged me on with shouts of encouragement because the French delegate was winning. Happily, perhaps because the kind waiters gave me smaller and smaller portions, I managed eighteen portions before giving up. My French rival ate nineteen and so won the prize. However, he was sick in bed the next day, while I was up and active in attending the Conference.

The Conference contributed to my learning about the psychiatric work being done in the various European countries. The papers given were probably largely above my head, but I sensed the personality and the philosophy behind each speaker's contribution, and my antennae were fully stretched. Amongst the nursing staff and the social workers (Assistant Socials) I was quite at home, and was able to explain the work of N.A.M.H. in the U.K., and its close relationship with the new National Health Service. It was a novel idea to them, indeed almost revolutionary, and my part in it was even more of an enigma. A "lady" interested in mental illness, and still more in subnormality, was something which was difficult for them to take seriously. However, I persevered, even if often overwhelmed by the enormity of my task, for at that time those associations and individuals who took an interest in mental health were doing so either in misdirected or in amateurist ways, and were not seeking to educate the public or to recruit volunteers in a campaign to dispel fear. In the 1950s the words mental illness and mental deficiency were almost taboo in most countries, including the U.K. I left the Vevey Conference slightly despondent, for I felt that no positive campaign to dispel fear had been launched, and that a spirit of laissez-faire was prevalent in the League. But at this multi-national get-together I made friends with whom I kept in touch during the many years I was to travel to conferences. Each in their way taught me something about mental health in their own countries and of the philosophy which lay behind their psychiatric work, so that I left knowing that I might have a role to play which would be stimulating for me and a positive use for my energy.

Belgium, 1952.

My next foray was in the autumn of 1952 when, together with Robina Addis and Mary Applebey, I represented the N.A.M.H. at the W.F.M.H. Conference in Brussels. This was my birth place, and where I had a sister-in-law, nieces and nephews, all now married and with children. They had rarely seen me since my second marriage, so I was therefore something of a stranger to them, and an object of some curiosity, for they had learned of my interest in the mental health services of the world and my contacts with juvenile courts, prisons and social work—an unknown world to them. Tragically I was to see the beginnings of a mental health problem in my family which, through negligence, not carelessness, later resulted in a suicide. A beautiful young married woman, wife and mother, was obviously in need of psychiatric care and her husband in need of advice. I made many efforts to suggest psychiatric help but was constantly confronted with a barrier, behind which was hidden mental suffering of which I was only too well aware. My nephew refused to admit his wife's illness other than post-natal depression, and in this he was supported by members of the medical profession who themselves had had no training in psychiatric medicine. I was powerless to make them understand and could therefore only watch in sorrow. All this showed me only too clearly the task facing any Association for mental health, the barriers that had to be broken down, the terrible fear to be overcome and the urgency of getting the message across to those who insisted on denying the existence of mental illness when it occurs in their own families. At this Conference, perhaps more than at any other, I knew I had a role to play because of my intuitive understanding and my work amongst professionals in mental health.

During the Conference Robina Addis gave a paper, as usual well prepared and delivered. There were the normal plenary sessions, technical sessions and group discussions in which I took part, but what remains in my memory is a visit to Gheel, the large colony for mental defectives in the village of that name some miles outside Brussels towards the Dutch border. The colony had started in Gheel as a place of pilgrimage to St. Dymphna, now the Patron Saint of Mental Health. An Irish princess, so legend has it, escaped with her Confessor, a holy monk, from the embraces of her wicked father, the king, whose queen (the princess' mother) had died and who in his grief decided to take his daughter for wife. In desperation, having failed to dissuade the king from his obstinate obsession, the monk and princess fled from Ireland to the coast of Holland and took refuge in a monastery. The king, in hot pursuit, caught up with them and murdered both his daughter and her escort. It was said that on reaching heaven the princess begged God to have mercy on her father, saying that he was only mad (deranged in mind) and not bad. Her request was granted and the statue and grotto put up in her memory became a resort for pilgrims whose minds were in some way deranged. Some miraculous cures took place and gradually, over the centuries, a place of refuge grew up for the hundreds of unhappy and simple folk who came to pray for relief and cure. Villagers, perhaps with an eye to business, took pilgrims into their homes and helped them to live peacefully on the land and to co-operate in agricultural work; farm work being given to

In the Way of Understanding

men while house chores, gardening and chicken rearing were the lot of the women. It grew over the years to an enormous co-operative undertaking. The villagers' understanding of the problems of the mentally defective and their need for repetitive work, as a gentle exercise of body and an occupational therapy became well known, and today it can be said that our supposedly new ideas of care in the community have their roots in this haphazard experiment. Now a hospital is incorporated in the scheme, the latest psychiatric methods are available, and a development which permits the transfer in the village of patients or paying guests who may be temporarily too disturbed to benefit from employment. A regular fee or wage is now regarded as essential, and the scheme forms part of the Belgian Health Service.

It would be beneficial if we in the U.K. were able to set up some kind of analagous service for our psychiatric patients, but the Belgian scheme has a tradition of hundreds of years behind it and has grown out of a religious belief nurtured over the centuries. The British community care scheme seems to me to have germinated from this experiment, and now awaits cultivation and flowering in a caring community with the help of a psychiatric team that is trained to understand the mentally sub-normal.

It was at this Conference, during a dinner party on the beautiful Grande Place in Brussels, that a member of the Executive Board of the W.F.M.H. suggested that I might join them on the Board. I was immensely flattered, having had no professional qualifications but only some years of experience and work with the National Association for Mental Health. At this dinner I was asked by, I think, Ewan Cameron—a controversial psychiatrist from Montreal—if I could discreetly discover from the head waiter where he and the other doctors could find the famous statue of the Mannekin Pis. Despite my Belgian blood I had never heard of this little boy, and when I saw him I understood why, for my adolescence had been a protected one. In my best French I consulted the waiter and he laughingly said that all visitors, especially the Americans and English, were crazy to see this fountain. He then gave us instructions about how to find it and thus ended a very amusing dinner party. Next morning my name was put forward for election and the proposal carried, I believe, unanimously. Perhaps it was thanks to the little boy!

U.S.A. and Canada, 1952 and 1954

I had been to the Eastern Seaboard of the U.S.A. on many occasions with my husband but in 1952, and now a widow, I went to New York alone to try to get some financial help for the struggling N.A.M.H. in England. It was a really horrific crossing on a small Cunarder, perhaps the worst and most spectacular I have ever experienced, even though I have crossed the Bay of Biscay eighteen times.

It might be of interest if, at this point, I digress for a brief moment to remind my readers, especially the younger ones, that I am writing here about thirty years ago when most people crossed the Atlantic by boat. In those days, those born into my station of life had large, heavy luggage—usually a dressing-case full of bottles, i.e. cosmetics, medicines, etc., as well as a cabin trunk the size of a small wardrobe, with drawers and hanging space. The latter was invaluable if you did not take your personal maid with you. During this particular crossing the sea was so rough that I found when I went to bed one night that my trunk was rolling about my cabin in an alarming fashion. Seeking help I was told it was not the steward's duty to look after roaming trunks, and that I had to await the arrival of an able seaman to lash the dancing wardrobe firmly in place. Not surprisingly, all the seamen were busy lashing together the important cargo, including some hundred motor cars, in the hold. While I waited I dared not get into bed because in those far-off days I felt it improper to be in bed and allow a man into my cabin other than the steward. However, finally I could wait no longer and got into my bunk where I felt safer away from the advances of the marauding trunk, and at last in came a glorious he-man, smelling of salt and sea air. He secured my trunk and assured me that the cars were no longer shifting around in the hold and that by morning the storm would have abated, which it did. During the day I had witnessed mountainous seas and from the Captain's deck

In the Way of Understanding

had seen the really frightening sight of a wall of water which made me feel rather as though I was standing on the steps of St. Paul's and expected to jump over the top of the dome! Miraculously, this little ship was so well navigated that each time we sank down into a trough we managed to float over the next wall of water and land safely in each succeeding trough, continuing thus for many hours. I confess to having felt very much alone and frightened and by night my nerves were shattered.

I arrived finally in New York 48 hours late and was given a royal welcome by my husband's friends, who were astonished to find me immediately immersed in meetings and pre-arranged appointments.

In a way I was leading a double life. The official reason for my visit was to collect funds for the N.A.M.H. in order to finance a British delegation to the W.F.M.H. Congress which was to be held in Toronto in 1954 and also to contact American and Canadian Foundations. But old friends insisted on seeing me and I had to stress that I was there on business as well as pleasure. Nevertheless my friends made me feel that in their view pleasure came first, and that mental health was only a passe-temps and unimportant!

I rather enjoyed this double life as my friends did give me a glorious time, and I appreciated every minute of it, especially as I had come from an England which was still in an austerity period. But I enjoyed even more the recognition given to me by the professionals in the Foundations and in the hospitals and clinics. Politics again entered my life, as all my business friends were Republicans whilst those in my professional milieu were Democrats. It was fun to listen and to be a fly on the wall, without needing to take sides, although at times I wondered if Roosevelt could really be the devil that he was painted by the Republicans.

On this mental health mission I was guided by Walter Stewart[1] in my approach to the various Foundations, as he had been Chairman of the Rockefeller Foundation and was at one time a close friend of my husband. He had been a Director of

[1] Walter W. Stewart, Adviser to the Governors of the Bank of England, 1928–30, formerly on the staff of the Federal Reserve Bank Board, U.S.A.

World Travels

the Institute of Advanced Studies in Princeton and, as we sometimes laughingly suggested, he must have corrected some of Einstein's sums before they were made public. He was a great man, a humble man, a good listener and a wonderful friend to me. He rehearsed every detail of my proposed interviews, giving me a thumb-nail sketch of the man or woman I was to meet. He took me himself to all my interviews and gave me courage, for I was shy and hated this begging business, and he gave me comfort when I came away with half promises.

At the Commonwealth Fund (the Harkness Trust) I was among many old friends. It was disappointing to hear that their Board had decided to pull out of Europe, as it felt it had given enough to child guidance, which was perhaps true. I tried to insist that Britain was not Europe but a half-way house to Europe but they were not having any!

Whilst in New York, and after negotiating with difficulty the buses and the Overhead Railway (now no longer in existence), I visited a Juvenile Court and was invited to attend a Domestic Relations Court. There I listened to case conferences dealing with clients from a mixture of races from all over Europe as well as, of course, from Africa and Puerto Rico. I was impressed with much of the work but was horrified to see some obviously mentally defective clients sentenced indiscriminately. However, I was comforted by a New York psychiatrist who was pushing for reforms.

In a child care centre—something on the lines of our Nursery Schools for Working Mothers—I discovered that no child learned to read before the age of six. As I showed some astonishment that a big boy of five did not even know his letters I was told that the U.S.A. authorities did not believe in early formal education. I tried to explain our nursery school principles and the Montessori, Frobel and McMillan methods which were anything but formal, but in their eyes I was a backwoodsman.

Of course I visited the N.A.M.H. Inc., an amalgamation, like ours, of the mental health movement throughout the whole of the U.S. They were holding their Annual General Meeting and I had to make an impromptu speech. Mrs.

In the Way of Understanding

Clifford Beers was present, the widow of the famous Clifford Beers, author of *A Mind that Found Itself* (Doubleday, New York, 1905) the story of his mental breakdown, his treatment in a mental hospital and his subsequent recovery.

Perhaps one of my most interesting visits was to Wiltwych School at Poughkeepsie for emotionally disturbed young boys and girls who would, it was hoped, be kept from appearing in a Juvenile Court. Mrs. Eleanor Roosevelt, now a widow, was interested in Wiltwych which was about an hour's run from New York and near the President's private residence in Hyde Park. Mrs. Roosevelt met me at the station and I noticed, as her hands took the wheel, how beautiful they were. The school was run on progressive lines; many of the professional staff were of different nationalities and races and the children too were of mixed races. All the children were emotionally disturbed and in need of understanding and psychiatric treatment.

I feel sure I saw the President's widow in the best possible setting, because these children obviously adored her and followed her about like puppies. The staff too respected her. She and her husband had taken a personal interest in the school from the time it was opened and often had children to tea and games at Hyde Park. I was impressed by what I saw and it gave me much food for thought when I got home.

I lunched at Hyde Park where there was a large party of house guests and others who streamed in for a meal. It seemed to me rather like Bedlam and I was surprised that such an intelligent woman as Mrs. Roosevelt, with so many outside interests, could stand the noise and strain of so much va-et-vient but my guess was that she found it difficult to be alone.

On returning to New York I spent a day at the Brooklyn After Care Clinic and Day Hospital, where I was welcomed by Dr. Carmichael, a delightful man, who, like others, treated me as a professional. We discussed problems of mental health in the Old World, and compared them with those of the New World. The problems seemed much the same; we were both aware of the apathy of the public and the reluctance of governments to spend money. I was envious of his success in after-care, which he himself considered to be only a drop in the ocean. This Clinic and Day Hospital was situated on the top floor of a big commercial store, so that those entering the store could have been either patients or ordinary shoppers and so were indistinguishable from one another. This seemed to be a very good idea. There were four such clinics in New York City, entirely paid for by New York State. There were many social workers, vocational counsellors and nurses out of uniform, and there seemed to be excellent co-operation with the New York social agencies.

The idea behind it all was an experiment in community care—an attempt to keep patients out of institutions and to give them a sense of security on leaving their psychiatric hospital. I was allowed to mix freely with the patients and one—an ex-alcoholic—took me in tow and gave me a pretty lurid description of the hospital in which she had been incarcerated for twenty years. During the coffee break, and afterwards in the cafeteria, I was asked to describe how mental health problems were dealt with in the U.K. It was an exciting and somewhat frightening experience to be quizzed by staff and patients on treatment in British hospitals, as I was not a doctor myself. Happily the Director, Dr. Carmichael, was most understanding and helpful during this ordeal.

I came away feeling that the alcoholic's description of life in a large mental hospital might have been matched by one from a similar patient in the U.K. but that the imaginative concept of a clinic in a large department store was one that the N.A.M.H. would have been hard put to advocate in England.

Another visit which I found rather charming was to Fountain House, situated in a nice, old brownstone house that had once belonged to Alexander Woollcott[1] and where *The New Yorker* was born. It was a delightful setting for this club house for ex mental hospital patients. The house had a pleasant patio and a small fountain—hence the name. The visit was most informal, and the patients referred to me as "that old toff from London"! There was musical therapy and a relaxed atmosphere but the staff were depressed, as they told me that in that district the clinical and social services were so poor that they

[1] Alexander Woollcott (1887–1943) American writer and journalist, author of the play *The Man Who Came To Dinner*.

In the Way of Understanding

often had to wait so long for treatment for patients that deterioration took place, and this led to eventual rehospitalisation.

I have always been interested in musical and art therapy, and feel sure both could be used to greater advantage in the treatment of mental illness. Alas, during my working life I have found that few psychiatrists understood this unless they happened to be musicians or artists themselves. Whilst in New York I took the opportunity to visit a Music and Rehabilitation Centre and the Musicians' Emergency Fund, Inc. and found them more advanced than our set-up in the U.K.; however, interest in both art and music therapy has gone ahead since those far-off days and they have been introduced into a number of British hospitals.

My visit to the U.N. building remains in my memory. Its site on the East River was impressive, and the imagination that had inspired the various nations to send gifts of carpets, furniture, curtains, paintings, and the Chagall window in memory of Dag Hammershold, gave me hope that world unity might one day be achieved. However, I felt the insecurity and bustle, though it was certainly exciting to see so many nationalities gathered together and to hear so many languages being spoken. Yet one longed for stability amongst all this talk and political gossip, and the words that Mackenzie King confided to his diary[1] when he was Prime Minister of Canada kept coming back into my mind: "I doubt if the U.N. can ever be other than a creaking house, with nothing of a solid structure about it'.

I went to see the Secretary General, U Thant, a sincere, humble man, who seemed to get much strength from his Buddhist faith, and who recognised the importance of mental health for the world.

While in New York I often stayed with the late Mrs. August Belmont, a good friend of mine. Eleanor Robson Belmont was born in Wigan, became a famous actress (Eleanor Robson) and a friend of Bernard Shaw. He wanted her to play in *Major Barbara* at one time, but for various reasons, alas, this never

[1] *Mackenzie King Diaries 1893–1931 and 1932–50*, University of Toronto Press 1974 and 1980.

World Travels

came off. She had a beautiful apartment overlooking Central Park, and on returning late from the opera or parties I would stand transfixed by the beauty of New York as seen from her apartment window high up on Fifth Avenue. Eleanor was the founder of the Opera Guild and a tremendous supporter of the Metropolitan Opera, and in many ways was its mother figure. It was a joy to stay with her as one was entirely free to lead one's own life. It was a highly civilised way of life now gone for me, with an excellent cook, caring servants and interesting guests who included politicians, bankers, opera singers and famous artists; in fact it was a truly wonderful existence with the added attraction of a beautiful and intelligent hostess who with her lovely voice could charm the birds off the trees. She died in October 1979 at the age of 100. She looked with scepticism on my mental health work, but with intuitive intelligence realised that it was my mission in life and was of importance to the world's stage. Her own particular interests lay in the theatre and in politics.

My sponsors in the U.S. arranged for me to visit Washington in 1952, and I visited the Security Administration Department and the Children's Bureau. The Bureau was conceived in 1900 but only became established in 1912 after the first White House Conference. Under the auspices of the Federal Security Agency I was allowed to visit the National Institute of Health at Bethseda in Maryland. In those days it looked like a huge village under construction; today, maybe, it looks more like a small town. It covered research into every known and unknown illness throughout the world. The mental health section had not yet been built, but when I visited it again in 1959 it had all the latest and the best in design, and I confess to having been very envious.

Dr. R. H. Felix, the then Director of the Institute, welcomed me and gave me a thumb-nail sketch of the mental health set-up as we stood together before a huge map of the United States. The slow but steady growth of mental health as shown on this map was sufficient proof of the good work this Institute was doing. I was given a wonderful picture of what the Federal Administration was trying to undertake, and it seemed to me a superhuman task. Many areas on the map were bare, and this made me realise the work that still had to be faced by N.A.M.H. Inc. and the various Mental Health Associations in the States who at that time had received little or no education in the problem of mental illness and mental sub-normality. The good work I had seen in New York and later in Boston had still to spread, and Dr. Felix's task was truly awesome. To be privileged as a foreigner and a non-professional to see the beginnings of this stupendous undertaking was thrilling, and I have kept a close watch on the development of the provisions for mental health in the United States ever since.

I was also given an opportunity to visit St. Elizabeth's Hospital, an 8,000 bedded hospital well known in literary circles as the place where Ezra Pound was incarcerated because of his political actions during the war. The Chief Nursing Officer took me from one barrack ward to another, and we must have covered many miles. My reaction was that of an insect caught in a spider's web. Everything was sterilised and orderly and the atmosphere oozed Iodoform. My heart bled for the old people in the geriatric ward when I saw them stream-lined in tubular furniture and wheel chairs. All was hygienic but nothing was home-like. Perhaps it was better than some of our scruffy old wards but I still wonder. If "the bigger the better" is the norm it was O.K., but now that we have learned that "small is beautiful" maybe my feeling of horror was not so strange. It made me all the more determined on my return to the U.K. to press for more care of the mentally ill within the community, and for smaller hospital buildings when hospitalisation became necessary.

I went to Boston and stayed with another friend of Mont's, a distinguished botanist, who gave me her friendship unstintingly. She was interested in my work and did not mind my using her lovely apartment as a hotel. It was perhaps one of the most beautiful private apartments on Commonwealth Avenue, with its spacious, high-ceilinged rooms, parquet floors, Persian rugs and a fine library of rare botanical books. The whole area is now changed and many of these beautiful houses are no more.

I spent one whole day at Framingham, just outside Boston an unusual reformatory for women where the Governor was a most remarkable character—in some ways a revolutionary

World Travels

The powers-that-be had tried to dismiss her because her politics were not those of the Government then in power, and at one time the matter had been a cause célèbre. To my surprise I found a white-haired, gentle and extremely cultured old lady who gave me the feeling that she was living in another world. Her great integrity and uprightness reminded me of Field Marshal Smuts. She had an inner peace that was quite uncanny and, although knowing her prisoners and facing the facts about them, she still believed in their fundamental goodness. We discussed her prison and others in the United States and in the world generally, and I was quite awed by her disregard of evil as such. She seemed to live with it and ignore it as if it did not exist. We went round the prison together and, if such places can be, it was a happy place. She had her keys and yet always left the doors unlocked behind her, much I am sure to the discomfiture of her staff.

I attended an assembly of all the students, as the prisoners were called, which took place in a hall with a huge stage. They sang to me and the officers gave reports of activities that had taken place, some of the students reading reports themselves. At the end I was asked to address them—not an easy thing to do on the spot and off the cuff. Then the students asked if they could shake hands with me. I found this moving, particularly when one coloured woman asked to speak to me alone and said "You have met the most wonderful Governor in the world, not just in the United States of America".

On returning to Boston I found an invitation from Dr. Erich Lindemann, Psychiatrist-in-Chief, to spend a day at his Massachusetts General Hospital. The invitation must have been prompted, I think, by Denis Leigh,[1] one of his students. I was welcomed as a long-lost friend, and treated as if I knew a great deal about the subject of mental health which he so ably discussed. I fell under his charm—a middle-aged, grey-haired, humble and gracious man with a twinkle in his eye. At the hospital there was close communication between doctors and nurses dealing with patients and with their families, thus

---

[1] Now Consultant, Maudsley Hospital and Secretary-General to the World Psychiatric Association.

giving training to those interested in community welfare. The staff were experiencing much opposition from old-fashioned physicians, nurses and Government Departments who still thought in terms of bigger and bigger hospital buildings, but they persevered and their work was much in advance of what we were doing in the U.K. at that time.

At a lunch party, guests from the caring professions included an Emeritus Professor of Psychiatry. I was suddenly asked, over coffee, to explain the National Health Service and the role of the N.A.M.H. within that setting, and also the proposed new Mental Health Act. This was quite a shock as I was totally unprepared. However I did my best to explain the composition of the then Regional Hospital Boards and Management Committees and how the N.A.M.H. fitted into this scheme. It was very difficult to get the Americans to understand that in our so-called socialist set-up there were still Boards of Governors and committees whose members were unpaid. The idea that these volunteers, laymen and women with no professional qualifications administered the hospital was quite incomprehensible to my audience, but after much questioning and answering I think I was able to make the situation fairly clear. Anyway, I got a tremendous reception before being despatched to the Wellesley Human Relations Service Centre which Dr. Lindemann had started twelve years earlier in order to study problems of the community and which was financed by the Grant Foundation. It was all extremely interesting, but I could not at the time see such a scheme being accepted in the English countryside, even though in a more humble way we were already making some progress in educating the community in the care of its members in need.

Later I went up to Toronto at the invitation of the Canadian Association for Mental Health to discuss the planning for the 1954 W.F.M.H. Congress which was to be held in that city. The then Chairman of the Canadian Association for Mental Health was Dr. Clare Hinks who was to preside at the Congress. Professor William Line, a Canadian psychologist, was at that time on the Executive Board of the W.F.M.H. and was taking a very active part in the organisation of the programme.

They were all rather shy of me and at first the atmosphere was strained, but after finding that I was not averse to rye on the rocks the stiffness wore off. I was surprised to find how much the C.A.M.H. wanted to be identified with the N.A.M.H. in London and how much they valued any suggestions I had to make—so very different from the attitude of the Americans.

This was to be the first big W.F.M.H. Conference and, as usual, the lack of money loomed large. The Organising Committee had made contact with big business and had found just the man whom they thought might be interested in mental health and who would put up money for running the Congress. He was asked to lunch to meet me and then came an ordeal, as I found that I was supposed to charm him and to get a cheque! The lunch was held in a fashionable men's club and I had learned, before the guests arrived, that besides being an industrialist of some repute he was a farmer with many acres of land and prize cattle. This was a happy discovery. One of my interests for many years had been my mother's farm in Lancashire and Mr. T. A. Miller, her Agent and Manager, had taken the trouble to explain his farming policies to me. I became keen and at that time knew quite a lot about Ayrshire cattle. I had been to cattle sales and as an interested pupil had learned a lot from listening carefully to the B.B.C.'s Saturday morning programmes "On your Farm".

My introduction to this tycoon was hardly auspicious from my point of view as he had been told that Lady Norman was now going to talk to him about mental health. When I heard this I quickly said that this would probably be dull for him and that I would rather hear about his farm. Then, for an hour, to the horror of Dr. Hinks and Professor Line, we talked of farming, discussing the respective merits of bulls and heifers and the benefits of artificial insemination. What luck it was that this man owned *Ayrshire* cattle, for I was able to impress him with my slight knowledge. As the time went on Dr. Hinks and Professor Line must have doubted the wisdom of giving me two rye on the rocks before lunch, but as coffee was served the tycoon said "Now to business. What do you want with me?" To the relief of all concerned I had truly landed him and later I believe he gave a considerable sum of money. He certainly worked to promote interest in mental health among the business fraternity in Toronto.

When the Congress took place in 1954 it was a great success and was attended by about 2,000 delegates from all over the world. The weather was good and the hospitality in the halls of residence on the campus was delightful. There was a fine delegation from the U.K. and Mary Applebey, the able Administrative Secretary of the N.A.M.H. went with me.

The late Sir Geoffrey Vickers, V.C. gave an inspiring address on "Mental Health and Spiritual Values" which is still remembered by many—not only by those who heard it but by those who read the published version afterwards. I made some notes and the following is the final passage of his address:

> . . . *By far the most significant discovery of mental science is the power of love to protect and to restore the mind. Every film-goer, every newspaper reader today believes that there is likely to be a causal relationship between the deprived child and the adult and adolescent criminal. He will accept on the authority of science that love can build for one child a haven of security in a mad world and can thus equip it to give back the same powerful influence in after life, whilst its absence may leave another imprisoned in self and capable of no contact with its kind but aggression. It is not often that the findings of science confirm the intuitions of religion in language which does not even need to be translated. This alone, in my view, entitles mental science to be regarded, not as a rival but as a partner in the eternal effort to realise spiritual values in the daily life of men and women—even perhaps in the policies of Governments.*
>
> . . . *Yet its most important promise, I believe, is the promise of helping us to conceive of mental health as a positive and dynamic condition of mind, to see the path towards it, to develop the will to achieve it. Mental health is not the same thing as spiritual vitality or spiritual vision but I do not believe that they will always belong to different Universes of discourse.*[1]

[1] The full published version of the Toronto Proceedings might be available from MIND.

World Travels

My own small contribution was an address on "Community Partnership in Mental Health and the Function and Organisation of Mental Health Services". The Congress was not all hard work and many friends were made.

During the time in Toronto I managed to escape with a friend to Stratford-upon-Avon, Ontario, a three-hour train journey. It was in the early days of that great festival, before the theatre was built, and an open stage was being used as in a circus. We saw a magnificent performance of *Oedipus Rex*. We had eaten nothing during our journey as there had been no restaurant or bar on the train, but the organisation running the catering for the festival gave us simple fare at long trestle tables. On the return journey my friend and I drank whisky from our flasks and got water from taps on the train. The day had been exciting and enjoyable, very interesting but most exhausting and it was 2 a.m. before we got back. Most of the theatre audience had consisted of women, as at that time Canadian husbands were suspicious of art.

Another interlude was a weekend with friends who had a small cottage by one of the big lakes and here I learned to swim in the nude—a novel and delicious experience for me. Mike and Marian Pearson had a cottage close by. He was Prime Minister at that time. At joint parties we all had great fun together with much discussion on world politics. I enjoyed listening to good talk amongst men and women of remarkable intelligence and although there was criticism of the part Britain was playing in world politics I was happy in the relaxed atmosphere which enabled them to say hard and perhaps undiplomatic things in front of me. I took this as a sign of real friendship.

The International Conference on Social Work had preceded the World Federation for Mental Health Conference and, by attending both, I was privileged to stay quite a long time in Canada and saw much of the campus at Toronto University. The Conference was opened by the Prime Minister, Mike Pearson. He gave a great welcome to the large audience of delegates who came from most countries of the world, and quoted Arnold Toynbee who said: "The 20th century will be chiefly remembered by future generations, not as an era of political conflict or technical inventions but as an age in which human society dared to think of the welfare of the whole human race as a practical possibility".[1] He pressed us all, including Governments, to accept this challenge.

Perhaps what I took back from both these meetings was the thrill of being with so many colourful personalities, and especially those from India, Pakistan and other countries whose representatives wore their national costumes. Sitting out in the quadrangle before an evening session was something I shall never forget; talking, discussing, laughing with representatives of all those nations. Their English was impeccable, especially that of the Indians who, not unnaturally, consider it their lingua franca. I received many kind invitations to go to talk about what the N.A.M.H. was doing in England and to give advice and help in so many countries. Alas, although I have travelled widely since those days, fate has never taken me to India.

Austria, 1953 ichabod

As a member of the Executive Board of the W.F.M.H., I was now able to view the horrific problems of mental illhealth and mental deficiency on a large canvas. The caring professions from far afield sent representatives to the Congress in Vienna in 1953, and a Russian delegate appeared unexpectedly and insisted on "taking the floor" and delivering long speeches—thus upsetting the planned agenda. Until this time Russia had shunned anything to do with our non-governmental organisation. The delegate gave papers containing detailed studies of mental handicap, brain damage and organic mental illness, but denied the existence of any form of emotional disturbance. When one of our delegates explained our progress in the U.K. on child guidance, the Russian cheerfully informed me that child guidance was quite unnecessary in Russia, as all children were happy there.

The policy of the W.F.M.H. was to demonstrate that a non-political gathering of multidisciplinary delegates could achieve something useful through discussion and exchange of

[1] No reference known.

views, the delegates being unfettered by their governments. This was a view the U.S.S.R. was unable to accept or understand. Wild rumours circulated amongst the delegates of appalling conditions in psychiatric hospitals and the incarceration of so-called mental patients for political reasons—not only in the U.S.S.R but wherever dictatorships existed.

The W.H.O., U.N. and U.N.E.S.C.O sent observers to our meetings, and at this particular Congress in Vienna in 1953 we were hearing reports about the plight of children in the 90 refugee camps in Austria, these contained something like 300,000 persons and 8,000 children—appalling figures but perhaps a mere handful compared with what the world was later to farce in Vietnam, China, and in so many other countries.

The beauty of Vienna and the gracious hospitality of our hosts, who had suffered so much from the war but still clung to their old fashioned civilisation, was heart warming to those of us still experiencing the austerities of post-war living. This was demonstrated for me by the attitude of the Austrian authorities who understood perfectly and were in no way offended by my attending the opera rather than an official banquet. There was a very nostalgic atmosphere in Vienna at that time, a looking back to the past, enigmatic, enchanting but unreal.

Interlude in Egypt, 1955

It had been a traumatic year for me because of leaving Plodge. I was physically tired moving into the Aubrey Lodge flat and began to realise I was starting a new chapter in my life and needed to recharge my batteries. So I decided to accept a pressing invitation to visit Cairo from Bonté Elgood, a much loved friend and relation of Mont's, who had lived most of her life in Egypt. Bonté (it was her Christian name and has a nice meaning in French) was the daughter of Professor Sheldon Amos, a judge in the Egyptian Native Courts. She became a doctor (at that time a very unusual profession for a young girl) and organised, at the request of Lord Kitchener, the Kitchener Memorial Hospital and Training Centre for doctors and nurses in Cairo, which was opened in 1923. She told me she

In the Way of Understanding

had many opportunities of appreciating his feelings for Egyptian women and children, and he had commissioned her to start a centre to train native midwives at a higher level than was possible at that time in the Egyptian government hospitals.

It was in the days before the tragedy of Suez, and in Bonté's house I met many interesting Egyptians and was able to visit museums and historical sites, such as the Tutankhamun treasures. It was a bit of a busman's holiday for me, as I also saw something of the heroic efforts made by the social welfare services to alleviate poverty and dirt. I spent time in a Juvenile Court, and was invited by the then President of the W.F.M.H., Dr. El Kholi, to meet psychiatrists and psychologists and to address a meeting of the Egyptian Medical Association. At that date I believe it was the first time a lay person had been asked to do so. The meeting was held in the House of Wisdom, Dar El Hekma, surely an appropriate title for the headquarters of the medical profession. Like most medicos in the world at that time they were curious about our National Health Service and asked intelligent and searching questions, which I believe I coped with satisfactorily: at least Bonté approved. The psychiatrists present wanted to hear about team work in child guidance clinics, and afterwards kindly arranged for me to see a nursery school and some work which was being done in Helouan for the mentally ill and mentally handicapped.

I felt especially priviledged to be invited into the home of a psychoanalyst, an ex Coptic monk and author of many religious and scientific books. He had invited some other Egyptian men and women so that I was able to savour another side of life in Egypt from the British one in which I was living. This is perhaps the only real way of getting to understand a little of the complexity of problems in a foreign country. They freely discussed their views (including political ones) in front of me so I felt I was learning something of normal Egyptian life.

On leaving Cairo I did not see Bonté again until after Suez when, despite her great age and her distinguished medical career, she was, like other British citizens, brutally arrested during the early hours of one morning and put into a common prison amongst criminals and prostitutes, the latter being horrified by her treatment. They were kind and solicitous for her welfare and even found a Bible to comfort her. Eventually she was expelled and forced to leave her home and all her possessions, her devoted Egyptian staff and, worst of all for her, her cats. At the customs she opened a small case containing her jewels and passport, together with the highest award for services to Egypt given her by King Farouk. The customs officer thought she might have stolen it, but when Bonté explained everything in Arabic he expressed sorrow and said that the situation was beyond his comprehension. It still remains beyond mine.

Jersey, 1955 and 1964—welcome perch on a fair island

On two separate occasions my flights took me to "Les Isles de la Manche", the Island of Jersey that came to the Crown through William Duke of Normandy, later William the First of England.

My first visit was as a result of an invitation from an ex member of the N.A.M.H. staff, a psychiatric social worker who had retired to Jersey and was shocked to see no recognition by the authorities or the public of mental illness as a handicap, even amongst children. She appealed to me as chairman of the N.A.M.H. to go to address a meeting which had been arranged by the Soroptomists Club of which she was a member. They were to make all the arrangements for my visit which would include hospitality at Government House. In accepting I was somewhat anxious that the authorities, and especially the redoubtable Bailiff who was still highly critical of the British Government's neglect (as he saw it) during the war, might think the N.A.M.H. was interfering in their domestic arrangements. I need not have had any such fears, for I was welcomed by all with whom I came in contact, including the Medical Officer of Health and the medical profession. They all stressed the crying need for recognition of the problems of the mentally ill, and bemoaned the lack of provision for the mentally ill and the mentally handicapped, especially amongst children. I was taken to see hospitals and schools for boys and girls and the few classes for backward children.

The meeting I addressed was a large one, thus denoting the

great interest in my subject. At the end it was resolved to try to found a Jersey Association for Mental Health. The Medical Officer of Health later persuaded the Public Health Committee to approve the establishment of an occupational centre and to appoint a psychiatric social worker. It was almost ten years before I was to return to support yet again my intrepid social work friend.

On my second visit the Constable of St. Helier had arranged a meeting of some 200 people in the Town Hall. The Attorney General proposed the formation of an Association for Mental Health and was supported by the probation service and by the medical profession. The voluntary societies were also represented, including one for spastics. The idea was opposed by some uninformed and reluctant voters who had always been against a Mental Health Act for the Island. However, very gradually, things improved on the Island and I like to think I did something to help a courageous group to get their views across through the media—although in many ways the success was chiefly due to the constant efforts of the retired psychiatric social worker who was always struggling for mental health problems to be recognised.

Germany, 1956—troubled landing in a divided city

I was to return to Europe in 1956, this time to Berlin, a divided city, where there was little nostalgia but much grim reality. The theme for discussion was "Mental Health in Home and School". This city was ripe for such a topic.

The Germans talked freely of their difficulties, especially of the division of their capital and the proximity of the Russian Zone. West Berlin had a population of 3½ million, of whom 40% were under the age of 50. Most women had to go out to work. The children had become nervous and insecure. Much damage had been done to the adults by the media in overstressing that life was one long struggle from birth to the grave, and depression leading to suicide was not uncommon. The children preferred to stay in hospital where they were better cared for and felt happier than they did at home.

This meeting was held in the Free University of Dahlen, and

members of the board included representatives not only from European countries but also from Hong Kong and Thailand. The U.S. representatives included the famous anthropologist Margaret Mead, and the WHO sent an observer.

As Vice-Chairman of the Board I was unexpectedly called on to take the Chair in the absence of Dr. Hoff, who had been called back to Vienna. I was pleased to perform this task because the subject of Mental Health in Home and School was one of my main interests. I might not have been so at ease if the subject had been one in which I had had little previous experience. It was hard work sitting in that Chair for up to seven hours at a time, coping with such eloquent members as Margaret Mead and also several vocal members whose English left much to be desired.

There were most interesting reports from various countries, but each delegate attempted to claim the lion's share of the time allotted for discussion. I had therefore to develop an iron hand in my velvet glove, and to curb my own interest and enthusiasm for all the new experiments which were presented to the meeting. Discussions were long and at times acrimonious, and the North Americans and English became somewhat exasperated by the verbosity of the Southern Europeans and their obsession with detail.

A new problem which raised its ugly head for the first time was the result of the huge increase in the diplomatic and consular services in all countries, and also the movement of big business and oil company personnel throughout the world. The question of schooling and the loneliness of wives, differences in food and climate, lack of communication, differences of language and habits; all had their effect on mental as well as physical health. To me this was rather a new thought, as no such problems or inhibitions had, as far as I knew, affected our Empire builders. Such difficulties had been faced with a stiff upper lip by the British pioneers, men, women and children, in India, Africa and Asia.

After four days strenuous work at Board Meetings the Conference itself opened, and I was glad to be joined by three representatives from the Bethlem Royal and Maudsley Hospitals, Dr. Denis Leigh, Dr. Wilfrid Warren and Dr. Staf-

In the Way of Understanding

ford-Clark. I was no longer alone, and felt supported by my three medical musketeers. I remember teasing Dr. Stafford-Clark after he had delivered a brilliant lecture in English. He had spoken far too quickly, his words sounding like bullets shot from a gun, and it was impossible for foreigners to comprehend. I like to think he took notice of my well-intentioned criticism, for ever afterwards his delivery was impeccable and his diction clear and was much admired by his listeners, especially on the B.B.C.

At plenary sessions we used simultaneous translations. English and French were the official languages chosen, as most members understood one or the other. The Latins felt inhibited, and hated the domination of those speaking English. Language problems still bedevil board meetings and seem insoluble, as instant translation is an expensive luxury.

One discussion group took place on the stage of the big Conference Hall. A packed audience listened with rapt attention while speakers from different backgrounds and professions argued forcibly. Margaret Mead was in splendid form, and the audience was electrified by a free-for-all and impressed by our tolerance. We were able to demonstrate to the Germans that an open discussion could take place between people of different nationalities who held very different views, and between professors and students, without inhibition or prejudice.

Perhaps the greatest benefit derived from such a Conference was the opportunity it offered members of the caring professions from many different settings to meet each other, to exchange and share problems and to visit each other's institutions.

I chose to visit a Juvenile Court, and found that the main difference between the basic principles in Germany and in our own country was that the child was guilty until proved innocent. This concept has since been changed.

One afternoon Dr. Krapff and I slipped through the dividing line between East and West Berlin in the Underground. It was perhaps a silly and dangerous thing for me to have done, but Dr. Krapff encouraged me and seemed sure that we should be undetected. Being an Argentinian and a W.H.O. official he was not worried. He also spoke three languages, so I took a chance and promised not to open my mouth. He stepped on my toe when we crossed the border, and then we got out at the Central station and started to walk through the ruins and through architecturally hideous blocks of flats, mostly built of dark grey concrete. There were no cars, few bicycles, and the women wore drab and shapeless clothes. There were no smiles or laughter, and there was little to buy in the shops except masses of flowers in a florist's shop and in the Underground station.

We went to the great Pinacothek Museum and saw the marvellous exhibits from Greece and Rome. We sat together in silence contemplating ancient glory and wondering about the future. I came back much moved, troubled, and in no mood to laugh.

Denmark, 1957—a watchful eye from a maiden's head

On the tenth anniversary of the W.F.M.H. the Board was invited by the Danish Society for the Prevention of Mental Diseases to hold their Congress in Copenhagen. Under the watchful eye of "The Little Maiden", the bronze statue by Eriksen, I entered the harbour of this free port and began again to live my double life. By the courtesy of the Danish National Bank the Governor lent me a car, and his secretary shepherded me in my free time through this beautiful country with its large and small farms, the Castle of Kronberg at Elsinore and the famous house of Hans Andersen.

In deference to our hosts the theme chosen for the Congress was "Growing Up in a Changing World", and the emphasis was set on the prevention of mental ill health. This Danish Congress was a landmark in the development of the W.F.M.H., for it was here that we found a father figure in Dr. Brock Chisholm. He had just retired from being the first Director of the W.H.O. and it was our good fortune that he was both willing and able to throw in his lot with us, and to succeed Margaret Mead as President. He was a little man in stature but towered above us in wisdom. He was tough though gentle and quiet in speech. He was unmistakably Canadian yet had a great understanding of the problems of Europe as well as those of North America, as well as a realisation of what was emerging in the Third World, and had a sympathy with the difficulties of South America. All delegates who came in contact with him, regardless of creed, politics or colour, put their entire faith in his integrity.

In his address to the Conference Dr. Brock Chisholm chose to concentrate on the phrase "The Changing World" as it appeared in the title of our discussions. Courageously, he challenged us to face our own need to grow to maturity so that we could in turn help our children to grow up in a world in which a revolution had occurred. No longer could strong nations rely for their security on their military strength. The use of atomic weapons meant that it was no longer possible to kill without being killed and that major warfare and suicide had for the first time in the world's history become synonymous. He foretold that to some nations the changes would bring anxiety and fear but that to others changes would bring hope: understanding must be the key to any solution and co-operation, not competition, between nations must be our aim for the future. He pointed out that none of the world's great problems could be solved from inside any one culture or any one group or sub-group, and was encouraged that some of the early steps towards integration had already been taken by the W.F.M.H.

I agreed with him when he stressed that the W.F.M.H. had already taken steps towards the integration of many nationalities and many professions. We were now much more of a multi-disciplinary team, as the nursing profession was now represented for the first time by Iris Marwick, a Chief Nursing Officer from the Republic of South Africa. She was a remarkable Scots woman from the Orkney Islands, the daughter of a wheelwright whose parents had emigrated to South Africa at the time when cartwheels were no longer in demand in Great Britain. Her father foresaw business opportunities in the Transvaal and other parts of Africa. Iris had trained as a psychiatric nurse and brought her expertise and much wisdom to our Board, with a freedom of speech which was unusual at that time among nurses when in the presence of doctors. She

World Travels

was then Matron of Tara Hospital outside Johannesberg, which was a training school for all the professions engaged in psychiatric medicine. She was a quiet, gentle creature with a spiritual philosophy and deep understanding of psychology, coupled with a tolerance of variants in psychiatry. This quality was not surprising in someone who had already learnt to live in a political situation alien to her upbringing. She had never felt any difference between whites and blacks, and this feeling played a part in her great work in training nurses of all colours.

Another newcomer to our Board at this meeting was the late Mildred Scoville, a pretty and elegant woman who came to represent social work for the first time. She was as charming as she was intelligent, and as one of the Directors of the Commonwealth Fund of America had often visited London to help the Child Guidance Clinic in Canonbury. Her diplomacy enabled her to extract from her reluctant Board continuing support for child guidance in the U.K., and for this I must salute her memory.

With the addition of these two stalwart women, who were both to become my great friends, the multi-disciplinary nature of the Federation was strengthened.

For members of the Executive Board it was not easy to find time to visit institutions in the host country, but I always tried to keep abreast of what was new in the prison service or in juvenile courts. I was particularly anxious on this occasion to visit the much criticised Institution for Psychopathic Criminals at Herstedvester, where castration was practised. Fortunately for me the late Dr. Peter Scott, the Forensic Psychiatrist from the Maudsley Hospital, was at the Conference, and arranged for me to accompany him on a visit. Dr. G. H. Stürup, the Director, took us round the Institution and we talked to staff and patients with the aid of an interpreter. An amusing incident remains vividly in my memory. Teasing me, Dr. Stürup handed me a small bagful of glass balls, asking me to guess what they were for. Only when the penny dropped did I colour up, much to the amusement of both Dr. Stürup and Peter Scott, and the latter never ceased to remind me of the incident.

Castration as a treatment is something which the medical

profession in the U.K. condemns almost unanimously, yet, having talked to some of the patients, I am puzzled by the horror which the practice provokes. I wonder whether the attempt to free psychopathic criminals of their violent sexual urges by surgery, even if it takes away their manhood, is not a small price to pay for ridding the world of this sexual violence. Provided of course the patients are willing, is it not perhaps more humane in the long run?

Back at my hotel I was shocked, particularly as a magistrate, to witness from my balcony overlooking the main square one of the first attempts of a rock and roll demonstration by youngsters on motor bikes, wearing black leather jackets and long boots. They were being attacked by the police with truncheons, and the Conference members who watched were alarmed by the violence shown both by the boys and by the police. The next day the incident was taken up with the Ministry concerned by the Danish Association.

The Danes were embarrassed that so many foreign visitors had witnessed the incident, but the Danish Association for Mental Health was grateful for the back-up given by the W.F.M.H. to the document being prepared for their Government. The Executive Board agreed that adolescent revolt was not confined to Denmark, as it was erupting in many countries, but that brutal repression was not the answer.

As was usual at Conferences, we had our social gatherings, and I still have a vivid amusing recollection of escorting Margaret Mead back to our hotel after a party. We were both a little tipsy. She had the help of her shepherd's crook and engulfed me with her famous cloak as we tottered across the Town Square, avoiding high-speed traffic and tramcars. As President of the Federation she had always had her feet placed firmly on the ground, but now, having relinquished some responsibility, perhaps she felt entitled to celebrate, even if it caused her feet to become a little less steady.

Northern Ireland, 1960—touching down on a troubled isle

It was in 1957 that I first went to Belfast, as I had been invited by the Northern Ireland Health Authority to open their exhibition on Mental Health Services in the Wellington Hall. This was before the formation in 1959 of their Association for Mental Health. Again in 1960 the Northern Ireland Health Authority organised a conference in the Sir William Little Hall in Queen's University, when I spoke on the "Changing Outlook on Mental Health". They were then considering their proposed new Mental Health Act. The legal profession were taking an active part in the setting up of the Association for Mental Health, just as happened in England in the early days of N.A.M.H. The Rt. Hon. Lord Justice McVeigh became the chairman and active leader. In 1965 he invited me to open a Conference on "Community Responsibility for Children and Adolescents with Behaviour Problems" and Dr. Jack Kahn Consultant Psychiatrist, London Borough of Newham was the main speaker.

Leading my usual double life I always stayed at Government House with my friend, Lady Wakehurst, the wife of the Governor General. She took a very real and personal interest in mental health problems, and was unanimously elected President of the Northern Ireland Association. I marvelled at her handling of this Conference of some 500 delegates from all over the Province, from Scotland, Eire and the Isle of Man. Her understanding and intuitive control of the large gathering of psychiatrists, psychologists, nurses, teachers, G.P.s and many interested lay members showed considerable skill.

The Northern Ireland Association, like its counterpart in Scotland, had its own identity, but worked closely with us in London and with the Mental Health Association in Dublin. Like all voluntary mental health societies all over the world it was non-political and non-sectarian. All the voluntary associations in Northern Ireland consisted of differing political parties and of different religious beliefs, but here under the mental health flag they were all the more united in their endeavour to work together for mental health.

During my three visits I went to several hospitals and clinics in different parts of the Province, and talked with patients and staff. In Belfast the late Prof. Gibson showed me with justifiable pride his new purpose-built psychiatric unit. This made me feel a little jealous, for the wards at the Maudsley badly needed upgrading at that time and we could not induce our Government to provide the money.

My contribution to the Conference had, I think, been useful and constructive, for I put the N. Ireland Association in touch with our many local mental health associations on the mainland; and the N.A.M.H. headquarters were to feel much closer to, and more understanding of the problems facing N. Ireland.

Since my last visit in 1965 much violence has erupted in Northern Ireland, as it has in many other parts of the world, but I know that the Association gallantly carries on with its headquarters in Beacon House in Belfast, providing a professional advice service for patients and their relatives. The Association includes Roman Catholics on its Executive Board as well as Protestants, and the staff are always appointed on merit with no questions of politics or religion. I was not aware on my visit of serious trouble, but looking back there must have been tensions which did not surface in the Association.

Now I can only keep them all in my thoughts, and hope and pray that the undoubted good work I saw being practised by a brave community will eventually bear fruit, and that a more positive mental health attitude to life will prevail, for I can bear witness to their courage and tenacity.

Nigeria, 1961

It is with deep sadness that I look back on the first Pan-African Psychiatric Conference which I attended in November 1961, at the invitation of Dr. Thomas Lambo[1] who was then Director of the Neuro-Psychiatric Centre in the Western Region at Abeokuta. So much tragedy has overtaken Nigeria since that date—civil war; the murder of that great statesman and Prime Minister of the Federation, Alhagi Sir Abubaka Tafawa Belewa, a man of international stature; not to mention the death by violence and by other means of many of the friends whom I made during my three-week visit. I quote the words which I wrote at the end of the journal I kept whilst in Nigeria:

[1] Now Deputy Director General, W.H.O.

World Travels

Nigeria has been described as a country in a hurry and that is true. They do not hope for things to be done next year, next month or next week, but tomorrow or, better still, today! There is immense vitality and enjoyment, amazingly rapid development and eagerness against a background of colour, wisdom and great friendliness. Population problems, the need for water supplies and living amenities, the need for a balanced economy, better standards of education, the eradication of malaria—apart from the dangerous political question of the Northern, Southern and Eastern regions—all this presents the country with an enormous challenge, the need for discipline and hard work and the necessity to stamp out corruption. I believe it is our duty and should be our pleasure to help these people in their first years of independence. We opened up the country and have a fine record in Nigeria, but there is still much for us to do and we should be proud to do it.

Who knows what went wrong, who was to blame? I can only describe the country as I saw it in 1961 and let some of the high hopes I had at that time seep through these pages.

I was invited to attend the Conference in Nigeria as Chairman of the N.A.M.H., and I was also asked to give a paper on "The Role of the Public in Mental Health Promotion". Robina Addis, who was Head of the Social Services Department of the N.A.M.H., was to give a lecture on "Social Work Training". On arrival at Lagos Robina and I were whisked off in a car by the then Governor of the Bank of Nigeria, Roy Fenton, and Mrs Fenton. He was the last Governor to be nominated by the Bank of England to a Central Bank, and had been a friend of my husband's. It was delightful to relax and see something of Lagos, and to meet the many expatriates working in that city, and to hear about the problems of transition before the complete take-over by Nigerians. I attended one glorious lunch party given by the Governor for his successor, a Nigerian who had worked in the Bank of England for some years. The Directors of the Bank came from the Western, Eastern and Northern regions, all dressed most colourfully in their native costumes, the Northerners especially so with huge headdresses—making those already big men look like giants or mediaeval knights—it was really rather frightening.

We visited some of the many voluntary and missionary schools for the blind and deaf, and saw good work undertaken by European staff, mostly British. But I especially enjoyed my visit to the 60 acre Federal Farm School at Ikedja, on which worked fifty men, whose after-care and oversight was carried out by Miss Grace Ingham from Burnley! She knew all about me and the Towneleys. She was a remarkable, dynamic personality with great physical courage. In her after-care work she travelled by Jeep with her dog and a Nigerian driver, sleeping in local rest houses if possible, or otherwise in a tent. She saw the terrifying Sardauna of Sokoto, Premier of the Northern Region, slept in his harem and reproached him for his various misdeeds, so she was not popular in Establishment circles. She told of the many mentally sick people who were in poverty and distress, and often in chains, and she hoped that out of the Conference would come a Federal and Regional Association for Mental Health.

Leaving the Fentons we motored to Abeokuta for the actual opening of the Conference, staying in a Government Guest House, formerly the Residency in Colonial days and now the Police Headquarters. This stood outside the town and on the top of a hill. It was not air-conditioned, but had electric fans and mosquito nets. We were joined by my old friend and colleague on the W.F.M.H. from South Africa, Iris Marwick, Matron of Tara Hospital, so we were a gay trio.

The Federal Minister of Health opened the Conference, and it was a dignified and formal occasion at which we all patted each other on the back and gave greetings from our various countries. I read a message of goodwill from H.R.H. Princess Marina, the then Patron of N.A.M.H., and from Rab Butler our President. About 200 persons attended this Conference, mostly hand-picked by Dr. Lambo, the majority being Nigerians from the three Regions, comprising doctors, nurses, social workers, educationalists, the rest being Europeans from similar professions working in different parts of Africa. The venue was the Neuro-Psychiatric Centre at Aro Hospital, Abeokuta, Western Nigeria and the Federal Government and

Iris Marwick and self in Nigeria

With Hospital staff, Singapore, 1965

Planting a tree, Singapore

Nigeria (L. to R.) Lady Mbanefo, Eastern region, self, Lady Ademola, Western region, 1961

Alhagi Sir Abubaka Balewa, Prime Minister of the Federation, with Lord Brain and myself

World Travels

the Minister of Health, on Dr. Lambo's advice, had invited specialists on mental health from the U.K., U.S.A. and Europe in addition to representatives from W.H.O. and W.F.M.H.

The aim was to present a rounded picture of psychiatry, and to discuss in terms of human values the effect of the amazing changes in the social, cultural and political life of Africa. The British team was of a high calibre, and included the late Lord Brain, the famous neurologist, and Professor Sir Aubrey Lewis from the Maudsley Hospital. Both delivered brilliant technical papers, and their mastery of their subjects made it all seem so simple. Sir Aubrey's wife, Hilda, spoke about her studies of children's problems in the U.K. and Dr. Peter Scott spoke about juvenile crime. As we sat under electric fans in the fierce heat, all these topics were seen against a tropical colouring, and we persisted in a constant effort to adjust our experiences to a strange environment. How did these things look in Africa? "The miracle of Aro", as Dr. Rumke from Holland described it, was explained by the fact that this Conference was held in Aro Hospital, where since 1954 Dr. Lambo had carried on his experiment of running a village community of mental patients. This gave a special flavour to discussion. We milled around, meeting patients as they walked to occupational therapy, or visiting them in the wards or at the out-patients department, and all this made us feel part of the hospital. It also gave us a chance to talk to all the other international delegates from North and South America, Europe, Africa and Asia, all very high-powered in their different professional settings but here relaxed and friendly.

We visited the village community where the Bale (Chief), surrounded by his Elders in lovely colourful clothes, addressed us with great dignity in the village square. He told us that he was taking the responsibility for fifty patients boarded out, each with a relative in charge, in this village of 500 persons. We visited the mud huts surrounded by dense bush. The hospital provided electricity and water, and a reception centre had been built so that the patients could be admitted at any hour. Doctors and nurses visited the patients, who came from a large catchment area. I was struck by the simplicity of the whole scheme. Here was what we in the U.K. were contemplating but

In the Way of Understanding

were still only talking about. One moving moment remains in my memory, when Dr. Rumke from Holland, that wise and kindly psychiatrist, examined a very mentally sick little boy who was specially cared for in the Bale's own home. We were all silent, and there was a hush whilst we watched spellbound the contact between the Professor, surrounded by the best neurological and psychiatric brains from Europe and America, and the little patient. Both seemed to be completely oblivious to the crowd around them. Such a demonstration of trust between a doctor and his patient left me feeling that this was psychiatry in its perfection.

Community care of the patients, who remained under the supervision of the hospital services, was the spearhead of development at Aro. At the time only 200 patients were in hospital, and 300 were boarded out. Other countries have much to learn from this scheme in a remote part of Africa, where patients are kept in touch with ordinary folk and thus avoid the danger of institutionalisation. Moreover, here is a good example of villagers accepting responsibility for the mentally ill and the mentally disordered.

Back in Aro, while walking one day with Dr. Lambo in the hospital grounds, I saw a senile old man tied to a tree, grinning and laughing. I was horrified, and said so. Dr. Lambo said that the old man's relatives were working in the hospital and as they wished to keep him at home they took him with them daily to work, visiting him often at his tree and feeding him. Dr. Lambo asked me if it was not better to do this than to dump him in a mental hospital, to vegetate and eventually die as we did in England. I had no adequate answer.

I asked Dr. Lambo why, as we passed, some nurses kissed his hand and others did not. He answered that those who greeted him thus were of his tribe and that he was their Chief.

Our visit to Lantoro a hospital, where certified patients and criminal lunatics were detained, was less happy. Patients were heavily sedated, and it was a sad sight. Dirty huts and a shortage of doctors and nurses made treatment impossible. Dr. Lambo and the authorities deplored this, but at that time little, if anything, could be done about it.

During the week of scientific and technical discussions at the

World Travels

Conference some of us were taken back to Lagos to meet the Prime Minister, Alhagi Sir Abubaka Tafawe Balewa. The House of Representatives is a fine modern building with beautiful doors made of local wood, and lovely carving. The P.M., a very handsome man, was dressed in white, and was of most dignified bearing. One was conscious of being in the presence of a civilised being of wisdom and understanding; in essence a citizen of the world. He was relaxed and most welcoming, although we were one hour late, whilst he was supposed to be the only punctual man in Nigeria! He spoke in English, and reminded us of the enormous financial burdens that faced the government of a new country. Health, including mental health, had many competitors for resources. He told us that he considered that Dr. Lambo was a true son of Nigeria, and that he would have been influential in any sphere of activity he had taken up. The Minister of Health took this opportunity of making an impassioned plea for his new health programme, saying how proud he was that this first Pan–African Conference was being held in Aro. He praised Dr. Lambo for his courage in getting so many distinguished persons together, and for his perspicacity in taking the lead in mental health work in Africa. Sir Russell Brain, as he then was, thanked the P.M. and representatives from America and Canada did likewise. Then a tribute was paid by Tigani El Mahi from the Sudan, a splendid psychiatrist who later became temporary Prime Minister in his own country during the visit of H.M. the Queen, at a time of unresolved political differences. There was some tension when Professor Gillis from South Africa made his speech of thanks, but he did so with courage and dignity, quietly and to the point. He stressed how much he had learned at Aro, and how glad he was to see so much being accomplished for a section of the public which was much neglected in his own country.

One afternoon, H.R.H. the Alake of Abeokuta, Sir Ladapo Ademola, gave a Reception for us. I gravely followed Dr. Lambo into the audience room as he fell on his knees and crawled up to the raised dais. What was I supposed to do? I wanted to do the right thing and give no offence, yet as a feminist I would not crawl to any man, black or white! In true

In the Way of Understanding

British style I compromised, and walked up to the Alake with as much dignity as I could muster in my short European silk dress, and bowed low to him. This old man of ninety then invited me to sit at his right hand. Conversation was difficult, as he spoke very broken English, but I understood from the interpreter that all H.R.H.'s different hats, displayed in a Maple's glass cupboard behind him, had immensely amused Princess Alexandra. She had tried them all on when she came to the Independence celebrations. On this note we laughed and joked, whilst Nigerians crawled and Europeans bowed low.

After the Conference Robina and I stayed in Lagos with the Lord Chief Justice of the Western Region, Sir Adetokumbo Ademola and Lady Ademola, who held the inaugural meeting of the Western Nigerian Association for Mental Health in their house. Robina and I felt proud to be at the formation of the Association, which looked so promising and was conceived in a most democratic manner. It was to be a Federal Nigerian Association, but other countries in Africa could join it and there were to be regional branches. They used a modified Constitution of the British N.A.M.H. Dr. Lambo said that they had £2,000 left over from the Conference, and Cornell University, which had been working in the region, gave them typewriters and some useful equipment, so they got off to a good start.

Later Robina and I flew to the Eastern Region to stay with Sir Louis and Lady Mbanefo, he being the Eastern Region's Chief Justice. During this time we visited an excellent approved school for boys, and a leper colony. This latter now mostly dealt with blind, deaf and dumb children, as happily leprosy is now dying out. The University of Nigeria at Nsuka was being built with Nigerian money and technical aid from the U.S.A. It was a remarkable achievement, and the first President of the Federation, Azikiwi, had given most of the land and was to be the first Chancellor.

One afternoon Robina and I set off with Lady Mbanefo for Onitsha, the town where she and Sir Louis had their private residence, and where they had been brought up as children at the local schools. This is on the Niger river, about a hundred miles from Enugu. We saw the long canoes on this wide, fast-flowing river, some closed but others uncovered with merchandise piled high, paddled or poled by fine-looking men. The market by the riverside was said to be the largest in Africa, and was an amazing sight which has to be seen to be believed. Booths were piled high with goods from all over the world. There were clothes of every colour, live chickens, and much fish, some dried and some alive in bowls. Crowds of happy, jostling people milled around and it was said that it was possible to buy anything from a pin to a Rolls Royce! Huge white cattle with big horns had been driven down from the North by Hausa tribesmen and were slaughtered on the spot—but happily not at the time of our visit. There was an open sanded arena where the cattle's throats were cut, and the blood ran down huge gullies into the Niger.

Lady Mbanefo led the way through this medley of humanity, all shouting and yelling at once. Foul stuff ran down the gullies, but at night they were flushed, and, according to the health authorities, were clean by morning. At one moment Lady Mbanefo bent down to a very old lady, typical of many squatting about, gave her a pound note, and said: "This is my husband's aunt". Later that afternoon, in Lady Mbanefo's house, we saw an excellent portrait, painted by a modern French artist, of an almost naked man, with feathers and a spear. This was Sir Louis' father, and his elder brother also wears this "dress" on ceremonial occasions as he is the head of his tribe. This illustrates the terrifying pace of change in Africa.

After our excursion to the market we had hoped for a quiet night, but the Chief Justice was dining with the local Scottish Society for the St. Andrew's night dinner, and we were invited. Tired as I was, I thoroughly enjoyed the excellent Scotch whisky and the haggis, and admired the white dresses and tartan scarves of the ladies, the men in kilts, the bagpipes and the Scottish music and reels. Sir Louis made an amusing and clever speech, comparing Scottish clans to Nigerian tribes in their squabbles and jealousies, and their disputes with the English, and it went down very well.

That night Robina and I mused for hours and talked of our amazing experiences—of Sir Louis, our host, of his father's picture, of his Cambridge education, of the latest novels and biographies from England, including the new translation of the Bible which we found in our rooms, and of all the contrast around us. He was very handsome, and wore London-made suits and shoes with colourful shirts, ties and scarves—in short, a truly remarkable person, and his wife was an enigmatic and handsome woman. Sir Louis was a Christian and took us to an Anglican service on Sunday. This was very impressive, with an excellent sermon, a full church and hearty singing.

It was with sadness that we boarded our plane for Lagos, seen off by our host and hostess. I seemed to have some apprehension or foreboding of what might happen before I would see those dear folk again. Tears welled up in my eyes and for a while Robina and I were too overcome to speak. Much later back in England I received a letter from Tom Lambo which reinforced my emotional bonds with Africa. He wrote "... having seen you in action so constantly and forcibly in this part of the world I feel you belong to us".

France, 1962—a joyful flutter

The W.F.M.H. visited Paris for its 1962 Congress at the invitation of the European League for Mental Hygiene, whose headquarters were in that city. For the first time I came to the Congress as an official representative of the Bethlem Royal and Maudsley Hospitals. I felt this was something of a triumph. I had gained recognition for the W.F.M.H., and my continuous work for the joint hospital had won recognition for me as a serious worker in world mental health. The U.K. was well represented by a number of delegates from many professions who were well known and friendly to each other, and they included observer delegates from the D.H.S.S. and the D.E.S. An old friend of mine, the late Dame Eileen Younghusband, joined the Executive Board representing British social workers. Those who remember her sense of the comic will not be surprised that she inveigled me to skip the official reception at the Louvre in order to take me instead on an unofficial tour of Paris by night, including some "bôites". The next morning Eileen excused our absence, saying, with that well-known twinkle in her lovely blue eyes, that to see life in all its aspects

World Travels

was good for those working in the rarified atmosphere of mental health.

Three memorable yet contrasting contributions to this Conference were given. The first was by Rajkumazi Amrit Kaar, former Minister of Health in India, who, in outlining the necessity for interdependence in mental health, presented us with an imminent Utopia where each country accepted its responsibility to be the keeper of the safety of all. Once again, Margaret Mead brought us down to earth from the idealistic and spiritual plane, and reminded us of the prejudices, misunderstandings and inequalities that faced all countries, including India. She confronted us with the struggles and hard work that lay ahead. It remained for Dr. Wilfrid Warren to offer wisdom, experience and practical suggestions to the Congress. He reviewed the foundation of the child guidance service in the U.K., giving food for thought to colleagues from many countries who were only just awakening to the importance of mental health in children.

Amongst the many visits to hospitals, clinics and institutions, the most important to me was a trip to La Verrière, a hospital pilot scheme which Dr. Paul Sivadon, the host at the Paris Conference, had dreamed about one evening in my flat many years previously. I was happy to see this in action, now that his vision had become a reality. He had been given the opportunity to train staff in his team-work philosophy at the same time as the architect was at work on the building, thus enabling all professions to draw together in their efforts to provide an ideal hospital. I believe that his dream had been fulfilled, and looking back after twenty years this building and the enthusiasm of the staff remain clearly in my mind. From time to time improvements may be necessary, but just as Florence Nightingale's principles for building a hospital are still accepted today, so will Dr. Sivadon's plan serve as a model for future generations, for his basic idea was sound; namely, the harmonisation of the individual with his environment.

The French were determined that we should not leave Paris before we had absorbed some of their history. The climax of the week was a Son et Lumière performance at Versailles, and I can still remember the light going out in the bedroom of Louis

XV as the narrator told of his death, and I could almost hear his famous words "Après moi le déluge".

Greece, 1963

My official journeys had never taken me to Greece, yet I had long been interested in what some people call the loveliest country in the world as a result of reading two quite different books. The first, *The Torch*[1], a delightful novel about Hippocrates, the father of modern medicine, was written by Prof. Wilder Penfield whom I had met in Canada. The second book, *An Affair of the Heart*,[2] by Dilys Powell, is about the little village of Perachora, which in old Greek means "beyond the sea". My opportunity to visit Greece came when two dear Norman cousins invited me to holiday with them and to share a car.

On the way to the Acropolis we walked up the steep Philippus hill, passing what was said to have been Socrates' prison. The hill was covered with small olive trees in flower, flowering thyme, and small roses which gave out an intoxicating perfume. My heart, like Dilys Powell's, became instantly involved, and I was drunk with the beauty of the Acropolis and the colour of its marble, which was like a mixture of many honies mellowed by the centuries. I was truly overwhelmed, and feeling humble and reverent I made my "prière sur l'Acropole". However, it must alas be said that the most dramatic and superb view of the Acropolis (particularly at night when it is floodlit) is from the top storey of the ugly Hilton Hotel.

The National Museum with all its beautifully arranged objets d'art, jewellery, sculpture and gold, the creations of a civilisation unsurpassed, made me realise that after the Dark Ages few of us in Europe ever recovered. The exciting statue of Poseidon (460 B.C.) was only brought up from the sea bed in the Twenties, and is almost intact. It is a beautiful figure of a man, vigorous and alive, and it took me under its spell. The many tourists wandering about as if in a dream seemed also to sense the timeless grandeur around us.

[1] Prof. Wilder Penfield, D.M., C.M.G., F.R.S., F.R.S.C., Harrap & Co., 1961.
[2] Penguin, 1958.

World Travels

On our way to Epidaurus we drove via Corinth to the little village of Perachora, the site where the late Humfry Payne began his famous dig in 1929. It was still remote, just as it was described by Dilys Powell, his widow, with only goat tracks which our car found difficult to negotiate. Through our interpreter we made known our interest in the village. There was great excitement and rejoicing amongst the villagers, and one dear lady brought out her best china and made coffee. She put a table out in the fierce sun, presumably still believing that we were sun worshippers—shades perhaps of Noel Coward's "Mad dogs and Englishmen go out in the mid-day sun"! Whilst we waited patiently on the patio amidst the honeysuckle and the exquisitely smelling flowers in pots, an old man came to say that he had known Humfry and his lady, and would forever remember them for their work, their understanding and their love of their labourers. Our hostess refused any payment for her hospitality, saying, "tell them in your country about us, that we are friends and have built a little museum in remembrance". So much for a good page in our history, not written by politicians or diplomats but by a dedicated archaeologist and his lady who were in love with their work, with Greek history and especially with those dear folk in that tiny village.

Then to Epidaurus, which is perhaps even more spectacular than the Acropolis, with its superb open-air theatre and its back-cloth of Wagnerian mountains. Here was a theatre for entertainment and education, a temple for healing the soul, and a stadium for exercising the body—only in Greece could all this be found together.

After visiting Sparta, Olympia and Delphi we made our pilgrimage to the Island of Cos, pausing in Rhodes—rather too sophisticated, and modernised by Mussolini. But in Cos our hotel was unpretentious and right on the beach, so we could go out from our bedrooms and swim by day or by moonlight. I could dream of Poseidon and feel the old gods around us, with nothing but Asia Minor and Turkey in the distance.

It was in Cos that Hippocrates, some twenty-four centuries ago, first practised the art of healing as a science rather than as a branch of witchcraft. In the great square of this small town stands the plane tree where, according to legend, the father of medicine taught his disciples. The trunk is roughly forty-six feet in circumference, and the branches are so heavy that they are propped up by pillars. In the centre of the island is the now-famous International Hippocratic Foundation (just being built when I was there), where physicians from all parts of the world can carry out research, meditate or relax, and have time to think about us, their patients, in a beautiful and peaceful setting.

We sailed back to Athens via Delos and Mykonos, both entrancing and seductive places, which made us wish we could have spent more time in each. There is so much to remember, and so much I would like to write, but guide-books can make dull reading so I can only beg all who possibly can to visit Greece, with enough time to absorb its atmosphere. To my medical friends I would say—make a pilgrimage to Cos.

Back in Athens I spent some time on the Agora looking up at the Parthenon, perhaps from the very place where Socrates had raised his eyes when on trial. This was the market place where he must have argued and laughed, and I remembered another book that had deeply impressed me, *Portrait of Socrates* by Sir R. W. Livingstone[1], which I think contains the best description of positive mental health that I have ever read (see Appendix).

This two weeks holiday in Greece had made a life-long impression on me, and I felt refreshed and strengthened. I took back with me a deep reverence for ancient history and the work of mankind.

On the flight home our pilot kindly dipped down low over the lighthouse on the headland near Perachora, so I caught a last glimpse of the Greece with which I too had had an affair of the heart.

The Netherlands, 1963

By this date the Netherlands Association for Mental Health had, after a struggle, built up an efficient and well-organised voluntary organisation—perhaps one of the best in Northern

[1] Oxford University Press, 1938.

World Travels

Europe. It was therefore a pleasure for the W.F.M.H. to accept an invitation to hold their A.G.M. in Amsterdam with the theme of "Population Problems and Mental Health". This was a burning question in Europe, for we were all facing the problem of overcrowding and its implications for our mental well-being.

At this big gathering the Minister for Social Affairs and the Burgameester of the city took an active part in our discussions, as did Dr. A. Querido, Professor of Social Medicine of the University of Amsterdam. He was then the Chairman of the Netherlands Association for Mental Health. It was not a voluntary association as we understand it in the U.K. or in the U.S.A. because it was started by professionals—doctors, psychiatrists, psychologists and social workers—amongst whom were only a handful of psychiatric social workers at that date. The State psychiatric services were fairly well organised, and Professor Querido had a scheme by which mental casualties at home or in the street were seen by a psychiatrist before receiving treatment in hospital, thus involving police and social work departments. This was in advance of most other countries, and the idea had much publicity.

Dr. Hans Rumke, whom I have already mentioned as a founder member of the W.F.M.H., worked hard with Prof. Querido to educate the public and to get them interested in forming a truly voluntary association on the lines of the N.A.M.H. This was an almost impossible task in those early days, as the professionals were afraid of involving untrained volunteers in mental health work. However, both these devoted psychiatrists persisted, and something very like the N.A.M.H. was started with a paid Secretary and a voluntary committee of professionals and lay members. This was a real triumph, and as a pilot scheme it was followed in different ways by other European countries.

Dr. Edward Hare, a consultant from the Bethlem Royal and Maudsley, was also at the meeting and gave a useful paper on "Mental Health in the New Housing Estates". Most European countries have acute housing problems. Housing authorities, because of lack of space, tend to cluster many houses close together on estates, or to build high-rise flats, without considering the grim implications for mental health which are involved in both these kinds of building. It was hoped that the architects, the officials and the housing authorities concerned might include mental health workers early on in their planning discussions. There was also the fast-growing population problem, for which the solution was not simply birth control.

A prominent member of the Association took me to a house in the town which was now used as a children's clinic, and was run by the Netherlands Association as a memorial foundation. As I stood in the main dining-hall, my guide pointed out a two-foot gap between the wall and the ceiling on one side of the room. During the Occupation this house had been used as a collecting centre for Jewish women and their children before their deportation to the gas chambers. They came from all over Holland to await the lorries which were to take them to the cattle-trucks at the railway station. It was in this room that the mothers had to make the decision whether to take their babies with them, or to hand them over to the care of the Dutch nurses who were waiting on the other side of the wall. No child over about six months could be considered, as the open space between its wall and the ceiling was too small an outlet. The decision to save a child's life had to be taken in silence, for fear that the Gestapo officers would hear and find out. So these heroic women would push their babies through the gap to the willing hands on the other side. The reader can imagine, as I did, the agony of mind that these women went through before their final decision. I was frozen with horror, and the experience of actually seeing this room, and the opportunity of meeting some of the workers who took part in this merciful rescue, are memories I still have with me from that W.F.M.H. meeting.

Hong Kong, 1964, 1970, 1971 and 1973

Hong Kong was to be like a magnet to me after my first visit there with Robina Addis. It has the most dangerous of airstrips, jutting out far into the sea, and as we landed in the dusk the whole Island was alight and looked like a diamond brooch hanging in the sky. The crossing by ferry from Kowloon on the

World Travels

mainland to Hong Kong Island on a balmy eastern night was spectacular, with the ships of the Royal Navy at anchor in the vast harbour all illuminated in celebration of the Chinese New Year.

During my first visit I stayed in the Mandarin Hotel. The decorations and furnishings were in the Chinese traditional style, in beautiful shades of yellow, red and black. The bedrooms were exquisitely planned, with silently sliding doors and built-in cupboards of sweet-smelling wood. I paid £5 a night without breakfast which in those days I considered an exorbitant price!

My first visit was to the Castle Peak Psychiatric Hospital, built in 1961 on the mainland about twenty miles or so from Kowloon. In those days this meant a lovely drive through glorious scenery. I was enchanted with the beauty of the place, but I was not allowed to indulge my aesthetic sense at the expense of my mission. Dr. P. M. Yap, the Maudsley-trained Professor of Psychiatry, was also in the car, and during the drive he took the opportunity to tell me of his depression because of the usual Government attitude to mental health, and the deplorable situation in Hong Kong. I was torn between delight in my surroundings and concern for his plight. However the Hospital itself was well-planned and was built on the villa system. Though part of it housed the criminally insane, my friend Dr. Walter Maclay of our then Ministry of Health had persuaded the Hong Kong authorities not to build a high wall. The splendid view inland was therefore unimpeded, although a deep ha-ha provided security and prevented any escape. I am sure that this invisible incarceration had much to do with the happy atmosphere that existed among staff and patients, and especially in the wards which housed the criminals. I was very impressed, and I very much enjoyed my welcome by the Superintendent, Dr. George Ou, who from that date has become a real friend.

My second visit in November 1965, with Denis Leigh as my companion, gave me even more pleasure as it was far more leisurely. However, the outward journey itself was not so pleasant. We were on our way to the W.F.M.H. Conference in Bangkok, flying Air India over Vietnam, when we ran into a severe thunderstorm. The thought of being forced down into what looked to be nothing but scrub, water and hills was frightening. There were quick flashes of lightning which could in fact have been flak and I was thankful for a calm landing. Denis and I received V.I.P. treatment when we were met by the British Council and by the smiling Professor Yap and Dr. Ou, who were now already old friends of mine.

Next day we motored through the New Territories to Castle Peak. We passed through a new resettlement area and through Kam Tin, a walled city with Hakka women in local dress with large hats with black frills to keep off the sun. After lunch we were taken to the Chinese border and into the Police Post. It was manned by only eighteen good-looking, young British policemen. They were unarmed, and faced Red China's 2,000 soldiers who were in pill-boxes, on the other side of some barbed wire. China was visible through the binoculars which they lent us. It was a lovely sight, with the sun setting on a line of hills and, in the foreground, endless artificial ponds for ducks and geese. Only the river divided us from the might of Chairman Mao. Then it was back again to Kowloon, through the market teeming with fortune tellers, medicine men, snakes, cats and chickens. The animals were for eating, and many were still alive.

Denis Leigh was of course visiting hospitals to talk to the medical authorities and to discuss psychiatric problems. While he was doing this I was taken to resettlement centres, to residential homes for boys and girls, all happy and well-cared for, and to a remand home for boys. These were said to find sleeping four to a room a nice change from being one of a large family all living in one room. They much preferred living in the remand home to going home. This was becoming a real headache for the authorities.

I discussed with Professor Yap the work of the Hong Kong Association for Mental Health. This needed more money and more support from monied people, of whom Hong Kong has a rich selection. But the traditional fear of the mentally ill among Europeans is a terrible barrier. They supported other charities most readily, but at that time the Hong Kong Association was, as elsewhere, the Cinderella of the voluntary services. This

World Travels

grieved me, and I would have liked to have stayed in Hong Kong for six months to see if I could have done something to get the support of the rich business men, and also of their wives, who seemed to have so much time on their hands.

Denis gave a superb lecture to doctors, nurses, students, occupational therapists, and so on, which I attended. He spoke of the latest developments in England, and was skilled at answering questions in a kindly way. He gave some of the shy Chinese men and women a real chance to share in the problems which he had dealt with in his lecture. As I look back I think it is not surprising that he was elected to be Secretary of the World Psychiatric Association, a post which he held for ten years. He is undoubtedly a born teacher, and a lover of these diffident foreigners from whom, however, he stands no nonsense, which is why he sometimes appears brusque. However, they must sense that for all his aggressiveness he has a loving heart, and many came to enjoy his teasing.

I stayed on after Denis had to return to England, and I spent a day in the Juvenile Court. This was run very much on our pattern, except that one Chinese woman magistrate distributed family planning pamphlets to the children for them to give to their mothers. The cases were mostly for hawking, a charge only too well known to the Court, and they were discharged with a small fine. Parents did not have to accompany their children, as most of them were working and all were terribly poor. Schooling was only half-time, so not unnaturally the children tried to earn an honest penny by hawking. It seemed impossible to prevent this and ridiculous to try to do so. The adult court was in an excellent building, and seemed well administered, with good interpreters provided.

I left Hong Kong with a feeling of helplessness and hopelessness. Here was this beautiful island, a jewel in the British crown, a hive of thriving business, full of very rich Chinese and Europeans, many of them millionaires, and yet I had seen the other side of the picture and I was disturbed. The social services and the provision of education and housing were most inadequate. Great tower blocks were being built without adequate play-space for children, against the advice of those who had already encountered this problem in England. Thus crime, petty theft and violence were on the increase. Training facilities for all the professions were very inadequate, and although another university was to be built in the New Territories, things were moving too slowly. The excuse for this, which had some justification, was the influx of thousands of illegal refugees with whom the authorities had to cope. In the late 1970s the situation must have been even worse.

Six years passed before I returned, and in that time much improvement had taken place in all the fields of the social services which had so disturbed me on my two previous visits. The W.F.M.H. were holding their twenty-fourth Annual Meeting and the theme, "Mental Health and Urbanization", was well chosen, for the history of Hong Kong has been a record of continuous urbanisation. I was to see a further example of this on yet another drive to Castle Peak. Where there had been such lovely scenery there were now ugly, sprawling housing estates.

The resettlement schemes were good in comparison with the terrible housing conditions of the past, but they reminded me sadly of Alcatraz in their prison-like architecture, and the crowding of people in skyscrapers was undoubtedly creating the problems of mental health which many had predicted earlier. This was only too clear to the Social Welfare Department, but somehow unimaginative architects, shortage of cash and inertia had won the day.

The Hong Kong Mental Health Association had done a marvellous job in organising this big Conference, and things were efficiently run with everyone happy and smiling. I had a heart-warming reception from my many friends in the movement. The Conference itself was a splendid exercise in communication, for Maudsley-trained men and women from all over the world had an opportunity to renew friendships, to talk of their time in England, and recount in an uninhibited manner their experiences since returning to their homelands. Their affection for Britain and their appreciation of their professors and tutors was very real. They were anxious to keep in touch and to know more of current developments at the Bethlem Royal and Maudsley. I had a lump in my throat, and also a prick of conscience, in receiving so much overwhelming affection and hospitality, for I felt that I had done little to deserve it.

On this occasion we were not staying at the Mandarin Hotel, so dear to my heart, but at the Hilton, a huge impersonal building. The concept was perhaps that of an Inn, as in olden days, with a bustle of coaches arriving full of visitors of all nationalities, weary, tired, or frustrated. In these days of big business travel there are loud-voiced visitors from Western countries, or soft-voiced visitors from the East, but always one finds hordes of them sitting on their luggage in the big reception hall. It is not a peaceful atmosphere, but it was useful for the W.F.M.H. to have all the delegates under one roof, with plenty of small rooms for meetings and an excellent cafeteria service. As one went up to different floors on a moving staircase, the shopping centre itself was a great source of entertainment, and the many cafeterias were useful places in which to meet friends. As was usual during such Conferences, I had to help my many men friends to choose presents for their wives and girl-friends, and this always gave me great pleasure. I hope I succeeded in my choice of gifts in giving pleasure to the recipients, and that I did not mar any relationships, matrimonial or otherwise! One dear friend chose a diamond ring for his wife, and another bought from the Communist store in Kowloon a whole trousseau for himself and his wife.

This was, alas, the last year of Professor Carstairs' presidency of the W.F.M.H. (see page 278). He had proved to be a first-rate leader—a canny Scot who had put the finances of the W.F.M.H. on an even keel. Communication with colleagues, with universities and with national associations all over the world had been much improved, and his wisdom and good judgment were universally acknowledged.

At this Congress I found myself caught up in educational problems. At the invitation of the Director of Special Education I met, at her flat, teachers of the deaf, blind, spastic, autistic and mentally handicapped, just as I had met social workers six years previously. These fascinating young Chinese men and women (some of them Inspectors) were eloquent in their praise of Britain and of what they had learned. They were grateful for their training and were especially anxious to talk about what the N.A.M.H. had done for them in its Education and Training Department. When I returned home, it seemed to me on reflection that the social workers and teachers, and perhaps the mental health workers above all, were doing remarkably good ambassadorial work—better perhaps than the career diplomats or the government-sponsored British Council.

This had been a good Conference, and the W.F.M.H. had a splendid turn-out from Australia, Israel, Japan, the U.A.R., Thailand, France, Italy, the Philippines, Canada, the U.K. and the U.S.A. Edith Morgan, now deputy Director of the N.A.M.H., was representing that organisation officially on the Executive Board of the W.F.M.H., and she also represented the social workers.

Perhaps the most important item discussed by the Executive Board was "Freedom of Conscience". In discussion it was agreed that:

> *There are many definitions of mental health but one thing they all have in common is the recognition of each man's freedom of opinion which is based on freedom of conscience—that is, his right to hold and to affirm his personal moral values. Freedom of opinion has been attained only relatively recently in some countries of the world; in others, it still has to be asserted, and in all countries it has to be vigilantly defended because deprivation of this freedom is both an affront to human dignity and a severe form of mental cruelty. Respect for freedom of opinion has been incorporated in the United Nations' Universal Declaration of Human Rights.*

(Resolution passed by the W.F.M.H. Board, Hong Kong 1971.)

A resolution incorporating this statement was forwarded to the meeting of the World Psychiatric Association in Mexico.

Again in 1971 Robina and I made a stop-over visit to Hong Kong on our way to Peking to stay with John Addis, the then Ambassador. We were lent a luxurious flat high up on the Peak with a most superb view, especially at night, when one felt as if one were looking at fairyland from an eagle's nest. Our many friends visited us and we went to the races—not my favourite sport but it was fascinating to see the rich at play, both Honkongese and Europeans. Having on other occasions peered into the less happy side of Hong Kong and noted the squalor, poverty and unspeakable overcrowding, I felt ashamed to be mixing with these affluent people, so oblivious of how the majority lived.

This time we drove through the new tunnel and used a helicopter to take us to and from the mainland. It was a far cry from my first glimpse of the diamond brooch I remembered from the plane in 1964. The view from the helicopter was fantastic and I enjoyed seeing the whole panorama of Hong Kong and its adjacent islands. But the tunnel, although useful, was boring, and one could have been in New York City or anywhere else.

In Hong Kong I was to come across so many lonely young women, the wives of the European business-men, many of them from the U.K. Their day-to-day lives seemed to be spent in enjoying themselves in swimming, yachting, sun-bathing, dancing, bridge, and so on, with Hong Kong or Philippine servants to care for their homes and children. I longed to channel all their energies into some kind of social work, if only a few hours a week, and help these young things get a glimpse of that other world, the real world of the island. The State services and the voluntary services seemed to be separate entities and to mistrust each other. This was the usual case of the "do-gooders" knowing nothing of the professionals, and vice versa. Here was a chance to bring together a team of young men and women so that they could discover another side of life in Hong Kong to that of making money. As with all such ideas it needed a leader.

The magnet drew me back to Hong Kong in 1973. This time I was travelling with Dr. Wilfrid Warren and his wife, Betty, on our way to the W.F.M.H. Congress in Sydney. Dr. Warren was to deliver the first memorial lecture for my old friend Professor Yap who, alas, had died suddenly in Mexico when attending the World Psychiatric Congress. It was a thoughtful paper on the subject of youth, written in classically simple English and

In the Way of Understanding

delivered slowly and with beautiful diction so that the many Chinese and non-professional friends of Professor Yap would not feel bogged down with psychiatric jargon and psychological theories. I remember he used one splendid expression "astringent psychiatry" which to me implied clean treatment which was not wrapped up in dubious analysis. The emphasis was on youth service and work among disturbed adolescents. A venerable Chinese figure in the audience was Professor Yap's uncle. He was dressed in his national robe and was accompanied by many of his family, so it was a moving occasion. Hong Kong psychiatric services and the Hong Kong Association for Mental Health will miss the cultured and civilised figure of the late Professor with his love of beauty (so well displayed by the work of many artists in his flat).

Betty and Wilfrid Warren saw something of that other side of Hong Kong which I have already mentioned, and were as shocked as I was. Wilfrid was able to discuss problems of student mental health in the new University, and the very necessary training of psychiatrists. He paid an official visit to the British Military Hospital and talked with the Surgeon Commander about the stresses that service families have to meet, and the social and psychiatric problems which are met among their children and adolescents.

Once again I said 'farewell' to this extraordinary, overcrowded island, and as we climbed up from that dangerous air strip I said my usual prayer "Please God, may it not hurt too much"!

Thailand, 1965

Anyone who has read the book, *Anna and the King of Siam*[1], or seen the play or film based upon it, must realise how thrilled I was to be flying from Hong Kong to that ancient and mysterious country, (now known as Thailand) for the 18th A.G.M. and Conference of the W.F.M.H. My companion was Dr. Denis Leigh. We were both representing the Bethlem Royal and Maudsley Hospitals, and we felt justly proud that so many

[1] Constable & Co., 1952.

Group of past Maudsley students in Hong Kong, 1971

Opening session, Hong Kong, self in chair

Bangkok, At a Palace garden party
(L. to R.) Dr. Estefania Aldaba-Lin, self, Miss Dolores Francesco

Queen Sirikit With the King of Siam

World Travels

of our Thai friends who had been trained at the Maudsley were now contributing to one of the best psychiatric services in the Far East.

I had expected the gentle courtesy and the ever-smiling faces of our hosts, but I was unprepared for the great efficiency of their organisation and the smooth running of the Conference sessions. This was surely due to the thought given to every detail, and to the imaginative and individual care taken in the preparations. One example of their concern for our comfort was the presentation of European dishes as well as of Thai cooking at each party, and even at the hospitals we visited.

From the beginning we were aware of the strong support given by the Government to education and health. The Prime Minister opened the proceedings, thus showing the Government's appreciation of mental health, and he also gave a dinner party and a garden party at his palace for all delegates and their wives and husbands. The ladies in their colourful national dress were a joy to the eye, and the calm solicitude for our comfort is something I shall never forget. It showed perfect manners—a demonstration of real civilisation such as we have forgotten in the West. Instead of shaking hands, the greeting is always to hold one's hands together and to bow to the person you are meeting. I accustomed myself to this and naturally reciprocated. I found their deference to age and seniority quite delightful: for example, a secretary bringing a message to the President in the Chair on the platform, would creep up on her knees and hand over her message.

The King and Queen received us at a garden party. His Majesty, who was very interested in religion, had attended the Mary Hemmingway Rees Memorial Lecture on Buddhism and Mental Health the night before. Unfortunately I had played truant and had not heard the lecture, so I was forced to improvise and to appear knowledgeable, and this made me listen carefully to the serious young man. His lovely Queen, Sirikit, also chatted to me about sending her young son, (aged I think about ten at that time) to an English Prep. School. Remembering my own experience of boarding school my heart bled for the boy, but his parents were taking his education and the education of their people very seriously. Their confidence in the English system of education was no doubt due to the influence of Sir Robert Morant (already mentioned in an earlier chapter),—"that supreme civil servant", as Harold Nicolson called him in his life of George V. Sir Robert was tutor to the Crown Prince in 1887 and held this position for seven years. The force of his personality made itself felt beyond the Palace. He wrote the first Primer ever used in Siam and created a system of public education for that country.

Khunying Ambhorn Meesook, Chairman of the Thai Association for Mental Health, and the organising influence of the Conference, was a senior official in the Education Department and a highly educated and intelligent lady. Amy, as she became known to her friends and colleagues, was now on the Executive Board of the W.F.M.H. and did much to bring understanding of mental health to the Asian countries. Her wisdom often contributed to the overcoming of the delicate situations which arose when difficult and even dangerous political problems confronted the W.F.M.H., with its commitments to the world of mental health. Her friendship has meant much to me, and I learnt to admire her courageous tackling of the enormous educational problems which arise in a developing country facing periodical political crises. She seemed to possess a spiritual serenity, and to impart it to others. She arranged for the delegates from Malaysia, Taiwan, Sarawak, Indonesia, Korea and Japan, mostly psychiatrists, to discuss their problems together, and compare notes with Thai doctors—taking advantage of the presence of Dr. Denis Leigh to gather advice and encouragement. This gathering of many nationalities for a free and open discussion seemed to me basic to the understanding and promotion of sound national and international human relations, and this is what the W.F.M.H. does supremely well.

I also had time to visit the colourful temples and shrines, the famous Emerald Buddha and the Marble Temple as well as the Temple of Dawn, and to see the monks in their saffron robes. An early morning visit to the floating market (around 6 a.m.), is difficult to describe to Europeans. The klongs (canals) are numerous and smelly, and presumably insanitary, but this is where thousands of Thais live with little apparent ill effect upon their health! Along these klongs are glorious silk markets with bales of beautiful coloured material, enough to make any woman with an artistic feeling for dress lose herself in a dream world of gorgeous fabrics. I could not help feeling how much most young women of today have missed out in never having known the luxurious feeling of real silk, crepe de chine or chiffon caressing their naked bodies.

The Philippines, Manila, 1965

Robina Addis and I touched down in Manila for a brief stay with her brother John, then Ambassador to the Philippines, before flying on to Sydney. We were invited to the Presidential Palace to pay our respects to the First Lady, the wife of the President. Everything seemed very regal and not what one would have expected in a Republic. During our stay John invited an old friend of mine to meet me. I was happy to be once again with Fanny Adama Lim, who had been a colleague in the W.F.M.H., and who was later to become President of the Committee of the International Year of the Child in 1979. She is a beautiful woman who looks most striking when in the evening she wears her full national dress. Having lost her husband in an air crash she was left to bring up six children with the aid of an extended family of grannies and aunts. She managed to continue with her pioneering work for mental health and education.

One spectacular drive, which took all day, was through picturesque Filipino villages and up over the Tagatay Pass to Baguio. The view was superb and one could see for miles over wild mountainous territory, and breathe delicious uncontaminated fresh air. John had a Filipino cook who gave us excellent well-cooked local fish, and prepared local vegetables and home-made bread. My breakfasts of fresh paw-paw or mango were a welcome start to the day, and although Filipino coffee is excellent I enjoyed my green tea with kaldmanze, a kind of lime.

There was a flourishing Association for Mental Health in Manila, and at that time an excellent secretary, Dolores Francisco, and a hard-working President in Dr. Jesus Tun. Robina and I were taken to their headquarters and met the enthusiastic Committee. It was arranged that we should visit a community after-care scheme and half-way house. This was a splendid pioneer venture directed by Dr. Sasana Reyes, a psychiatrist, a very keen and alert person. She told us simply yet clearly that her scheme was to "help former mental patients to prepare themselves for a new life": in other words community care—a very new and untried concept in the Philippines. About 30–40 men and women selected by the mental hospital had come for training, and were living in a Nipa house (a raised hut of bamboo and reed). This had the usual large room under the house, and open to the four winds, where patients, chickens, dogs and lines of washing all shared the space. Many arrived very scared after years of life in mental hospitals, which were described to me as prisons with nurses who were rather like wardresses. The freedom and peace of this village of nipa huts was initially strange, but eventually healing. There was psychotherapy, drug therapy and family counselling, and the residents—no longer called patients—were helped to take an interest in the arts and in their church. There was work for both men and women in the rice fields, and they learned to manage piggeries on a Danish system. This was obviously an excellent pioneer venture, and a visiting Egyptian psychiatrist who was with us said he would like to try something on these lines outside Cairo.

I was impressed by the work undertaken by the Filipino Association for Mental Health, for with so many scattered islands there has to be much travelling and the same problem bedevils education. It was said there were 7,000 islands, some very small. John made extensive tours to meet the local people, travelling by boat and plane, and was doing a magnificent job of communication and of showing the flag.

The nation is made up of a mixture of Chinese, Spanish and Americans, and naturally it comprises much of the good and bad in each. A conservative Roman Catholic church did not help. Some of the people's practices seemed to me careless and cruel, and I felt for the little horses pulling large two-wheeled carts with such tight bearing reins, and for the miserable-looking mongrel dogs picking up garbage. Chickens were tied by their legs, and there was much cock-fighting.

Philippino half-way Housing Scheme, self and Dr. Reyes

Manila group workers with Robina and myself

Robina and self with Philippine Association for Mental Health Executive Board

N.A.M.H. Dinner 1962

(L. to R.) Miss Mary Applebey, Dr. T. P. Rees, The Lady Adrian, Lord Butler, H.R.H. Princess Marina, self, Lord Feversham, Lady Butler

World Travels

John's friends were most kind to us, and one house which I shall always remember belonged to Mr. and Mrs. Lindi Locin. He was the architect of this beautiful house which was panelled in a variety of woods, had windows made of shell, and contained well-designed modern furniture which married happily with many old Spanish pieces. There were rooms full of rare porcelain, and there was a feeling of years of civilisation in the atmosphere that reminded me very much of Plodge. This was one of the many occasions when I wished that Mont had been with me, for he would have understood and admired the use made of beautiful furnishings and rare woods.

Before I flew on to Sydney, Robina had heard that she had been awarded the O.B.E. in the New Year's Honours List. I was particularly happy to be present on this occasion, as I knew so well the caring and selfless attention she had given to all who came to her for help, whilst at the same time never neglecting her large family, and the many demands they made upon her.

Australia and Singapore, 1965

> *And we shall say to all the world*
> *That kinship conquers spice*
> *And he who fights the British Oils*
> *Must fight the British Rice.*

The little jingle that heads this chapter ended an after-dinner speech of thanks given by Professor Otto Klineberg at the W.F.M.H. Congress in Sydney in 1973. I was so tickled by it that I begged him to write it down on the back of my menu card, and while he did so he told me that he had heard it in 1940, in a radio report of a speech made by the Australian Foreign Minister, Mr. Evatt, after the French surrender. (Those who have trouble in understanding it may be helped by the reminder that many Australians pronounce the word race as if it were rice.)

Otto was one of those highly civilised and Europeanised Canadians who spoke fluent French and German as well as many other languages. He had been an active supporter of the W.F.M.H. since its formation, and I grew to love him and to admire his wisdom and his ability to grasp the core of an argument and to put it down succinctly on paper. An argument that might have raged for a long time in Committee was often quickly resolved after Otto had brought his clear mind and deft pen to work upon it.

Our deep affection for one another played a considerable part as we graduated to become joint Honorary Presidents of the W.F.M.H. His sense of the comic in any situation makes me look back with great pleasure on our many years of working together. He was a little man in stature but, like Brock Chisholm, he certainly had a great heart.

My interest in Australia was aroused before I married Mont because I had met at Plodge a remarkable and lovable lady called "Aunt Sib"—her full name being Sibella Macarthur Onslow. The Macarthur Onslows were somehow related to the Normans, and Mont was fond of the whole family, but especially of Sib. She stayed at Plodge when in England and kept him in touch with her kinsmen. They in their turn came to visit Mont, endlessly seeking his advice in all manner of ways. The owned a huge estate, Camden Park, some miles outside Sydney, which had been granted to John Macarthur by Lord Camden for the purpose of establishing and increasing the breed of Merino sheep which he had imported in the latter part of the nineteenth century. If Australia could be symbolically represented by the names of her first free pioneering families, Macarthur would be one of them. Sibella's great-great grandfather, John, fostered sheep breeding and the wool industry, defying much mockery by experts. Sib was a remarkably intelligent lady, well read and passionately devoted to her forbears. She was charming to me, and Mont had a real affection for her. As in the case of Mrs. Markoe of Bar Harbor, Maine, I am pretty sure he had also asked her advice on the marriage that he was slowly contemplating.

The Macarthur Onslows were not a harmonious family. Greater feuds and quarrels existed between them than in most other families, and Mont, a friend of each warring character, made up his mind to try to heal what seemed an insoluble

World Travels

problem of money matters. He often said "When I retire, Honey, I am going to take a year off, or if necessary two years, and live in Sydney to knock those dear folks' heads together and put some sense into them". It was not to be: Sib died in 1943 and Mont in 1950.

So it was with pleasure that I accepted an invitation from the Chairman of the W.F.M.H., Professor Alan Stoller, to be the guest of the Mental Health Authority of Victoria State in Melbourne in 1965. After arriving in Sydney and being cherished by the Macarthur clan, I talked with the then Professor of Child Health, Professor Stapleton, in his gothic university and met many Maudsley-trained psychiatrists. They all told me that the New South Wales Association for Mental Health was going through a bad time, and that it seemed unable to get across to the public the importance of mental health. Besides the questions of mental illness and mental deficiency, it was also concerned with the problems of divorce, suicide, smoking and alcoholism. He thought I might do something to help! I therefore agreed to broadcast a talk on the work of the N.A.M.H. in the U.K., and was interviewed by an astounding lady of seventy, one of Australia's leading radio personalities at that time.

There was, according to Prof. Stapleton, a conflict between the voluntary societies and the statutory services. In the early days the Government made itself responsible for the social care of ex-prisoners and others in need. Later various welfare societies modelled on the U.K. pattern were founded and prospered. They grew in strength and did noble work of a pioneering nature but as time passed the problems became too big and the statutory authorities were forced to step in. The voluntary societies resented this so-called interference. I sensed this myself when I visited the New South Wales Association for Mental Health.

Most evenings I was entertained by different members of the Macarthur clan, and one weekend I went with Denzil (later Sir Denzil Macarthur Onslow) and his clever doctor wife to Mont Gilead, Campletown, their home not far from Camden. The property was vast, with miles of paddocks and stubbly parched brown-yellow grass, as there had been no rain for months. The view from my window over Camden and the Blue Mountains was magnificent. Denzil showed me all the old family portraits and miniatures dating back as far as 1820. He also took me to the famous rotolactor, a machine designed to milk 2,000 cows twice a day to supply Sydney with milk. To me it was horrible factory farming, and I preferred my visit to the ninety acres of fruit orchards. The property covered 15,000 acres of land, all that was left of the original 54,000 acres.

Camden Park itself is an old-fashioned Colonial house with a portico and pillars. Inside it is lined with cedar wood, now unfortunately varnished. The beautifully carved shutters (there are no curtains) had charm for they could be closed from the inside, and the outside shutters were green to keep out the fierce heat and sun. The garden had been planted with loving care, with oleanders, plumbago, hedges of rosemary and wild geranium, some tulip trees, eucalyptus and many other lovely trees. While I was in Camden, Winston Churchill died and we older ones in the clan listened sadly to the funeral service on the radio, thinking back over the years.

In Sydney I visited the Victoria Hospital, one of the oldest in the city, part of it designed by Florence Nightingale. Friends of the Hospital numbered about 300 and these men and women volunteers were doing all sorts of jobs with the enthusiastic approval of doctors and Matron. Apparently they had an initial interview and, if accepted, were given one month's trial. If not satisfactory after this time they were dismissed. They had a strict rota, a uniform and there seemed to be no trouble in liaising with professionals or with the unions. This scheme for hospital volunteers was ahead of our own, and our Volunteer Centre came into being much later.

After two fascinating weeks I took off on my assignment to Melbourne as the guest of the Mental Health Authority of the State of Victoria. Dr. Cunningham Dax and Dr. Gordon Russell, together with Prof. Stoller (author of the Australian Mental Health Act), organised my busy programme. I found Melbourne a fine city with many trees—plumbago, hibiscus, frangipani, huge white magnolias and red castor-oil trees. I stayed at the Windsor Hotel opposite the Houses of Parliament. It was delightfully old-fashioned—early Victorian, and very comfortable. During the visit I stressed the connection with my Regional Hospital Board and rather played down my connection with the N.A.M.H. I could feel the tension, as in Sydney, between the statutory authority and the voluntary sectors. The latter did not like the professional workers and felt that all their past good work was being taken over. But maybe the time had come for a change, and the State service seemed to be alive and to be doing a good job. A new Mental Health Act was in force, and the teamwork in the Mental Health Department seemed excellent. I spent some time in a Day Hospital and talked, over tea, with the doctors and nurses, who questioned me about the Regional Board and our Health Service in general.

One evening I dined with the late Sir Arthur Stephenson, the famous architect, who specialised in the planning of hospitals. He was a most charming old gentleman who put me completely at my ease, and we talked of almost everything under the sun whilst eating well and drinking excellent wine. He was not complimentary about hospital building in the U.K. and said that the best was in the U.S.A. There, he said, they were realistic, and had a completely different philosophy and outlook, with good team work between administrators, doctors, nurses and other staff before any building was begun. He said: "In England you yap, yap for years, and by that time wages have gone up and doctors and administrators have had new ideas which fail to become incorporated. So when the building is up it is already out of date"!

It was helpful to be able to talk to Alan Stoller about the 1973 Congress which was to be held in Sydney, and I was happy to think that I was to return to this country with which I had already developed a love/hate relationship. Sometimes I was charmed by the old-fashioned nonsense of their supposed love for the 'old country', but at other times I was conscious of their brashness, and even brutality, as recounted to me by a visitor to the farms in the Northern Territory. There money and yet more money was the uppermost aim of the farmers, regardless of what it might mean for the cattle.

My next visit to Sydney was in 1973. I attended the

In the Way of Understanding

W.F.M.H. 25th World Congress, which had the theme "Cultures in Collision"—a very apt subject, as the Israeli-Egyptian war was breaking out just as the Congress met. Dr. Louis Miller, the Israeli delegate, hurried back to Jerusalem looking very sad and ill. The late Dr. Wagdi, our wise Egyptian delegate, had failed to get a visa from his Government to attend our meeting. The Executive Board passed a Resolution of sympathy which was telegraphed to both warring nations, in the hope that their Governments might soon get round a table for discussion.

The first plenary session took place in the new and now-famous Opera House, with its impressive setting, but I have reason to take a jaundiced view of the occasion. I had to take the Chair. On the platform of the huge stage stood a small table, four chairs and one lectern. Dr. Jabvala, a prominent Indian architect, was to give us a lecture with slides showing the problems of mental health caused by bad housing in his country. Unfortunately the lights failed and the loud-speaker was inaudible. Many in the audience, including all those on the platform, could neither see nor hear. Things improved slightly, but I was thankful when it was all over.

Thus my introduction to the fascinating Opera House was a fiasco, but it is a building for an age, not a decade. It is a very grandiose concept and from the outside it looks like an ancient ship in full sail. Had it been placed alone in the beautiful harbour it would have had a glorious setting, but alas, warehouses and other buildings seemed to overshadow its beauty. I thought the inside unattractive, but the smaller theatres and the concert hall are good, and the whole conception and decoration are functional, modern and just right for a young country. The fine woods lining the walls are beautiful and a real feature of the whole complex.

One of the sessions in the Congress was devoted to discussing the aboriginal problem, and Professor German from Uganda (Maudsley trained and now living in Perth), together with a few of us, went to a clinic run by a young Scottish doctor who was dedicated to his work. He was delighted to be able to pour out his heart to us on the iniquities of the treatment of the aborigines. We met some of the latter, and talked to them, and were shown a co-operative housing project. The Aboriginal problem, too long neglected by the Government, has now become enormous, and a Minister for Aboriginal Affairs has been appointed. The population is increasing, and to date stands at 120,000—most of whom live in great poverty, fecklessness and indolence. They have tribal habits which are difficult to shed—for example their belief that doors in a house are evil. Doors supposedly imprison the spirits, and so no door or enclosure is welcome. This means that a mixed housing scheme is difficult—yet segregation or apartheid is not a realistic solution.

Perhaps the most interesting session for me was one at which Hayes Gordon was the speaker. He was a Governing Director of the Ensemble Theatre, an actor, producer and singer. He spoke on the effect of the mass media on mental health. The theme of his lecture was that good actors can evoke the required feeling from an audience at any particular time, and that this can be dangerous. To illustrate his point he had brought with him his two leading ladies, on whom he called to act a scene from Neil Simon's play *The Ginger Bread Lady*. This is about an alcoholic who is just out of a mental hospital, and is crying for help from friends and relatives too self-centred to understand her. At nine o'clock in the morning with no props or make-up, the two actresses stood amongst us and brought home to us, more vividly than any speaker could have done, the despair of an abandoned alcoholic. Hayes Gorden stressed that this powerful technique could be used for good or evil, and was a serious responsibility for directors and producers. His message was important also for the medical profession, which already uses psycho-drama and role plays as curative techniques in the field of psychiatry. The instant release of such strong emotional feelings is as great a responsibility for the therapist as it is for the drama director. Once again my appreciation of the value of creative art in therapy was reinforced. My visit to the actual play, all alone in a none too savoury part of Sydney, was more than exciting. Afterwards the taxi I had ordered to take me home failed to turn up. No bus or underground was available but, happily for me, when everyone had departed two actors took pity on me at the stage door and conducted me back to my club in a more civilised part of the city.

It was some eight years since I had been to Camden Park, and when I visited it again after the Congress the changes which I found saddened me. Awful suburbs and petrol stations had been built, and had encroached through the glorious pastures to within five miles of the house itself. There was also a commercial airfield, and somehow the charm I had once sensed was no more.

After this I joined up again with Dr. Warren, who represented with me the Bethlem Royal and Maudsley Hospitals, and together we flew on to Singapore. I saw something of the social services there and met the Chairman of the Singapore Association for Mental Health, with some very enthusiastic young psychiatrists, nurses, social workers and others, who again were all Maudsley-trained and proud of it. No programme had been organised for me as I had merely tagged along with Dr. Warren, who was making an official visit. However the authorities soon found much work for me to do and many interesting places to see. This included some high-density housing where I found them making the same mistake as in Hong Kong—150,000 persons were crowded into thirty-storey flats. There was no room for children to play, whilst schools, churches, clinics, cinemas, shops and swimming pools were all included in one complex. The detriment to mental health caused by all this herding together had not been recognised, despite the warnings and experiences of other developing countries. There was an obvious lack of good mental health facilities in Singapore, and the young consultants were hoping for great things from Dr. Warren in overcoming officialdom and in stressing the need for more children's clinics and especially for child guidance provision. It seemed to me that we in the U.K. have a great responsibility for training people in these different disciplines. Young men and women return to their developing countries from the U.K. full of enthusiasm, only to discover the heavy hand of bureaucracy and much professional jealousy. Consequently they soon became lonely and frustrated, and turn to lucrative private practice among neurotic Europeans and those of other races who are ready to pay high fees. A follow-up service is required, and the Maudsley and other training centres should remember that there is more to training a young doctor from a developing country than just teaching him medicine and then sending him home to sink or swim. It will be some time before training facilities are available in the developing countries, and until that day comes we in the West have a grave responsibility.

I learnt much about mental health problems and the part that local Associations for Mental Health could play in promoting understanding, and I felt that local psychiatrists, nurses and social workers appreciated the support that Dr. Warren and I were able to give them.

The hospitality we received was superb, and during the all too short period of our visit I tried to listen, and to encourage all those kind, laughing young folk. I even planted a tree in the grounds of a hospital in memory of what they regarded as a well worth-while visit. It is when one is back home, with all the facilities that are available there, that one remembers guiltily what needs doing elsewhere, and recognises, like Rhodes, that there is "so much to do and so little time to do it".

Czechoslovakia, 1966—planing down with anxiety

An historic event in the history of the W.F.M.H. was an invitation by the Czechoslovakian Psychiatric Society of the Mental Health Society to hold a conference in Prague in 1966. The moving spirit and the chairman of the Organising Committee was Dr. Joseph Prokupec, a very serious and sad man whose face spoke only too clearly of the tension faced by those living under a Communist regime. I felt much drawn to him, and in his presence I was almost ashamed of my easy way of living and my freedom of speech. On the Executive Board we were such a happy band, calling each other by our forenames and laughing and joking together, and I felt that we must have puzzled our remote and formal colleague who had joined the Board for the first time. I was uneasily aware of tragedy behind those gentle grey eyes.

Delegates from all corners of the world flocked to this

meeting, as it was a unique opportunity for them to meet colleagues from behind the Iron Curtain in the beautiful and historic city of Prague. The Government of the Socialist Republic welcomed the W.F.M.H., saying that they considered it a great honour to have so many members from so many countries, and that they hoped we would discuss our experiences openly and exchange our views. They felt that in so doing we could then be united in our endeavour to promote harmonious relations between all peoples and to secure the peaceful co-existence of all nations in the world. This was in August 1966. Two years later Prague was invaded by Russian tanks, and their progressive leader and Prime Minister, Mr. Dubcek, was forced to resign.

The opening address was given by the President of the W.F.M.H., Chief Sir Samuel Manuwa, looking most handsome in his colourful Nigerian dress. He was at that time First Commissioner of the Federal Public Service Commission in Lagos, Nigeria.

H. E. Joseph Ployhar, Minister for Public Affairs, gave a magnificent reception for us in the flood-lit Czermin Baroque Palace and in the great Hradcany Square. Robina and I slipped out for a moment onto a small balcony overlooking the Square and we could visualise the splendour of the old days, with carriages, powdered footmen, and the aristocracy in lovely evening dress. An old waiter who spoke French happened to come out onto the balcony, and he said he remembered much of the past splendour and shook his head sadly.

Gossip had it that our host had a doubtful reputation, being an ex-priest and a glutton. He certainly did produce an excellent buffet. At the reception I was close to becoming a secret agent, because before leaving London I had been given a letter to deliver to a stranger who was to make himself known to me at this social gathering. He did so by calling me by my name and by mentioning the name of his friend. In the midst of the crowd I handed him the letter and he vanished.

At a meeting of the National Associations for Mental Health, affiliated to the W.F.M.H., I was asked to take the chair. Dr. Prokupec caused a slight stir by attending, despite the fact that Czechoslovakia had no voluntary association for mental health. This is because voluntary associations do not exist behind the iron curtain. He gave us, quite briefly, a review of the statutory authorities for mental health work all over his country. He then told us, rather humbly, about a private meeting between representatives of the Socialist Republics of Czechoslovakia, Jugoslavia, East Germany, Hungary, Poland and Roumania, all of whom wished to affiliate individually to the W.F.M.H. He added that this could take place only gradually, for they would each have to go back to their own countries for further discussion. We welcomed the suggestion, which removed some tension that had undoubtedly been felt between the W.F.M.H. and the Socialist Governments, all of whom were suspicious of voluntary organisations. Dr. Prokupec came to this particular meeting in order to slip in this proposal, since he did not wish to bring such a controversial matter before the General Assembly or at the closing session. The hopes that this resolution would be further discussed by the countries concerned seem to have drifted away into the air, for as far as I know nothing ever came of the suggestion. It did however show how anxious was the medical profession in each Socialist Republic to become more integrated with world affairs.

Following this meeting I was included in an invitation from the administration of the Czechoslovak State Spas to take part in a two-day excursion to their world famous West Bohemian Spas of Carlsbad and Marienbad. We went by coach through a lovely country of valleys, hills and forests. The hospitality was generous and the hotel accommodation lavish, and I was fascinated to return to places which I had known before the Second World War, such as Carlsbad with its memories of the Kaiser, its hotels now turned over to holiday resorts for the people. The Kaiser's suite of rooms and his bath had been kept intact, as were those of King Edward VII at Marienbad. On visiting the hotel bedrooms I noticed expensive fur coats, perfumes and dressing table ornaments of a kind not usually seen in hotels, workers' camps or ordinary homes. The question in my mind was always "Is this really for the workers, or is it just for top civil servants and Commissars?" However, we all enjoyed ourselves and were interested to see the curative springs still in use, and the many famous Edwardian hotels which had survived two wars.

Peru, 1967

The W.F.M.H. held its twentieth Annual General Meeting in Lima, at the invitation of the Peruvian Ministry of Health and Social Security and the Ministry of Education, together with the Peruvian League of Mental Hygiene and the Peruvian Psychiatric Association.

I flew to Washington, where the Executive Board was holding a preliminary meeting before flying on to Lima. It was important for me to attend this meeting, as the following year the Congress which was to celebrate the twentieth anniversary of the founding of the W.F.M.H. in 1948 was to be held in London. I went to report on the plans being made by the N.A.M.H. in London for this event, since I had to get the co-operation and approval of the Executive Board. This meeting was also a turning-point in the life of the W.F.M.H., as the grand old man, Dr. J. R. Rees, who had contributed so much to the Federation, was no longer an active member of the Board. Many of us thought that after twenty years we should perhaps have a change of emphasis, and a new look at the way in which psychiatry, nursing and social work were evolving so rapidly all over the world. We had suggested that Morris Carstairs, the young and dynamic Professor of Psychiatry at Edinburgh University, be asked to be the new President.

We were booked into an unpleasant hotel, where I felt like an ant in a computer. When I entered the room where the Executive Board was meeting I sensed an atmosphere of doom. The older members of the Board were bemoaning the loss of the past in long speeches of anxiety about the uncertain future. Suddenly Morris Carstairs electrified the Board by saying bluntly that he could not understand why he had been asked to be President of an organisation at which he had always laughed. He told the members that their so-called research was a joke amongst serious researchers, and that many of his younger colleagues had asked him why he was joining such an outfit. However, he said he believed in the W.F.M.H. as a multi-disciplinary organisation and in what it might yet do—but not under present management! He was frank in his constructive criticism, and he ended by saying that he would quite understand if they no longer wished to consider him as their next leader. Tableau! I was truly proud of him because he had the courage to say what many of us had been thinking.

We broke hurriedly for lunch and Morris and I crept away to a small bar. We were terribly short of money as the pound had slumped and we had very few dollars. Some of his supporters found us and came to congratulate him, but I felt very depressed in case his frankness meant that he would not be elected as President. Later when we resumed our meeting, it became clear after endless talk that we would have to take a vote. Morris dived for the door! He need not have done, since the decision was unanimous in his favour, and I was happy that I would have his support in London for next year's Congress.

Dr. Griffith Edwards and Dr. Eric Carr joined me on the flight to Lima, where we were representing the Bethlem Royal and Maudsley Hospitals. From the moment of our arrival we realised that the arrangement of the meeting in Lima was disorganised. No one knew who was organising it—the W.F.M.H. with its headquarters in Geneva, or the Peruvian League for Mental Hygiene in Lima. The result was chaos. I was calm and happy because I felt that the London Congress could not possibly be as bad as this one. However Dr. Griffith Edwards spoilt my peace of mind by saying: "We allow for this at a first conference in Lima: no one will excuse any inefficiency in London!"

The opening session was attended by the President of the Republic with full military honours. Guards in highly colourful uniforms were posted at intervals. I felt the Brigade of Guards would never respond in like manner to our N.A.M.H. meeting at the Albert Hall!

The plenary sessions were held in the Hall of the large Ospedale del Seguro Social del Empleados—which was rather like holding a meeting in Grand Central Station, New York, and just as noisy. I took the chair for a meeting of all the

In the Way of Understanding

National Associations present. Representatives aired their grievances about the W.F.M.H., but it was a difficult meeting because of the noise and the va-et-vient all around us. I was forced to act dictatorially, which did not please the more vocal members. However, I was happy to have the opportunity of meeting representatives who were likely to be coming to London the following year, and of hearing ahead of time about some of their problems.

The theme of the Conference was "Mental Health in Rapidly Growing Populations". I was particularly interested in the lecture dealing with mental health in Latin America, as it was my first visit to that part of the world. Work in hospitals for the psychiatrically ill was being developed in Peru, but all too slowly (one hospital I visited was of the snake-pit variety). Provision for children, adolescents and the sub-normal was practically non-existent. I felt the frustration of all concerned, for although the authorities were alive to the problems they seemed either unable to understand them or were unwilling to tackle them.

However, our meeting in Lima was worthwhile, because it threw a spot-light on the needs of the mentally sick, and from the platform and in the media their problems were made known to the general public. This gave great support to all those who had seen the strides made recently in the western world, and who had been trying to get the ear of Government and people with very little success.

As usual, there were many Maudsley-trained doctors and nurses present, and they were glad to talk with Dr. Griffith Edwards and Dr. Eric Carr. They wanted to keep in touch with the Bethlem Royal and Maudsley Hospitals and the Institute of Psychiatry, as they felt lonely and out on a limb, with little support in their own countries.

In this land of striking contrasts we were taken to see something of the city of Lima. We drove through shameful slums, called Barridos, to the beauty of surrounding mountains, where we lunched at a country club for rich Peruvians and drink-seeking Americans. This club was renowned for its cocktails, and I had a 'Gentle Murderer', consisting of lemon juice, cointreau, kirsch and gin. It was very potent and was served in an imitation baby's bottle, complete with teat! We wondered what Freud would have made of this!

I left Peru with regret, since I had not had time to go to Cuzco with its monumental ruins or to see the lost city of Machu Picchu.

Venezuela, 1967

It was a great thrill to be travelling alone to Caracas at the invitation of the Venezuelan League of Mental Hygiene. Dr. M. A. Poleo, whom I had met at the Maudsley when he was working under Dr. Denis Leigh, had suggested my going to Caracas to give some lectures to the professionals and the public on the promotion of mental health. This was to stimulate them and to try to lift them out of their lethargy, and it was a challenge for me.

My first introduction to the uphill work of all those engaged in hospitals, social services and education came at a children's hospital. Here Dr. Lya Imber de Coronil, the first woman doctor in the country and the head of the hospital, took charge of me and introduced me to her team. They poured out their problems, and told me of their fight with the Government for resources. Dr. Coronil, who had worked in Great Ormonde Street, said that public health treatment and medical care in Venezuela had only started in 1936. There were only three psychiatrists in the whole country, and none of them were interested in children. When Dr. Coronil became head of the hospital in 1958 she had pressed for reforms, had hoped for a child psychiatrist and had asked for a child psychological service and for a social worker.

After going round the hospital and seeing the miserable conditions I gave my talk to the doctors and nurses in the lecture theatre, and it was very well attended. I explained our Health Service and our mental health services, and spoke about child guidance—including of course the N.A.M.H. and its local Associations. I was bombarded with questions, and Dr. Coronil acted as my interpreter.

Later that day I went to a day hospital, a neuro-psychiatric centre of training and a so-called Child Guidance Centre, all in one building. The splendid, enthusiastic staff and the children serenaded me, and danced to an old-fashioned band led by a blind man. It was most moving, and I found that the doctor-in-charge, Dr. Gonzalez Milean, had been trained at the Maudsley and was delighted to see me. He said that he found his work frustrating because the Ministry of Education and Health could not see the importance of training nor of special school education.

Next day I was taken to the Military Hospital of 1,000 beds, with only twenty beds for psychiatric patients. Dr. Fernando Risquez was in charge—another Maudsley man. He took me to meet the Head of the Medical Department of the War Office, a splendid chap covered in gold braid and medals. We had a friendly chat and Dr. Risquez, who spoke perfect English, translated what I said into Spanish and was delighted to have me help him in his fight for better conditions for his patients. This hospital had been built in 1960 but the psychiatric department resembled Old Bedlam. I sensed that it might be all important to get psychiatry and psychology on the military map, as the Army are the rulers and what they do and say is copied later by the civilian administration. He must have thought the visit important for he kept me for nearly two hours.

I made other visits, wrote an article for the Venezuelan medical journal and spoke on the radio in support of the need for further resources. At a farewell party given by Dr. Poleo at his lovely house, which had an indoor garden of orchids, I was given a beautiful orchid brooch—the emblem of Venezuela. I was asked to take messages back to the Maudsley, for so many who were trained there look back to it with deep emotion. As I left their luxurious house, full of rare things, I wondered what my host and his wife must have thought of their Camberwell lodgings when working at the Maudsley. I departed from Venezuela with some sadness, as I had seen their frustration and listened to their problems, but did not feel that my visit had done more than scratch the surface. I seemed to be running away without having given very much—but I left with an enormous bunch of orchids, and was taken for a film star when landing in San Domingo and New York on my way home.

World Travels

United Kingdom, 1968

Flying home alone gave me only a short time to consider what was uppermost in my mind—the London Congress. I longed for the old days of the leisurely sailing of the Atlantic when one had time to relax and to think out problems in depth. I needed time to adjust from being the fêted guest of so many conferences, and to prepare myself to assume the responsibility for the N.A.M.H.'s welcome to the W.F.M.H. in London. But on this hurried flight I began to wonder why people should travel thousands of miles to sit in a hall and be lectured to, when they could read the same material in books and papers sent through the post. I answered my own question—a Congress is an event, a happening which must stimulate, provoke, challenge and overthrow. It is surely a meeting place for the exchange of ideas rather than a machine for dispensing data. How could I bring this to pass?

Then I realised I was not alone. Whilst I was in the sky, on the earth a selfless team was already hard at work under the able leadership of Mary Applebey, the then General Secretary of the N.A.M.H. As she was already so committed to the heavy workload of the Association, she delegated to her deputy the organisation of the programme, and so Robina Addis assumed full responsibility for the essence of the Congress, i.e. the scientific papers. The headache of the general administration was to be borne by Edith Morgan, Head of the Social Services Department. Frances Dean as Head of the Training and Education Department co-ordinated the visits to hospitals, clinics and centres of special education, leaving Mary Thomson the all important task of arranging social hospitality under the guidance of Molly Butler.[1] Eric Carr, one of the psychiatric advisers to the N.A.M.H., was to be Chairman of the Congress Organising Committee, and Professor Griffith Edwards was to be Chairman of the Scientific Programme Committee.

Before my wings touched down at Heathrow I was reassured that with such a dedicated team we could achieve our ends. I also knew that the committees would be encouraged by

---

[1] Second wife of the late Rt. Hon. Lord Butler of Saffron Walden. K.G., P.C., C.H. 1902–1982.

In the Way of Understanding

the approval of their plans which I had submitted to the W.F.M.H. and by the support they would receive from the new President, Morris Carstairs.

Homecoming for me on this occasion was both exciting and nostalgic, for it had been decided that the venue of the Congress was to be my old home, Plodge, now known as Holland Park Comprehensive School. The new school hall gave useful accommodation for plenary sessions, and the numerous classrooms provided space for groups and working parties. The old home was to shelter me once again as Congress President, and provide office accommodation and reception rooms.

The theme chosen by the Programme Committee and approved by the Executive Committee in Washington was "Keys to Progress—Mental Health Education". This gave scope for all disciplines in the Federation to participate. I could not have been happier with the selected subject as it covered not only the training and education of professionals in the field but also dealt with the education of the public as the first move in overcoming the fear of mental illness—an ideal I had always advocated.

I began to feel the threads of my life drawing together in this Congress. One thread which was still missing was not to be drawn into the web until the Dean of Westminster agreed to hold a service to pray for "New Light on Human Needs".

Applications to attend the Congress were so numerous that it was considered necessary to hold the opening ceremony in the Albert Hall—and this enabled me to offer our many voluntary helpers and supporters free tickets to the opening ceremony. It was our way of saying thank you to our own workers from all parts of the country. The problem of hospitality was uppermost in my mind because of the welcome I had received all over the world. So while others occupied themselves with the scientific content of the meetings my task was to ensure that our visitors would feel at home. With thousands of participants this was a big job which Molly Butler shouldered heroically, and together with Mary Thomson she arranged, amongst other activities, two Government receptions—a visit

World Travels

to Windsor Castle and a night at the Festival Ballet. The children of the participants were not forgotten. A reception centre with a full-time leader and with helpers able to speak several languages provided supervision activities, visits and excursions. Those who have organised any conference will realise that co-ordination and agreement of final plans are not achieved without pain and grief, but the sharing of effort was compensation enough.

By the end of July final plans had been settled. In early August we were shocked to hear that our Patron, Princess Marina, was seriously ill and would be unable to open the proceedings. How her young daughter gallantly took her place has already been described in my chapter telling of Two Royal Ladies.

Delegates gathered over the weekend, all set for Monday's official opening, but on the Sunday afternoon something took place in Westminster Abbey which had never before been included in any Congress. We met for an Ecumenical Service, and all faiths and none met together under one roof. Christians, humanists, Jews, Muslims and Hindus read the lessons. I felt we had touched the heart when a non-believer from Denmark who had drifted into the Service, merely wanting to kill time, told me he had been moved as never before. The Abbey was packed, and after the service many outsiders bombarded our stewards with questions about mental health. Surely this was a new way of advertising.

The following morning at the Albert Hall Lord and Lady Butler, Professor Carstairs and I met Princess Alexandra, who was greeted by a fanfare of trumpets as we processed right down the aisle and through the centre stalls onto the stage, where she bent down to shake hands with that grand old man, Dr. J. R. Rees, the founder of the W.F.M.H., before taking her place on the platform. Having listened to my words of welcome, the Princess gave her mother's message which paid tribute to the great work of the W.F.M.H. Then the Rt. Hon. Alice Bacon, the Minister of State for Education, opened the first session of the Congress, and Professor Carstairs gave the Inaugural Address. He began his challenging speech by reminding us of the practical humanitarian tasks which claimed our immediate attention if we were to alleviate the suffering caused by mental illness. He stressed the need for the education of doctors and other professionals and looked forward to the day when medical scientists would be as alert to emotional disturbance as to the presence of a tumour. The W.F.M.H. as a non-governmental and voluntary body must act as a pressure group to overcome ignorance and hostility and to change the attitude of the public towards mental illness. He devoted the second part of his lecture to the concept of mental health: "The realisation of man's highest potentialities". Through the vision of poets, philosophers and religious leaders, such as Teilhard de Chardin, whom he described as "the poet of the evolutionary process" he led us from primitive tribes to "the birth of a new global concept of man" whose basic values had been affirmed in "the Charter of Human Rights". Education, now a basic human right, would provide the launching-pad for the next upward surge of man's development, which must be towards self-knowledge.

We poured out of the Albert Hall heady with intellectual stimulation and reeling from such a daunting challenge to the soul of man and crossed to the Commonwealth Institute where Molly Butler and I had arranged to provide meat for the body. The meat was there awaiting us but the catering staff were missing, either from strike action or mere misunderstanding, leaving hastily-summoned volunteers to unpack and distribute food to the "five thousand".

After the spiritual togetherness of the Abbey Service and the triumphant opening at the Albert Hall, there was, at least for me, the anti-climax of facing the day-to-day work of a Congress President in Holland Park School. This was particularly poignant for my office was in the very house I had "willed myself never to forget" when sadly I left it in 1954. Happily I had grown an extra skin since then, and anyway it no longer looked like the home I remembered, despite the words on the plaque: "Here from 1904 to 1950 lived Montagu Collet Norman, Baron Norman of St. Clere, who was Governor of the Bank of England from 1929 to 1944 and fashioned for his pleasure this house and garden". But James Burton, that old stalwart who had been with me in good times and bad, was waiting at the front door to greet me and to act as Master of Ceremonies. He had come back from retirement to support "her Ladyship" and to welcome his friends in the W.F.M.H. whom he had known over the years. Protocol was important to James as with perfect manners he ushered visitors into the presidential presence. Preference was always given to those he had known of old, and he questioned the credentials of all new faces, however distinguished their office might be. Lillian, my housekeeper, had her role too at the first-aid post, in caring for delegates who had lost buttons, gloves or simply had tired feet. Both these gallant souls helped me to keep calm, to remember the things I had forgotten or left undone, and to entertain modestly in the flat. I wanted my old friends of the Executive Board, the founder members of the W.F.M.H., to look upon my flat as a smaller edition of the "Plodge" they had once known.

This week, which had taken so long to prepare, seemed to pass in a flash. I rushed from social breakfasts at Plodge to seminars and sessions which covered subjects ranging from child psychotherapy to the training of nurses in under-developed countries and the education of a community in the changing attitudes to mental health. Robina Addis and her Committee had certainly provided us with a rich diet of food for thought, and also with one therapeutic shock in the form of a stage drama with audience participation. As Morris Carstairs challenged us to increase our self-knowledge, so Adrian Mitchell, the author, and Albert Hunt, the producer, challenged us to question our beliefs and to study the gods we have created for ourselves. Reactions were mixed. One nun said the play was good but *un peu trop*. A psychologist walked out after ten minutes saying that although he was an atheist he would not have God talked of in that way! "A profoundly religious play" was another comment. Surely the reactions to the Congress as a whole were as varied as the responses to the play. We had seen the gods we had invented and our reactions would have been difficult to send through the post.

At the final sessions the focus was on the future, but we also looked back to the past to honour the man who had carried so heavy a burden for twenty years. The house rose to give a standing ovation to that grand old man, J. R. Rees, and so the London Congress concluded.

The Holy Land, 1969—Interlude

In the year following the London Conference Mary Thomson, who had worked so hard to ensure the success of our hospitality, invited me to join a pilgrimage to the Holy Land which was to be led by her husband, the Rev. Ian Thomson. I joyfully accepted. The impact upon me of the history of Christianity, as told by Ian on the very spot where it started, was enthralling. I had been afraid of any tawdry and "holy" marketing atmosphere, but even this could not damp down the reality. I do not believe that it is possible to understand the Bible story, or to visualise in any depth the writings in the Old and New Testaments, without having visited this turbulent land, even for so short a time as we did. The gradual growth of Christianity unfolded itself clearly as we visited the historic remains, and the truth of the story seemed to come out naked in its stark reality. Looking back over the centuries it was logical to wonder how it had survived, yet here was proof. "Be still and know."

Ian took a Communion Service early one morning at the Garden Tomb. The Tomb has a curious history and is called "the Place of the Skull" because of a geological formation of rock. For various archaeological reasons it is now thought possible that it is the burial place of Jesus. General Gordon was convinced of its authenticity.

The Garden of Gethsemane, lying alongside the Church of All Nations, is also moving with its twelve huge olive trees, which are said to date back to the time of Jesus. It was in these gardens, so peaceful and so beautiful, that I rested and allowed the great historic events to seep into my mind. Some years later, when I visited the Garden of the Tomb with Morris Carstairs he was moved to say that if he were a believer it would be there in that Garden that the Christan message would whisper in his ear and reveal the mysteries of the past.

Of the many shrines of historic interest I liked best St. Anne's, where it is traditionally said that Our Lady was born.

This is a Crusader church, beautifully restored and very simple. In 1860 it was offered to the British Government for an Anglican church. The offer was refused, presumably for financial reasons, and because the Establishment with its Victorian taste wanted to build its own cathedral. Alas, the latter is not a thing of beauty, and looks incongruous amongst the glories of the past. The British Government bought Cyprus instead, so perhaps this millstone is a sort of retribution for a lack of aesthetic vision.

Research and excavation are going on outside the church, and it is thought that the Pool of Bethesda may have been on this spot. It certainly had a wonderfully calming and healing atmosphere as one browsed in the ruins remembering the words "Take up thy bed and walk".

On Maundy Thursday that saintly man Archbishop Appleton took a party of two to three hundred people to the Syrian church of St. Mark, the possible site of the Last Supper and the Upper Room. We had a Syriac Christian service with the Gospels read in Aramaic, our Archbishop taking part with the Patriarch. It was dark inside and was therefore all the more moving because we had no lighting apart from candles and torches. We proceeded along the road that supposedly Christ took to the Garden of Gethsemane. We paused to read the appropriate Gospels and then left the Old City and the Wailing Wall, which were floodlit and looked very beautiful. It was all done in silence and was therefore most impressive. However, in some ways it was terrifying, and I could imagine Jesus weeping as he moved towards Gethsemane. We still weep for the sins of the world and the horrors of violence and intolerance.

The walk through the Kidron Valley was steep and difficult in the dark, and this gave one time to reflect upon the way that had led to Calvary and the slopes of the Mount of Olives. There the Archbishop blessed us. We prayed in the Russian Orthodox church, where we listened to the glorious deep bass singers, and then went to the Roman Catholic Church of All Nations. This is modern but has good mosaics given by Christian churches all over the world. I shall always remember that night as the walk was long and steep and I had the first

In the Way of Understanding

beginnings of arthritis in my knees! Truly a Via Dolorosa.

Bethlehem moved me, and during the drive there we saw shepherds leading their flocks, just as in the olden days. Despite the many tourists I felt as if I were alone and very much at peace in the grotto beneath the church. This is now under Greek Orthodox guardianship and is where the stable is supposed to have been. We prayed and sang the beautiful hymn "Dear Lord and Father of Mankind", and although there is much that seems tawdrily ornate, and the stone walls are covered with embossed leather and embroidery, somehow at that moment we pilgrims were very much as one in our simple faith.

In the Roman Catholic Cave of Innocents nearby—very plain, just rock—there was a wonderful crucifix. It is perhaps modern and is carved out of olive wood. The cross is just crude wood but the figure was evidently carved by someone who knew anatomy to perfection—a tragic figure, the body sagging and the ribs falling in while the arms seem only just able to hold the body, almost crooked in shape: carved surely from the heart...

Here, in this land enriched by the story of the Old and New Testaments, I realised how much I had missed out in education and in the history of religions. I tried to make up for it by using my eyes and my ears and by letting my vivid imagination run riot. The sordid trimmings, the fanaticism, the dirt, the smell in the Holy City itself, the buying and selling, the yelling, the horrifying squalor, the noise (made worse by modern transistor radios)—none of all this seemed to matter. I felt spiritually revived, and as a picture of Martha and Mary came into my mind I was happy that for a short period I had "chosen the better part". Within a year the practical Martha would have to take over at the W.F.M.H. Congress in Israel.

Israel, 1970

The W.F.M.H. Annual General Meeting in 1970 was held in Jerusalem but we were all housed, alas, in a hotel some miles outside the town. This made it almost impossible to visit the Old City during the short periods when we were free. Morris

Carstairs, the President, gave an excellent opening lecture at the Hebrew University, taking as his theme "The Trauma of Threat and the Stimulus of Challenge". This was very appropriate, as Israel was at war and lived in conflict. He taught us to see that to be threatened induces trauma, but that when an active, constructive role is found, what had been a threat can become a challenge and a stimulus.

I already knew something of the Mental Health services in Israel. On a pilgrimage to the Holy Land the year before I had met Dr. Louis Miller, the Director of Medical Services, who was now a member of the Executive Board of the W.F.M.H. and our host at this meeting. He organised the many plenary and technical sessions in such a way that this large gathering of international and inter-disciplinary delegates could have the opportunity to discuss their special interests with Israeli colleagues. We heard fascinating talks on Israeli educational aims, the treatment of children and adolescents, the deprived child and the Kibbutz society. We were eager to learn of the problems arising from children being so regimented, and separated from their parents at so early an age. Though we discussed the difficulties they had encountered our hosts assured us that the Kibbutz incorporated the best ideals of communal living. No profits were made, all was shared, and supposedly everyone lived happily together. Here we were aware of coming under political propaganda. This was noticeable and unpleasant, but we were stimulated by hearing of the efforts and energy that were put into building so many services in a new country. There were many theories expounded, and Dr. Wilfrid Warren and I representing the Bethlem Royal and Maudsley, and with our backgrounds deep in the old child-guidance movement in the U.K. and the U.S.A. had much to turn over in our minds, and we listened with interest and some apprehension.

We had individually conducted tours and I went with Dr. Samuel Cohen to the new purpose-built psychiatric hospital of 200 beds at Errath Hashin. This is a splendid building in lovely country overlooking the City. It had Wolfson money and no expense had been spared. I was much impressed, and not a little jealous. The Hospital had a doctor/patient ratio of one to

In the Way of Understanding

three, and a teaching programme for students at the Hebrew University. I also visited the Hadassah Hospital Medical School where I saw in their small synagogue the incredibly beautiful stained-glass windows designed by Marc Chagall.

The subject of "Mental Health as a Responsibility of Society" seemed to dominate the Conference. Its truth was only too obvious in Israel, where waves of immigrants from differing political and religious backgrounds had arrived in the country at the same time. The authorities were so aware of the size of the problem that one had to admire their courage.

Some of us were given a meal by one of our colleagues who lived in the Old City in a house overlooking the Wailing Wall. This intimate visit gave us a closer insight into the Israeli way of life than we could have been gained from any of our large gatherings. On the way back to the hotel and passing through the Jaffa Gate, I could not help remembering the story of how General Allenby, at Colonel T. E. Lawrence's suggestion, dismounted from his horse and, after addressing the populace, entered bareheaded to walk through the Old City.

Uganda, 1970

I had always been anxious to visit Uganda because of my mother's connection with that country through her husband, Sir Gerald Herbert Portal, K.C.M.G., C.B., who had been Queen Victoria's Agent and Consul-General at Zanzibar. He had been entrusted by H.M.'s Government with the leadership of the first official British expedition to Uganda in 1893. He died in London, two months after his return, of some kind of fever—presumably caught while on this expedition. He wrote two books: *The Mission to Uganda*[1] and *My Mission to Abyssinia*[2], both of great historical interest in view of the subsequent tragic events in that part of Africa.

After my mother's death in 1950 I had given the manuscript of *The Mission to Uganda* to the University of Kampala. I had heard that it was preserved in the University Library at Make-

[1] Published by Edward Arnold, for India Office, 1894.
[2] Edward Arnold, 1887.

World Travels

rere College and accessible to students. It was therefore with pleasure that I accepted in 1970 an invitation to give a paper there at a workshop sponsored by the W.F.M.H. and the Commonwealth Foundation on "Methods of delivering Mental Health Care".

On landing at Entebbe Airport it was with some emotion that I thought of the mission in 1893, struggling through bush and scrub and thorn trees to reach a place which, in those days, must have been only a cluster of small huts. Sir Gerald gave the name Port Alice (after my mother) to this little settlement at the foot of Ntebe river, and now known as Entebbe.

As I write, and after such happenings as the Israeli rescue at Entebbe and the dictatorship of Idi Amin, I feel closely associated with my mother. She would have been unhappy and disillusioned at the disintegration of all the high hopes of those in the mission to Uganda, and the failure of all the tender, loving care of those many pioneers who gave their lives for a better world in Africa.

My mission, however, was an altogether different one during the five working days which I spent at the Mary Stuart Hall of Residence at Makerere College, Kampala. It was unbearably hot but, unlike the 1893 mission, I had plenty of pills against malaria, plenty of cool drinks and many aids against mosquito bites as well as the luxury of cold showers. The organisers and hosts of the Workshop were most welcoming to me, but warned that besides the paper which I had been invited to give I was also expected to give a lecture to a mixed audience of interested people, with the hope of stimulating the small and struggling Ugandan Association for Mental Health.

At the first session of the Workshop it was agreed that it was too simple a matter to make hard and fast distinctions between developed and developing human societies. Professor Allen German[1], our host, ended one of his talks by saying:

> *The days are gone for good when one could comfort oneself with the thought that mental ill-health was something that is a problem only in developed societies. This is*

---

[1] Professor of Psychiatry, University of Western Australia, (Maudsley trained).

In the Way of Understanding

not so. A very serious look indeed must be given to the place of psychiatric services in the overall medical provisions of developing countries, and present attitudes, which at times border on the complacent, must yield to the more realistic assessments of mental health needs, based on the actual situation existing in our populations and in our hospitals.

At the session entitled "Psychiatric Auxiliaries and Voluntary Associations: their Role and Training", at which I introduced my paper, I showed the need for more psychiatric social workers, and gave as my reason: (a) doctors do not necessarily know the viewpoint of their patient; (b) the psychiatric patient may often be not only the victim of social disturbance but may also return to an essentially hostile environment. In the discussion that followed, one member of the audience felt that much more research was needed into the personality of the psychiatrist!

During these five working days the mental health services of Tanzania, Ghana, Ethiopia, the Sudan, Kenya and Nigeria were all discussed, and the mistaken belief that psychiatric disturbance in children did not exist in Africa was scotched.

I went to Butabica hospital for men and women with 900 beds, including 300 for criminal patients. It had lovely grounds but a very unhappy atmosphere. Anyone who has visited psychiatric hospitals in England or, for that matter, in any part of the world, will know what I mean. The sick in mind and those whose minds have not developed, those who are mentally ill or handicapped, are all lumped together in one huge building. This engenders an atmosphere of hopelessness, and the visitor will immediately visualise the problem magnified a hundred-fold all over the world. Here in Butabica hospital the situation was no different, despite the lovely surroundings and the sunny weather. Patients, men and women alike, all uniformly dressed in shifts of some drab, grey cotton material sat around, just staring. The uniform dress, much criticised by Professor German and his psychiatric team, was said by the police authorities to be essential for identification purposes should any patient or prisoner abscond. Africans, usually so gay and carefree, were subdued and horribly apathetic. It will take some years for more enlightened policies to change this treatment. Even now, in the eighties, after all that has happened in Uganda and in view of the tribalism that still seems to prevail, I am even more unhappy about the future of mental health in that unhappy land.

At the end of the Conference I was invited by Mr. Woodcock the manager of Barclays Bank, and his wife to stay with them and to see something of the country. We went up to Fort Portal, which was another pilgrimage for me. The mountains of Ruwenzori, the range which separates Uganda from the Congo, were fine and fierce in the evening sun. They are usually enveloped in cloud but we were fortunate that day, and I was much moved on reaching the hotel to find framed citations to Gerald Portal and his brother Raymond in the Manager's office. They read as follows:

SIR GERALD HERBERT PORTAL, K.C.M.G., C.B.
Her Majesty's Agent and Consul General at Zanzibar was entrusted by Her Majesty's Government with the conduct of the first Official British Expedition to Uganda, which left Mombasa on the 2nd January 1893. He died in London two months after his return. In virtue of his report Her Majesty's Government decided to annex the territories, which had been conceded under Royal Charter to the British East African Company, and to construct the Railway to the Central Lakes.

CAPTAIN MELVILLE RAYMOND PORTAL
—*the Loyal North Lancashire Regt. who accompanied the Mission, together with Colonel Francis Rhodes and Major Roderick Owen, both of whom in later years found their death in Africa, died of malarial fever at Kampala, on May 27th 1893. These two brothers—'Par nobile fratrum'— intrepid in adventure and wise in counsel, were eminent for qualities which endeared them to their contempraries at School, at College, and in the Public Service. Their names should ever be remembered in the Great African Colony, to preserve which for the British Empire they freely gave the glory of their manhood and the high promise of their lives.*

In the Way of Understanding

I visited the Town Clerk of Toro, the province in which Port Portal was situated. He was most interested in my connection with the Portal expedition. He insisted on calling Sir Gerald my father, which would have made me over a hundred, but Mr. Woodcock begged me to accept the relationship, since an explanation would have been too long and too complicated! The Council Room still had a photograph of Sir Gerald at one end and one of Elizabeth II at the other. The Head of the Police had by this time appeared, and he insisted on taking me up to the Fort—a little mound of stones presumably put up when the expedition left in 1893, and named Fort Gerry. It bore the inscription: 'Fort Gerry, founded 1893 and renamed Fort Portal, 1900'. They asked me who Gerry was and were delighted to know that 'Gerry' was a diminutive of Gerald, whose daughter I was supposed to be!

Interlude in Taizé, 1971

> *Keep us, O Lord, today in the*
> *joy*
> *simplicity*
> *and compassionate love*
> *of the Gospel*
> (Les Presses de Taizé, Taizé Commune, France.)

An insatiable curiosity and a longing to visit as many places in the world as possible had entered my blood at an early age, but was intensified as I grew to maturity. This urge was stimulated by my desire to help the mentally sick and handicapped all over the globe, but when I was not travelling on this absorbing business I still wanted to go places and to meet the people who were doing interesting things. Therefore, when a friend returned from Taizé in Burgundy and told me of the ecumenical work being done there I decided to seek spiritual refreshment.

I discovered in Taizé an ecumenical centre founded after the war by Brother Roger Schutz, together with a handful of like-minded souls of different nationalities and denomina-

Royal Tomb,
Kampala, 1970

Self at
Fort Gerry,
renamed
Fort Portal in
1900

World Travels

tions, and including some Roman Catholics. As time went on the Monastery had become a magnet for thousands of young people, who formed a Council of Youth which included participants from Africa, Asia, the U.S.A. and Latin America. It was like a people on the march, determined to support a radical rebirth of the People of God, so that the Church could be in tune with her universal mission and a link of communion between men and women from all over the world.

It turned out to be a glorious holiday for me. Taizé surpassed all my expectations. The weather was hot and sunny and the great plateau, surrounded by hills and pine forests, was peopled with thousands of boys and girls, young men and women and a sprinkling of the more mature like myself, all milling around or sitting under trees in small groups. They reminded me of the places in the New Testament where Christ is discoursing with his disciples and friends, and framing a new way of life.

I was travelling with two younger companions, but on our arrival I went alone into the vast church at midday. Even then it was too small to hold the congregation, and I believe it has now been enlarged to accommodate the great throng which comes here from every part of the globe. Those present were so reverent, just sitting on the floor in meditation, whilst some who might have been of Buddhist or Muslim persuasion were bowed down with their heads on the floor in complete silence. The atmosphere was impressive but the place itself was spartan, with just a plain stone altar table, good modern windows (made by the monks), roughcast stone walls, a kind of cord carpet, no pews and very few chairs. There was a huge Byzantine crucifix behind the altar, and a painting on wood of the Virgin on one side of the church.

The Sunday service was packed, and I had difficulty in squeezing myself on a bench between two young nuns. Many young people had been more than kind in helping me up and down steps. We were on a kind of raised platform, so I had an excellent view of the thirty or so monks in white habits who were sitting in a circle, with the Abbot, like Christ, in the centre. Lessons from the Old and New Testaments were read in French, Italian, Spanish, German and English. The Prior

In the Way of Understanding

celebrated communion for the monks, and then they came amongst the congregation bringing the bread and wine and moving slowly in pairs. There was no hurry, and the huge throng, sitting on their haunches and then standing gravely, took communion from the monks in different corners of the church. The Roman Catholics and the Orthodox went down to a communion service in their respective crypts under the church.

The encampment or village was very clean and tidy, and the living quarters and washing facilities were wonderfully organised in squares, rather like an Arab village. The young wore the usual jeans and T shirts, their hair normally untidy but not over-long. All seemed normal and healthy, radiating a "Foi Vivante" and there was little noise, no pop music or radios, no violence and no overt sex play.

Roger Schutz, with whom I had a short conversation after the service, was a holy man and an admirer of Teilhard de Chardin. He had piercing grey eyes and parchment-like skin, and he radiated peace. In 1974 he received the Templeton Prize, the object of which is to "stimulate the love of God on the part of mankind and pioneer a breakthrough in religious knowledge". I left with a feeling that I had witnessed something very real in the lives of all these young people, all maybe strugglers against evil in their own different worlds.

2,000 delegates from the Youth Council in Taizé came to London just after Christmas in 1981 and converged on Westminster Abbey, Westminster Cathedral and St. Pauls. Various churches and organisations gave hospitality, and the week's visit was a huge success and made even the media notice a resurgence of faith in a godless world.

China, 1972

> *"The World is progressing, the future is bright and no one can change this general trend of history."*
> Quotation from Chairman Mao Tse-tung (Little Red Book)

In 1972 I paid a memorable, but all too short visit to Peking with Robina, as the guest of her brother John our first Ambas-

World Travels

sador to the People's Republic of China after the re-opening of the frontier. Since those days many visits of cultural and educational value have been paid to this remarkable country, and many books of descriptive and historical interest have been published, so I will only record briefly my personal impressions as one of the privileged few allowed to enter China while it was still a mystery to the rest of the world.

Robina and I crossed the border from Hong Kong, carrying our own luggage, leaving behind us the British soldiers looking so young and smart as we faced the solemn little Chinese soldiers dressed in their drab uniforms and all carrying fixed bayonets. There were no other tourists and we felt apprehensive as we parted with our precious passports. However, we need not have worried as our visas had been granted thanks, to John who was highly respected and admired by the Chinese Government for his knowledge of their language and history and as a collector of Early Ming porcelain.

This was a private visit; the W.F.M.H. had no impact on post-revolutionary China and thus its Honorary President hesitated to implicate the Federation or the British Embassy by asking for information or opportunities to visit their institutions. However, the Embassy Public Relations Officer, having elicited from me my personal and professional interests, kindly organised visits to a Nursery School and to a Special School for Deaf Children. I was struck by the cleanliness, efficiency, discipline and God-like devotion to Chairman Mao whose portrait hung on the wall of every classroom and dormitory. In the school for the deaf I witnessed the practice of acupuncture and was surprised to see no sign of pain even in the children's eyes as the needle was inserted behind the ear. Fifteen pupils were said to have been cured in one year and sent on to normal schools.

My most illuminating visit was to a Progressive Agricultural People's Commune, run on Soviet lines. This has since been disbanded because the people (peasants) were not happy in such a disciplined environment! The leader, a bright young man, lean and strong and with piercing eyes, showed me among other things the Public Health Centre where two "bare-foot doctors" administered Western as well as Chinese medicine and referred sufferers from serious illness to hospital.

He then showed me the hostel for old folk who had no families to care for them, and who before the Cultural Revolution had been broken-down rickshaw-men, street cleaners or slaves of bad landlords. A bound-footed, toothless old lady of seventy was amazed to find that I was older than she was, although presumably her life had been harder than mine! The old people were welcoming, and smiled as they said how happy they were thanks to Chairman Mao. Here they rested while the workers toiled at forestry, duck-farming, market-gardening and much else. Had it been possible to do without an interpreter, I would have enjoyed a discussion with my intelligent guide, for he showed real interest in British farming.

China was to me a country of contrasts: the beauty and peace of the Forbidden City, the Great Wall and the Ming Tombs were indescribable, and made one more aware of the restless bustle and noise in the streets with endless propaganda blaring through loud speakers.

The Chinese sense of colour was my delight; the grey green and vivid blue of their mountains appeared in their paintings and porcelain, and was even reflected in the uniforms of the army and in the suits worn by the workers.

I was amused to find how seriously the Chinese took their recreation. For instance, couples in boats would row formally with no fooling such as one would see on the Serpentine, and certainly no sex play was ever visible! I only saw one young man holding-hands, and then it was with two girls, one on each side of him. Girls are advised not to marry until they are twenty-four and the advice is obeyed, but as the Pill is fostered by the State, sex must surely surface somehow, somewhere!

The visits to places of archaeological importance remain vividly in my memory: one was the bridge of Wanping Hsien village, described by Marco Polo in 1276 and restored by Ming in 1444 and in 1648 by Ching. It was also the place where in 1937 the Japanese fought the Chinese in a bloody battle. The old walls still surround the village.

The other was the site of the dig near the village of Chow Kow Tien where Teilhard de Chardin, the famous Jesuit palaeontologist, carried out his excavations more than forty years ago. He uncovered the Peking Man, Homo Pekinesis, and revolutionised prehistoric studies. The Chinese are continuing his great work, but I found it sad that no mention was made of the early dig of this scientist-priest.

Back in Hong Kong, I reflected on Louis Heren's ending to one of his excellent articles in *The Times*. "It was all too good to be true, but it was true, China is a very perplexing country". This is a right description, for I felt as if I had been participating in a fairy story, a charade, or even a dream.

1972 was a dramatic moment in time, a great change from starvation to abundance. Looking back, I am thankful to have witnessed the rebirth of a great nation, almost an emergence from the womb.

South Africa, 1976

Readers may remember from my previous references to South Africa that I have a deep love for the country, and also perhaps some understanding of the problems which face its population of Coloureds, Indians, Afrikaners and English.

My first encounter with mental health in South Africa was in 1948 when I visited Tara, the first psychiatric hospital for whites. It had just been opened by Dr. Hyme Moross and was administered by that remarkable Matron, Iris Marwick, who was later to become my colleague and friend on the Executive Board of the W.F.M.H. In course of time she became the Chief Nursing Officer to the Department of Health in Pretoria. She was succeeded by Iris Roscher, whom I met in Sydney in 1973 when she gave an excellent lecture, with colour slides, of nurses at work in hospital and up country in community care, showing the great progress made in the training of black and white students. After talking with Iris Roscher I wished I could see some of this work, and also visit once again the country which Mont and I loved so much. Since 1948 South Africa has changed its government, left the Commonwealth and become a Republic. The system they have imposed, called apartheid, is evil, yet I believe that some of those who are caught up in all its horror could be encouraged by talking to workers from the free world, and especially those who have to administer a system which they abhor.

It was after the Sydney Conference that I received an invitation from the South African Council for Mental Health to be their guest, and to give the Morris Ginsburg Lecture on the theme of "From Child Guidance to Child and Adolescent Psychiatry" at their Annual General Meeting in Durban. This was a most attractive proposition, so I consulted Professor Tsung-Lin, the then President of the W.F.M.H. He strongly urged me not to accept, because as I was Hon. President of the W.F.M.H. it would be thought the organisation itself was approving apartheid. I also consulted Dr. Tom Lambo, later Deputy Director General of W.H.O. He was also most emphatic that I should refuse, and even telephoned me from Geneva to this effect.

It was a blow but, having asked for advice I felt bound to abide by it, and so I told the South African Council that as Hon. President of the W.F.M.H. I must refuse for political reasons. In 1975, however, after much communication between Iris Roscher and myself, I did accept another invitation. This time I made it clear that I would only go as an individual who was highly critical of their system of apartheid and that I was in no way representing the W.F.M.H. or the N.A.M.H. In Durban Iris Roscher took charge of me and was a real Nannie, and made all my travel arrangements for a heavy four weeks programme.

My first engagement was to attend the Conference and A.G.M. of the Council for Mental Health and to meet all the representatives of the Government Departments: Health, Social Services, Education, as well as the Bantu Administrator and representatives of the Provinces, all of whom were white. There were however several black and Indian social workers in the audience.

In the evening on which I gave my lecture, I found the occasion very trying, because there was a mayoral reception beforehand and several hundred people had to be shaken by the hand, all of whom wished to talk to me. This was followed by speeches of welcome from the platform in both English and Afrikans and prayers by a chaplain in English and by a Lutheran pastor in Afrikaans. By the time all this was over and it came to my turn the audience seemed frozen and I felt cold too! However I did my best to warm them up, and my friends were pleased, but I myself still remain doubtful. I had of course made it quite plain in my opening remarks that although my connection with the W.F.M.H. and N.A.M.H. was a close one, I was in no way representing them officially and that any opinions I expressed would be mine alone.

Durban is very English, and in my hotel facing the sea I felt very much as if I were in Brighton. My son, Peregrine Worsthorne, happened to be in Durban at the same time. We had many arguments when we met with my social worker friends, and I teased him for accepting so readily the indoctrination of the Government—something which he hotly denied! Nevertheless his eyes were not seeing what I saw, nor were his ears hearing the other point of view so clearly as mine, so I found his subsequent articles in the *Sunday Telegraph* somewhat disappointing—not that I wanted wholesale condemnation, heaven forbid, because the problem is bedevilled by politics and there are two sides to every question. My friends, many of them Afrikans, Bantu and coloured, all endeavoured to show me their own particular point of view.

There is much devoted work being done for coloured retarded children in the slums and back streets of Durban. There were some black social workers, but all too few, and there is only one black psychiatrist working in the University Hospital, a miserable old building with only twelve psychiatric beds. Most psychiatrists in South Africa are state employees and thus they are muzzled.

Up in Pietermaritzberg I attended a big conference of doctors, nurses and social workers from various parts of Natal which was held in the Tower Hill Psychiatric Hospital with 2,000 beds. Here I had to give a talk about mental health in England, after which there were some very interesting questions from a mixed audience of doctors, nurses and ancillary staff, both black and white. In Fort Napier Hospital nearby I found many relics of the British troops in the Zulu War, because it had been the Commanding Officer's residence. There was also a large hut which had been built in India during

In the Way of Understanding

that period and had been brought over piece by piece and erected as a theatre for entertaining the troops. It is now listed as an historic building and is used for therapy. Pietermaritzberg was a fascinating place, and very Scottish in background. There is still a statue of Queen Victoria, and the Union Jack was flying over the Victoria Club. Surely life is stranger than fiction?

In the many clinics, hospitals and schools I visited all over the country the cry was always the same "Why don't more people like you come out and see us? We are lonely, and your holding aloof does not help us, the workers. Tell people to come and see what we are trying to do in mental health and other ways."

I spent about four days in Richmond and drove up into the Drakensberg mountains, which are about 4,000 feet high—all very hazy with what they call a "blue veil" which is just like smoke. I found it all very beautiful, with the little villages with their kraals, and with blue smoke coming from their rondavels, so picturesque and unobtrusive. The Africans surely have an artistic sense.

While motoring back to Durban airport my hostess drove past many villagers who were walking wearily along the roadside, but she dared not give even a poor, tired old man a lift as no white woman was allowed to take an African into her car.

Down in Cape Town I stayed in luxury at the famous Mount Nelson Hotel (where I had stayed many years previously with Mont) which is a little way outside the town and has a beautiful garden under Table Mountain. It had bitter-sweet memories for me, as had the breathtaking drive up Table Mountain and round the Cape in perfect weather with not a cloud in the sky.

My guide who took me on this trip gave me details of the horrors in the coloured areas, where clinics are stoned and fear is in the hearts of blacks, coloured and whites. He said that the police had even thrown petrol into the home for retarded coloured children.

It was in Avalon, one of the disturbed areas at that time, that I talked with social workers and with the press. I visited homes

World Travels

for retarded coloured children with their devoted coloured staff. There were great placards on the hoardings saying "Love means Violence". One could feel the tension, hopelessness and frustration in their work, which was but a drop in the ocean of misery. The leader of the Black Sash movement gave me unpleasant details of the disturbances and of the problems of the aftermath. Coloured doctors and nurses in the hospitals were much distressed by the violence of their own kind and found it hard to understand.

It was a moving experience to talk freely to all these workers, so forlorn and unhappy, who could see no light at the end of their black tunnel. The white matrons, too, disclosed to me in private their grave concern for the huge nursing staff throughout the Union, who could work so happily together if only the Government would leave them alone.

My next stop was Johannesburg, and then I went on to Pretoria by car and I paid my respects to our Ambassador. He was more than welcoming to me, despite being at the time busy with Dr. Kissinger. The Ambassador gave me sound advice, as I was becoming alarmed at the amount of help with hotels and travel that the Health Department and Ministry of Information were giving me, and I wondered what they might expect in return.

Perhaps the highlight of my visit was a dinner with Mrs. Suzman of the Opposition Progressive and Reform Party, who was at one time a lone Member of Parliament. She was an interesting woman, not pretty but very well dressed and with eyes that looked you straight in the face, a good bone structure, grey hair; she was certainly a dynamic and clever person. We had twenty minutes talk together after dinner, and I begged her to meet Iris Roscher and to see for herself the work of the nursing side of the Health Department. I had been told she had been asked many times to pay visits to hospitals and training centres but had always made some excuse. It was a delightful, civilised evening in a lovely house with beautiful pictures and objets d'art, Persian carpets, and so on, but somehow I was not happy. After this and many other delightful parties which I attended, I often wondered as I left, perhaps after midnight, what had happened to all the black and coloured waiters.

In the Way of Understanding

Perhaps they had had a long walk home, or at best had taken a bicycle, but there was always the danger of having mislaid or even of having forgotten their pass, and of ending up in the police court. I was told that they would then be fined and for employers this would involve much annoyance.

The Ministry of Information were very proud of their hotel training school, which had a rather terrifying young German in charge. It was run on strict lines, since the black boys came to it straight from their bush homes without ever having seen tables, knives, forks, chairs, cups or saucers. They learnt parrot fashion, with no idea why things had to be done in a certain way for the crazy whites. The boys looked sad and scared. They had worked intensively from 7.30 a.m. to 10 p.m. but with the certainty of finding a job afterwards. It seemed a far cry from a cosy family in a mud rondavel and must have been pretty frightening. I suppose they were the brothers of the girls who went in for nurse training, which was so much better organised.

The Ministry of Information also arranged a weekend break for me at Mala Mala Game Reserve, and it was rather a relief to be in a car with some good-looking and healthy young Rangers, and amongst four-legged animals. Here I had time to rest in the intoxicating silence of Africa, in beautiful surroundings and in a peaceful rondavel with every modern comfort. However, I was not at peace myself, for I felt as if I were swimming in a muddy ocean, swept at times by waves of tension and emotion, and certainly in deep waters. I began to feel alone and insecure.

It was early Spring, with everything burnt and brown, and with both animals and humans awaiting the rains in this glorious Veldt country. My memories took me back to such days at La La Panzi, my mother's lovely kraal in the Drakensberg Mountains at Tzaneen.

In the Lebowa Homeland I spent two nights in Groothoek psychiatric hospital just at the time when the transfer of all health services to black administration was being carried out. The Lebowa Government was to have one health authority, and a comprehensive health service combined with social services. The Dutch psychiatrist-in-charge seemed to me to have much understanding and sensitivity towards the local culture. In his treatment he used Bmolope dances in which movement, drama and expression combine to establish services geared to the condition in this homeland. This homeland now appears to have a cadre of well-trained black general and psychiatric nurses, both male and female, copied from the original idea put forward by Dr. Hymie Moross and Iris Marwick at Tara Hospital in 1948.

The provision for geriatric patients showed much imagination. They were housed in small rondavels with thatched roofs, as in the villages. It was like a village, not an institution. Couples, whether married or not, could live together. One old lady of 104 seemed to be the pet of the whole hospital although she had become a lively squirrel with other people's belongings.

I went to see a medicine man at work in the village. He was functioning in a reasonable way and was on excellent terms with both the hospital itself and the psychiatrist-in-charge. This seemed to me to show much common sense on both sides.

I think that much good is being done by the Department of Health, although I know there is one highly controversial question concerning the transfer of some of the black long-stay deteriorated patients to a privately administered concern. However, I was impressed by the structured activity programme in a cultural setting. These patients were housed in some old mining huts on the Reef which had been suitably upgraded, with sufficient washing and sleeping arrangements. They compared well with their village life and with conditions in long-stay institutions in many parts of the world. Patients were dressed in gay coloured clothing and seemed lively and cheerful—at any rate they were not just sitting and staring, such as I have, alas, only too often witnessed at home and on my travels. They were expressing themselves through drama and movement in the famous Molope dances. This sophisticated therapy is practised in Western hospitals, too, and it reminded me of the way in which our young folk jig along and jive. However these Africans do it with so much more freedom and grace.

In the Way of Understanding

Before leaving this "Beloved Country" I made a pilgrimage to the Smuts Memorial Trust at Irene, about ten miles from Pretoria. General Smuts used to walk to work from here every morning, much to the dismay of all those concerned for his safety—the police and his secretaries. The old homestead has been left exactly as it used to be, with tin roof, ugly Victorian furniture and iron bedstead. Ouma's[1] sold attaché case was still on her bed, as she used to sleep with it. The impression one gets is that the owners cared nothing for material things, nor for art or beauty, only for the bare necessities of life. Spiritual values mattered, were indeed all-important, and this creed was basic to this supremely happy couple and their family. The great honours that he was given, and the important people that he met, never corrupted his soul, and the spirit was supreme in his life. His ashes and those of Ouma are scattered up the hill (or "Kopje" in Afrikaans) that lies behind the house, and this is now a place of rest. The entrance is built of stone under thatched arch, and there are stone benches for resting and praying before one proceeds up the hill. "Be still and know" is written in fine lettering on a plain stone set into the floor, and it is all very moving. There was indeed a feeling of peace, and the Memorial Fund were striving to keep this so, despite the hundreds of tourists who come from all over the world—much to the surprise of the Government who expected that the name of Field Marshal Smuts would soon be forgotten. How silly can governments be? Perhaps this shows more clearly than anything I have written the spiritual isolation of the South African Government.

In my interviews with the press I stressed many of the hard things that I have written here. Some of them appeared, but my broadcast in Durban was censored. However, I know that the nursing profession, with all its great tradition of caring, is led by a gallant and courageous woman. I believe that even under the impossible situation in which it now finds itself, it could still point a way to a solution in which all races could work together in harmony in the relief of suffering. So beautiful a country must never be allowed to believe that Love means violence. I went, I saw and listened, with no immediate

[1] Wife of General Smuts.

result, but if enough people were able to go and do likewise I believe right could conquer might.

Canada, 1977

Despite my advancing years I decided to fly to Canada yet once more—this time over the Pole in a jumbo jet, which was a thrill in itself. We dropped down for a few minutes in Edmonton, and then flew on again over the Rocky Mountains to Vancouver, over lakes shimmering in the sun—a truly spectacular sight. The W.F.M.H. Congress was held on the campus of Columbia University outside the city, and the theme was "Today's Priorities in Mental Health: Knowing and Doing". Professor Tsung yi Lin of Taiwan (Professor of Psychiatry at Columbia) with whom I had a long friendship was the President that year. He had arranged for delegates to be housed in the University's splendid halls of residence and for me, as Hon. President, to have a small suite. This enabled me to entertain old Executive Board members and friends, many even coming for breakfast! It was also nice to have the facility for informal meetings and discussions in a peaceful atmosphere, as the campus, though lovely, was vast. I had not expected to take any active part in this Conference but to my surprise my dear friend, Tsung yi Lin, in his presidential address told the assembled delegates about a note I had once passed to him during a difficult stage in the early development of the W.F.M.H. This note contained the little French poem which had been my theme song since childhood and which appears on the first page of these memories. He likened the Federation to my bird perched on fragile branches having the courage to sing, knowing it had wings. Was it just a coincidence that these words which had so often given me courage were now to be used to inspire the World Federation?

There was quite a flurry in the dovecotes when Mrs. Rosalyn Carter, wife of the then President of the U.S.A., accepted an invitation to address one of our plenary sessions. A sweet and humble little lady, she told us she came as a dedicated lay person and as chairman of the President's Commission on Mental Health. In some of her research she had

In the Way of Understanding

found that about 70% of Americans sought help for emotional and social problems from non-professionals, as she felt this should be faced by the professionals in her audience. She said that prejudice and fear concerning mental health are ever-present in the minds of lay people. This is certainly true even today, and the stigma attached to mental illness is still holding back progress. In a lovely, soft Southern voice Rosalyn Carter made a passionate appeal for all of us to work for a common goal and for a more caring society. She wisely emphasised that Euro-American standards of treatment could not be imposed on other parts of the world, and that we needed to tailor our services to ethnic and racial minorities.

At a big dinner given for her I had the opportunity to ask her to adopt my baby, the one which I had nurtured with so much care since 1948. She looked startled, as well she might, but I explained how someone in her position could do so much if she would take a lead in W.F.M.H. affairs. At the next Executive Board meeting Mrs. Carter's name was proposed as President of the W.F.M.H. but, to my surprise, there was much opposition. Politics and jealousy dominated the discussions, and when I pointed out that I had been elected Hon. President while I was a U.K. representative, I was told that my years of service had counted and not my nationality. Argument went on, in a rather unattractive fashion, but the heat was taken out of the discussion by dear gentle Brother Gerard, a missionary from Zambia. He said that when he read that Rosalyn Carter was to address our assembly he had to ask who she was, since he himself was only a back-woodsman from Africa. The matter was settled by Mrs. Carter herself when she declined the invitation.

More exciting, but no less controversial, was a two-hour debate between Professor Morris Carstairs and Ivan Illich, the philosopher, economist, writer and ex-priest who now lives in Mexico. Illich condemned the surrendering of personal responsibility to a priesthood of professionals. He lashed out at teachers for insisting that no-one should become a useful citizen unless they had years of schooling, and he also sniped at the media for destroying the dignity of words. He believed that the modern practice of medicine is to be deplored, since it makes it impossible for people to care for themselves. Professor Carstairs argued, in his gentle manner, for the survival of mental health professionals, saying that Illich's bookishness had removed him from the reality of the world in which all have to live, and that his views on pain and suffering were forms of Stoicism which were not what most of the world wanted. It was a lively discussion, and the debate was summed up by that great man, teacher of psychiatry in the U.S.A., Karl Menninger of Topeka.

It was a nostalgic meeting for me as this was to be the last time I was to see Margaret Mead. We had become very close, though I was still nervous of her sharp tongue and her erudition. She would often come and sit next to me at board meetings and whisper "You try to tell them, I feel I have said enough"! Over the years we had many sparring matches, and when after one of her excellent lectures I had ventured to congratulate her she quickly replied "So you have forgiven me for that inadequate contribution I once gave on child guidance?" She had a curiously soft and feminine side to her all too arrogant exterior.

Bidding farewell to so many old friends and new, and cheerily saying "See you at the next Congress" left me wondering. Life is uncertain, and with advancing years who knows what is to come?

Austria, July 1979

The W.F.M.H. Congress which was to be held in Salzburg in July was too much of a temptation for two old stalwarts like Robina and me—both founder members with their roots in child guidance. It was the International Year of the Child, and our old friend from The Philippines, Dr. F. Aldaba-Lim, its President, was to give the opening address.

The theme which ran through all four days naturally concentrated on children. Thus "World Wide Dilemma for Children and their Families", "Rights of Children", "Changing Environment of Families" were some of the topics which were discussed. There were also workshops which attracted professionals in child care and education from all over the world.

In the Way of Understanding

Robina and I had both been to Vienna, but the beauty of Salzburg, the home of music, called to that side of our natures which is attracted to the arts. Salzburg is one of the cities I feel that I could return to time and time again.

The framework of this Conference took its usual form; plenary sessions, group discussions—now called topic workshops—but there was one change which I welcomed. This was a youth panel run by the sons and daughters of the participants. They told us of their experiences in living with their parents, and to my surprise these young people were conservative in their views, and took very seriously the problem of growing up. These were adolescents, some of whom I had known as babies, and it was a thrilling experience to watch them on the stage, freely discussing the problems we were battling with: I hope that this "youth session" will be incorporated into future conferences.

Since our last Conference in Vancouver, Margaret Mead, that vital and dominating character, had died. She had been a tower of strength to the W.F.M.H., as one of its founder members who rarely missed any of our conferences. Tributes to her memory were paid by many of her friends, and a memorial lecture was given by Benjamin Spock. An excellent film of her life, made in the U.S.A., was shown and for those of us who had known and admired her it was moving to see that small, dumpy figure in her red cloak and with her shepherd's crook, walking away into the unknown as the film ended.

The Executive Board had changed completely from its small cosy membership of roughly fifty, which included advisers and representatives from W.H.O., U.N.E.S.C.O. and similar organisation. Now there were over a hundred delegates who came from Africa, Asia, North and South America, Australia, Canada, New Zealand, Japan and South Africa, but the East European and the U.S.S.R. countries were still shy, whilst the Republic of China sent no representative at all. So as to make the huge gathering more manageable, the delegates were now grouped into geographical regions for discussions. Even so, the members on the Executive Board were vocal and discursive and to my mind over-nationalistic as well.

In the early days we had tried to confine our attention to

World Travels

mental health and its maintenance, as well as to mental illness and its care. Now the Board Meetings were long and prolix, as is only to be expected when members come from so many continents and countries, and possess strong nationalistic emotions and differing ideologies and cultures. The Third World was well represented and very vocal, and keen for us to share in the tremendous problems which faced them. South Africa is in a difficult situation; she is a member of the African region but is deeply suspect and something of a rogue elephant. So the cosy and élitist club I had joined in 1948 is now a veritable league of nations, voluntarily meeting together to show their concern for mental health.

This was my last Executive Board meeting, and after the four-day conference and an Executive Board Meeting which lasted five hours I was none too sure of my own mental health! Most of the time was taken up discussing a new Constitution, and with my past experience of trying to crack this hard nut I could sympathise with our Chairman, an experienced Canadian lawyer, who was having no woolly psychological ideas upsetting his proposed administration.

After this marathon, Robina and I took off to a small, restful kurhaus on the Wolfgangsee in order to sleep and to eat, and to enjoy the beautiful scenery and excursions on the lake. We believed that we had earned this holiday. What remains in my memory is that Austria, despite the War and the changes around her, seemed to me essentially unchanged. The people's manners are still beautiful; their women-folk—even when not wearing traditional dirndl dresses—are exquisitely turned out and well-tailored. I saw no Austrian hippies nor the universal jeans. The well-mannered children in their happy play showed no signs of anger or violence. It was all very peaceful and old fashioned. It is a true civilisation which has somehow survived, and I pray it will never lose its identity nor let itself be overrun by an alien one.

Retirement

20

Retirement

In the process of growing older and by the application of common sense we learn to adjust to situations, and learn to take to ourselves advice we ought to give—and would give—to others. We learn to cope with problems and to become less vulnerable.
    Cardinal Basil Hume, O.S.B., *Searching for God*,
        Hodder & Stoughton, 1977, p. 146.

Living memory seeps imperceptibly into history and leaves the bitter-sweet emotion of a life-time. Trying to piece this pilgrimage together has been difficult and even unsatisfactory with lapses in memory but enough is remembered I hope for the reader to get a picture. I have only attempted to write lantern slides in a rough time sequence.

A moment of truth came for me when I gave up my car. My reactions were becoming slow, my eyesight dim and my hearing imperfect and I therefore felt myself to be a hazard on the road. Both my oculist and my general practitioner seemed delighted that I had reached this decision alone as each assured me they would not have had the courage to tell me for fear of hurting my feelings. I parried by telling them I considered it wrong not to tell patients the truth, thereby not taking them into their confidence and not treating them like adults, and particularly when other members of the public using the roads could be in danger.

Car-less my life was restricted and I felt a loss of independence even though I am lucky enough to live in a city with adequate public services and walking to and from bus stops and underground stations is a useful exercise. But now there was to be no more easy travelling for weekends with family and friends, with luggage containing clothes for all weathers and occasions (so necessary in England) tucked in the boot of the car; and no more lifts for car-less friends providing companionship, nor morning visits to Kew Gardens on a Sunday when I had often had that glorious place to myself. In many ways this obviously wise decision became more and more a

In the Way of Understanding

reminder that old age was creeping up on me, and this had to be faced squarely and cheerfully if I was to be mentally healthy—something I had been trying to preach and work for and now needed to be put into practice!

My retirement from the Regional Hospital Board was a natural break, as the old hospital authority was to be succeeded by a new form of health service administration after thirty years, with all members retiring automatically.

Now I was busy "just living" as opposed to dying, as at the time when I left Plodge, with all the problems concerning lawyers, settlements, distribution of furniture, etc. Everything was different now without James[1] and Lilian. Some "dailies" came and went, careless of me, with eyes on the clock and hands ready for the weekly pay packet. Unfortunately at my birth, the art of cooking was forgotten by my fairy godmother and an cute dislike of dust and untidiness substituted, and this made for hard domestic work coming rather too late in life. But my life is still an active one though diversified. I have no settled working hours, but time to enjoy friends, time to think, to read, to see plays, hear concerts live and on the radio and to look at wonderful historical programmes on the television such as *Civilization*, Bronowski, and the *Journey of the Beagle*, Alistair Cooke's America and Edward VIII & Mrs. Simpson. For the retired living alone, I believe television to be a boon. News coverage, music and plays have revolutionised entertainment for senior citizens and can alleviate loneliness and give opportunities to participate in so much: interest, laughter and tears at the press of a button—something never dreamed of in the days of my youth. I am thankful to be alive to benefit from the miracles of science.

Writing this book has forced me to think, to look back and take account of the thread running through my life, the desire for more mental health in the world and the realisation of the vital importance of something still universally eschewed. The years have gone by in a flash, the early ones when I craved a profession, the nonsensical ones of Paris, Monte Carlo, yachting, etc., followed by my more mature days when after my

---

[1] Died in his sister's home in Blackburn in 1979. I sadly attended the funeral of my friend and loyal servant.

second marriage I found security and understanding and fulfilment in a useful way of life.

I have learnt from what some may call my junketing around the world that the prevention of mental ill health and suffering is not only the responsibility of the caring professions. But with the pooling of resources and co-operation help is more and more available. No one profession can expect to care for the whole world of human frailty but sufferers can be taught to live with problems and many mentally healthy people have a part to play.

By listening with intelligence to what people have told me and now with time for reflection I have learnt through experience in the courts, amongst the underprivileged, through visiting mental hospitals, schools for the mentally ill and handicapped, and wards for the aged and dying in many countries, that the writing is on the wall. Therefore we must have more research and unified action. Leadership must come from those in authority or else we perish in apathy and violence. Science and religion must overcome their antagonism and unite and this must include psychoanalysts and those engaged in physical medicine.

Ordinary people in every country have an immense responsibility because each individual has the power to achieve what seems to be the impossible if one cares enough, takes the trouble to look and listen and then voices an opinion. At Taizé I saw serious minded youth searching in dialogue for the higher power which the various religions in the world were unable to explain in a manner they were able to comprehend. There is however light at the end of the tunnel. More and more National Associations for Mental Health are gradually emerging. The W.F.M.H. is recognised in every country and has the support of W.H.O. and the World Psychiatric Association.

Mental illness is no longer a tabu subject as it was in my early days. I would never dare mention mental health when asked about my activities but spoke of my interest in social work. Today fear has largely been overcome by more understanding and perhaps the media has helped. Films such as *One Flew Over the Cuckoo's Nest* and the *Snake Pit* and television shows such as *Mayberry* have undoubtedly given the public a

In the Way of Understanding

wider vision of mental illness than they had in the past, evoking compassion in place of fear. Government enquiries have revealed some of the malpractices in mental hospitals and have caused the public to demand better conditions. As a one-time magistrate I am now encouraged by the work of progressive Governors of prisons and borstals and the bravery of their comments in the press.

At the memorable party at the Grocers' Hall to celebrate my 80th birthday it was a unique occasion for me to mix together the extraordinary variety of my friends who had given me support, my family, present and past Governors and Directors of the Bank of England, and a conglomeration of Lords and their Ladies, some professors and a generous number of professional colleagues. It was a truly motley gathering or a multidisciplinary team to all of whom I wished to say thank you from the bottom of my heart. At this party my two sons and their wives and children were my mainstay in welcoming the guests, and it may then have been the first time they realised the double life I had lived. This book tells little of their stories and contributions to my life but I have watched their peregrinations with admiration and some pride, Simon as Her Majesty's representative in the County Palatine of Lancashire, carrying on the devotion to duty in the best traditions of the Towneleys throughout the ages. In this capacity he has consented to become the first President of MIND's Regional Division, thus helping to fan the small wind of change blowing in this County. His dear wife Mary has in her busy life found time to give weekly riding lessons to the mentally handicapped from Calderstone Hospital. This carrying on of the torch has given me great satisfaction. My younger son Peregrine, gifted with the pen of a ready writer, has successfully carved himself a niche in the precarious world of journalism and his daughter, Dominique, has graciously given me my first great grandchild, Adam, for which I am well pleased.

In retirement I also have the Norman family who have been a constant prop and justify the prophecy Mont made in a letter to my mother at the time of my marriage, namely that "Priscilla will find a new family who will welcome and cherish her".

London Congress, 1968
(L. to R.) H.R.H. Princess
Alexandra, self, Dr. Morris
Carstairs, Lady Butler

Peregrine

Her Majesty the Queen with Simon and Mary, 1980

Epilogue

21

Epilogue

"Where shall I begin please Your Majesty?" he asked: "Begin at the beginning" the King said gravely, "and go on until you come to the end. Then stop."

Lewis Carroll.

When I was in doubt and in a deep depression while writing these memoires, a friend gave me a quotation from the diary of Père Roger of the Taizé Community, which gave me courage: "La découverte de toi-même sans personne pour te comprendre peut provoquer une honte d'exister qui va jusqu'a l'auto-destruction, mais pour l'évangile il n'y a que des hommes a l'image de Dieu—Aime ton prochain comme toi même, si tu le déteste".[1]

It has been like putting a jigsaw puzzle together with many pieces missing in my memory, and I have often wondered in reverence at the discrepancies in the Gospels and have not been surprised because in my writing there has come a greying in memory as the years go by. I only wonder there was not more diversity amongst the Apostles considering they wrote in later life and under many difficulties with little research material available. I only marvel and rejoice they had survived the vicious attacks made by writers and lesser souls down the ages and, to me, the Acts of the Apostles reads like the truth from fading memory and dimming eyes of four different men. So when Denis Leigh told the guests at my 80th birthday party that I had a "deep faith" I realised I had not mentioned what this had meant to me all these years.

What Denis said must have seemed incongruous or even inappropriate to my sons and any Roman Catholic of the old school present. It will have been noticed that even as a child I was protesting inwardly against the extreme views of the Roman Curia as preached at that time and as practised by my

---

[1] Prieur Roger Schutz, *Diary*, Communauté de Taizé, Cluny, France.

In the Way of Understanding

mother. In my heart of hearts I never accepted hell and damnation, or the infallability of the Pope and the arrogance of the Roman Church in their belief that they alone had access to the truth. This has always been an anathema to me. Tradition and an inherited background of religious education was not easy to escape from without deeply hurting my mother, but my chance came in 1933 when after I obtained a divorce I married Mont. I took the plunge not without agony of spirit, for I knew this was a parting of the ways and that mother would be heart-broken, angry and even ashamed. She had, poor lady, already been hurt by the defection from the Roman Catholic faith by her Aunt Alice O'Hagon (née Towneley), and of her husband Lord O'Hagon, Lord Chancellor of Ireland. They rejected the infallability of the Pope in 1870, and it is impossible now to believe that Roman Catholics were in those days forbidden to read the Authorised Version of the Bible! The O'Hagons lived in the time of Darwin's evolutionary theories and the last straw was I suppose the appearance of *Origin of Species*[1] and *The Descent of Man*, the culmination of years of doubts and the liberal views expressed amongst progressive Christians, discussed in depth by the Towneleys with their many visitors to Towneley Hall, for example Huxley. This skeleton in my mother's family cupboard was never referred to except in a cynical and derisory way by my mother and the true and unhappy story was only revealed to me by Kathleen de Beaumont, Lord and Lady O'Hagon's daughter, in 1961. Just before her death, she wrote down for private circulation at my suggestion, the thrilling but painful account of these happenings in *My Memoirs*. The Towneleys and O'Hagons suffered greviously from the not unnatural harsh judgment of the Roman Catholic Church at that time and the bitterness and passion engendered amongst many Christians of all denominations. Happily since the unprecedented activities of that saintly Pope John XXIII we have travelled far from the evil days of the power of the Curia Romana and the future under the present Polish Pontiff John Paul II, himself having experience of persecution, shows some hope. I see light at the

---

[1] Charles Darwin, John Murray 1859.

Epilogue

end of a dark tunnel though I doubt if I shall live to see a complete reversal of many of the beliefs which are anathemas to many despite the leadership and ecumenical thinking of Cardinal Basil Hume.

To be fair, I was never persecuted or made the victim of Roman Catholic Church authorities, perhaps because I was too small fry compared to the Towneleys but they may have sensed that my views, strongly felt and acted upon, were balanced by a great respect and even admiration for a faith rarely questioned by the majority of the faithful, yet held deeply by the thinking minority of brave souls like Galileo, Cardinal Newman and Teilhard de Chardin and many others whose hearts were broken by obedience; just as today many cannot adapt to the new ordinances and look back nostalgically to the days before Pope John.

Mont had an inborn fear of the political influence of the Roman Catholic Church and viewed their nefarious practices down the ages with horror. He often expressed his sentiments angrily, to the amusement of his brother Ronnie and his saintly wife who were also suspicious of papal pronouncement but nevertheless were on the side of those who rejected the infallability of the Pope. So in my protesting thought I now felt free and gladly joined in Anglican worship at Much Hadham and elsewhere, not that even here I found the answer. Far from it. But at last I sensed freedom to question. I enjoyed the beautiful language of the King James Bible and the liturgical prayers of the *Book of Common Prayer* in English. I also read *The Bible Designed to be Read as Literature* edited and arranged by Ernest Sutherland Bates (William Heinemann Ltd) a magnificent compilation which fed my starving soul and famished spirit. I now knew that "in my Church are many mansions" and that the Roman Church was but one of many.

It must have been while on the Juvenile Court Bench that I heard from my colleague and later dear friend, the late Dame Eileen Younghusband, of the World Congress of Faiths, founded by her father, Sir Francis Younghusband in 1936 and at that time a startling innovation in the religious world. At a meeting in the Queen's Hall, London, there were I believe besides Christians, Buddhists, Hindus, Moslems, Jews and

In the Way of Understanding

other faiths assembled by Sir Francis from all parts of the world. In Tibet he had had a transforming vision which made him see everything anew, a wonderful and clear view as from the peak of a mountain range. I found kindred spirits in the various religions gathered in the Congress of Faiths, or l'Union des Croyants as it was called in France, and later joined the Executive Committee where Kathleen du Beaumont, my cousin, was an active member. Eileen was close to me in my work as a magistrate and had taught me to temper justice with mercy and to understand the meaning of wise social work in the professional and voluntary fields. Working so much internationally she had learned the art of communicating with people and understanding their various religious beliefs. She was among my many friends who insisted on my writing this book.

After Mont's death I came across by accident a review of the *Letters of a Traveller* by Pierre Teilhard de Chardin (Wm. Collins, 1959) translated from the French by Bernard Wall, with a glorious introduction by Sir Julian Huxley. This book echoed so much of what I had been feeling and had been unable to express. Sir Julian Huxley's introduction told me that "here was a remarkable human being, at the same time a Jesuit priest and a distinguished palaeontologist who had effected a threefold synthesis—of the material and physical world with the world of mind and spirit; of the past with the future; of the variety with unity; the many with the one." Pierre Teilhard de Chardin's book *The Phenomenon of Man* was hard work, but his thought came as a spiritual illumination. He was reviled and exiled by his superiors in Rome but loved and supported by like-minded spirits, many of them Jesuits. He received the Legion of Honour for his work as a stretcher-bearer in the 1914/18 war, did much scientific work in China and elsewhere, and during the 1939/45 war, and died suddenly in New York on Easter Sunday 1955. He was forbidden to publish during his life time so his books only appeared after his death. His work is now acclaimed universally, and his ideas are exercising a powerful influence on thought

---

[1] Pierre Teilhard de Chardin, *The Phenomenon of Man*, Collins, 1959.

Epilogue

in the religious and scientific worlds, and even Roman Catholics now cash in on him.

I joined the Teilhard Centre for the Future of Man, an Association of those interested in this great prophet and his works. I was on the Executive Committee for many years and took part in their lectures, discussions and groups, reading with pleasure the excellent *Teilhard Review*, published three times a year. In this milieu and on the Committee I got to know another Jesuit priest who became my friend, and mentor, Tom Corbishley. He was a distinguished preacher and the first Roman Catholic in history to preach in St. Paul's Cathedral and to be invited to say Mass in the Katherine of Aragon Chapel in St. George's Chapel, Windsor. This was during a conference I attended in St. George's House, which is now a conference centre where clergy and laity meet to discuss contemporary problems.

To quote the words spoken at a service of remembrance held in Westminster Abbey (May 1976): "We think of him perhaps above all as a pioneer of a particularly attractive kind, one who simply could not resist holding out the hand of friendship to fellow Christians of all denominations. He had the engaging habit of letting his head follow his heart in this direction and many of us are the richer for that. At times he stretched the traditional discipline of his Church to breaking point in his eagerness to welcome his friends, but never in a spirit of defiance or rebellion but rather as one who believes that the Church is truest to herself when sometimes she ardently breaks her own rules."

Tom certainly held out the hand of friendship to me at a time when I needed it badly and maybe he also stretched the traditional discipline of his Church in my favour for not only did he give me the Bread of Life in the privacy of the Chapel in Farm Street, but at Dyneley he encouraged me to take Communion with my family in their private chapel where he was celebrating Mass. Alas we both realised too late that our hopes for understanding were perhaps naïve and mistimed. As usual I was in too much of a hurry and too passionate. Tom's death left me bereft and once again I had to struggle alone, but I had seen the spirit of God in his face, the well-remembered smile, the wry wit, the firm words, and above all his sense of humour which at times I feel is not far away.

In the Teilhard de Chardin Association, as in the World Congress of Faiths, I have sensed what Teilhard and Tom would have approved of—a drawing together of the great religions of the world under one roof, a convergence once referred to by Teilhard as a "Summit movement", perhaps a summit of divine spiritual aspirations which I find wonderfully helpful.

> *I have considered the days of old: and the years that are past. I call to remembrance my song: and in the night I commune with mine own heart, and search out my spirit.*
>
> Psalm 77, v. 5 & 6.

Appendix[1]

Sophrosyné is usually translated "temperance", less commonly "self-control", "sobriety", "sanity", "balance". None of these renderings is adequate. To understand *sophrosyné*, think of the vice to which a quick, sensitive, emotional people like the Greeks are most liable, and the virtue which they most need. Their danger is excess. *Sophrosyné* is the quality which enables them to walk safely along the narrow knife-edge between the precipices of extremes.

Next, think of this quality as having a range far beyond temperance (as we use the word). *Sophrosyné* stretches out and tends to become the whole of virtue, an inner harmony of the soul, a reasonableness which reveals itself in every action and attitude. It saves the individual from physical excess, from extravagance of thought and word, from the arrogance that exaggerates his capacities, and the ambition that overleaps itself. The Greeks would have found it absent in the drunkard and the debauchee, but also in Luther and Napoleon and in some more recent national heroes, in the advocates of the class-war, in militarists and extreme pacifists, in the optimists who thought that the world would be regenerated by science, and in the pessimists who despair of civilisation. It is an especially difficult virtue for politicians; no one finds it easy in times of social and political tension; and in war-time it vanishes almost entirely—especially among civilians.

Finally, conceive a quality which is positive. This removes it far from the barren slackness which is neither hot nor cold, from the type of Liberalism which Matthew Arnold described as moral indifference without intellectual ardour, and from a mere colourless self-control. It is, in the literal meaning of the Greek word, "soundness of mind". Restraint is of its essence, but is felt, not as restraint nor as a drag on natural instinct nor as an infringement of liberty, but as that natural service to right reason which is perfect freedom. Indeed *sophrosyné* is, or ought to be, pre-eminently the virtue of an educated man. Plato describes those who possess it by saying that they are

---

[1] From Sir R. W. Livingstone, *Portrait of Socrates*, Clarendon Press, Oxford, 1938.

"stronger than themselves"; the source of their strength over self is the wisdom that is the essence of *sophrosyné*.

Sophrosyné can take, as we have seen, many forms. These dialogues contain perfect examples of two of them. The close of the *Phaedo* shows it in the art of writing, the character of Socrates shows it in man. A good, though not quite perfect, example of it among our own countrymen is Sir Thomas More.

Index

Abeokuta, 242
Aborigines, 273
Acropolis, 250
Adam, Dr. C. H., Warden of all Souls, 112
Addis, Sir Charles, 152
Addis, John, 260, 265, 298
Addis, Robina, 151f, 209f, 212f, 241, 246ff, 254, 260, 265ff, 276, 283, 287, 298f, 311ff
Ademola, Sir Adetokumbo, 246
Ademola, Sir Lapapo, 245
Adrian, Hester, 147
Adrian, Lord, 147f
Affair of the Heart', 'An, 250
Agora, Athens, 252
Aldaba-Lim, Dr. F., 311
Alexander, Misses, 167
Allderridge, Patricia, 175, 182
Allenby, General, 292
Appleby, Mary, 138, 142, 212, 226, 283
Appleton, Archbishop, 289
Aro Hospital, Nigeria, 243ff
Armistice, 31
Ashwell, Lena, 102f
Association for the Psychiatric Study of Adolescents, 200
Astor, Nancy, 54
Athens, 250, 252
Atkinson, Mrs. Creswick, 110
Aubrey Lodge, 167, 171
Austria, 311ff
Avalon, 304
Ayrshire Castle, 225

Bacon, Rt. Hon. Alice, 285
Bagnold, Enid, 37
Baldwin, Sir Stanley, 99
Balkmanaugh, 119
Bank of England, Governors of, 87f
du Beaumont, Kathleen, 326
Beers, Clifford, 218
Belewa, Alhagi Sir Abubaka Tafawa, 240, 245
Berlin, 232–4
Bertie, Lady Alice Josephine (mother of the author), 8, 12, 18ff, 44ff, 51, 120, 166
Bertie, Evie, 20
Bertie, Sir Francis, 25
Bethesda, Pool of, 289
Bethlehem, 290
Bethlem Royal and Maudsley Hospitals, 174–185
'Bible designed to be read as Literature', 325
Birthday Honours List, 190
Black Sash Movement, 305
Blampied, Miss, 109
Brain, Lord, 243, 245
Brittain, Vera ('Testament of Youth'), 24
Brompton Oratory, 42
Brooklyn After Care Clinic, 218
Brouckère, Monsieur de, 12
Brown, Miss, 144
Burton, James, 45f, 120, 122, 166, 169f, 286f
Butabica Hospital, Uganda, 294
Butler, Molly, 283f
Butler, Rt. Hon. R. A., 155, 157, 187, 285

Cairns, Sir Hugh, 117, 119
Caledonian Canal, 40
Camden Park, 268ff, 274
Canada, 309ff
Canadian Association for Mental Health, 224

In the Way of Understanding

Capell, Lady Iris, 111
Capes, Dr. Mary, 200
Carlsbad, 277
Carmichael, Dr., 218f
Carr, Eric, 283
Carstairs, Morris, 259, 278f, 285, 288, 291, 310f
Carter, Mrs. Rosalyn, 309f
Castle Peak Psychiatric Hospital, 255
Castration as a treatment, 237
Cavell, Edith, 23
Cavendish Square Convent, 18
Chagall, Marc, 292
Chaplaincy to Bethlem Royal and Maudsley Hospitals, 182f
de Chardin, Teilhard, 125, 300f, 326f
Charles II, 187
Chelsea Borough Council, 53
Child Guidance Report, 58
Child Guidance Council, 60, 63, 78, 81
China, 298, 301
Chisholm, Dr. Brock, 157, 235f
Churchill, Lady Gwendoline, 20, 22
Churchill, Jack, 22
Churchill, Sir Winston, 21
Citizen's Advice Bureaux, 115
Clarke, Dr. Stafford, 233f
Coetze, Mr., 122
Cohen, Dr. Samuel, 291
Collet, Sir Mark, 81, 98, 119
Copenhagen, 235
Corbishley, Fr. Thomas, 327f
Cos, Island of, 251
Court of Appeal, 132
Cowes, 39
Czechoslovakia, 275–8
Czechoslovakian Psychiatric Society, 277

Dahlen, Free University of, 232
Darwin, Charles, 324
Dean, Frances, 283
Delano, Moreau, 79
Diaghilev Ballet, 19, 37
Divorce, 49
Doodle-bugs, 120
Douglas, Mrs. Lewis, 155
Drakensberg Mountains, 304
Draper, Ruth, 91
Duncroft, 144
'Dyneley', 45, 166, 327

Edwards, Dr. Griffith, 279, 283
Egyptian Medical Association 230
Eightieth Birthday Party, 320
Elgood, Bonté, 229f
Epidaurus, 251
d'Erlanger, Catherine, 37
European Mental Health League, 209
Errath Hashin Hospital, Jerusalem, 291f
Evacuation from London 1939, 110, 113

Farouk, King, 231
Fenton, Roy, 241
Ferrier, Kathleen, 90, 150
Feversham Committee, 64, 115, 187
Filipino Association for Mental Health, 265f
First Communion, 13
Fleming, Alexander, 117f
Forel, Dr. Oscar, 210
Fort Napier Hospital, 303
Fountain House, 219
Fox, Dame Evelyn, 61f, 115, 121, 138
Framingham Reformatory, 222
Francis, Miss, 145
Fraser, Mr., 45
Fraser-Gamble, Miss, 117
Freud, Anna, 156

Gater, Sir George, 52, 58, 60
Gerard, Brother, 310
German, Professor Allen, 272, 293
Gestapo, 254

Index

Gethsemane, Garden of, 288f
Gheel, 213
Gibson, Hugh, 23
Gibson, Professor, 239
Gillis, Professor, 245
'Ginger Bread Lady', The, 273
Gooreynd, Alexander Koch de, 42, 47f
Gordon, General, 288
Gorden Hayes, 273
Greece, 250ff
Groote Shuur, 124
Groothock Psychiatric Hospital, 306

Hadassah Hospital, Jerusalem, 292
Halpin, Miss Kathleen, 110
Hammy, (greyhound), 52
Hare, Dr. Edward, 253
Harkness Trust, 217
'Harmony in Grey' (Whistler), 167
Hayward, Mr. Leader of L.C.C., 167
Heath, Mr. Edward, 88
Helmsley, Lady, 42
Hennuy, Mademoiselle, 13, 16
Henriques, Sir Basil, 131
Hinks, Dr. Clare, 224f
Hippocrates, 251
Holloway Prison, 130
Holy Land, 288ff
Hong Kong, 254–262
Hong Kong Association for Mental Health, 256, 258
House of Wisdom, 230
Hume, Cardinal Basil, 325
Huxley, Sir Julian, 157, 326

Ibberson, Miss D., 114
Ikedja, Federal Farm School, 242
Illich, Ivan, 310
Ingham, Miss Grace, 242
Institution for Psychopathic Criminals, 237
International Conference on Social Work, 227

International Hippocratic Foundation, 251
International Year of the Child, 311

Jabvala, Dr., 272
James I, 187
James, Lord, 146
Jersey, Island of, 231f
Jersey Association for Mental Health, 232
Jones, Professor Kathleen, 135f
Jones, Miss Margaret, 145

Kaar, Rajkumazi Amrit, 249
Kahn, Dr. Jack, 239
Keeling, Miss Dorothy, 115
Keppel, Mrs., 41
Kholi, Dr. El, 230
Kibbutz, 291
King George VI, 101
King, Mackenzie, 220
King and Queen of Thailand, 263
Kitchener Memorial Hospital, 229
Klineberg, Dr. Otto, 267f
Krapff, Dr., 234

Lagos, 241
La La Panzi, 122f
Lambert, Leon, 8
Lambo, Dr. Thomas, 240, 244ff, 302
Lantoro Hospital, 244
Lawrence, Lady Isabel, 51
L.C.C., 51
Leigh, Dr. Denis, 255ff, 262, 264, 323
Leitner, Dr. Zoe, 117f
Lennox, Cosmo Gordon, 18ff, 37, 41, 44
Leslie, Capt. Norman, 24
'Letters of a Traveller', 326
Lewis, Sir Aubrey, 174, 185, 243
Lewis, Hilda, 243
Lim, Fanny Adama, 265
Lima Conference, 278ff
Lin, Professor Tsung yi, 309
Lindemann, Dr. Erich, 223
Line, Professor William, 224f

Lister, Lady, 171
Locin, Mr. Lindi, 267
London Congress, 283
Loneliness, a personal view of, 164–6
Lywood, C. A., 133f

McClay, Dr. Walker, 141
McMahon, Sir Henry, 39
McMillan, Margaret, 53, 55
McVeigh, Rt. Hon. Lord Justice, 239
Magistrates, 129
Maitland, Sir Alexander, 150
Makerere College, 293
Mala Mala Game Reserve, 306
Malevoz, 211
'Mannekin pis', 214
Manuwa. Chief Sir Samuel, 276
Mapother, Dr. Edward, 176
Marienbad, 277
Markoe, Mrs., 78ff, 268
Martin, John, 121, 124
Marwick, Iris, 122, 236, 242, 301
Mason, Dr. Pamela, 145
Massachusetts General Hospital, 223
Maudsley, Henry, 176
Mbaneto, Sir Louis, 246f
Mead, Margaret, 156, 233f, 238, 249, 311f
Meesook, Khunying Ambhorn, 264
Menninger, Karl, 311
Mental Health Emergency Committee, 115, 121
Mental Treatment Act, 129
Mercier, Cardinal 15
Milean, Dr. Gonzalez, 282
Miller, Jonathan, 197
Miller, Dr. Louis, 272, 291
Miller, Mr. T. A., 121, 225
MIND, 138, 146, 320
Mitchell, Adrian, 287
Montessori, Madame, 55
Moor Place, 76, 97, 115, 117
Moran, Lord, 117ff, 156, 264
Morant, Sir Robert, 21

More, Sir Thomas, 330
Morgan, Edith, 282
Moross, Dr. Hyme, 301
Mount Gilead, 269f

National Association for Mental Health, 137, 151f, 155, 208, 231
National Association for Mental Hygiene, 187
National Council for Social Service, 112–149, 162
National Institutes of Health, 221
National Museum of Greece, 250
New South Wales Association for Mental Health, 269
Netherlands Association for Mental Health, 252ff
Neimeyer, Sir Otto, 138, 142
Nigeria, 240–8
Night clubs in Hamburg, 164
Nijinsky, Vaclav, 37
Norman, Mrs. (mother of Montagu), 82f, 166
'Norman Circus', 195
Norman, Lady Florence, 76, 84, 98, 115
'Norman House', 145
Norman, Montagu, 73–85, 87f, 93f, 98f, 115, 117ff, 161, 268, 320, 325
Norman, Ronnie, 76, 83, 98, 115
Northern Ireland Health Authority, 238
Nurses' Homes, 181
Nursery Schools, 53

Oedipus Rex, 227
O'Hagon, Lord, 324
Onitsha, 246f
Onslow, Sir Denzil Macarthur, 269
Onslow, Sibella Macarthur, 268ff
Ou, Dr. George, 255f
Our Towns: a close-up Report, 113

Paine, Mr., 176
Pan African Psychiatric Congress, 240

Index

Pavlova, Anna, 36
Payne, Humfry, 251
Peacock, Sir Edward, 162
Pearson, Mike, 227
Peruvian League of Mental Hygiene, 279ff
'Phenomenon of Man', The, 125
Phipps. Mrs. William Wilson, 52
Pinacothek Museum, 235
'Plodge', 76, 87, 89, 114, 120, 161, 166–9, 284, 286
Ployhar, Joseph, 276f
Poleo, Dr. M. A., 281
Poor Law Re-organisation, 53
Pope, Infallibility of, 324
Pope John Paul II, 324
Portal, Sir Gerald, 8, 69, 292f, 295
Portal, Capt. Melville Raymond, 295
Portal, Rosemary, 50
Portal, Sir William, 39, 69, 73, 75
Portal, Wyndham, 50, 69, 73
Poseidon, Statue of, 250
Pound, Ezra, 222
Powell, Dilys, 250f
Powell, Enoch, 140
Prince of Wales, 41, 65
Princess Alexandra, 189f, 246
Princess Marina, 146, 181, 186ff, 242, 285
Printemps, Yvonne, 26
Prison Officers, 134
Prokupec, Dr. Joseph, 275
Protection de la Jeune Fille, La, 16

Queen Elizabeth, the Queen Mother, 101, 187, 191
'Queen Elizabeth', H.M.S., 40
Queen Mary, 101, 187
Querido, Dr. A., 253

Reading, Lady, 109ff, 112f
Rees, Dr. J. R., 153f, 207f, 285, 288
Rees, Dr. T. P., 141
Reith, Sir John (later Lord), 102f
Repond, Dr. 211
Reyes, Dr. Susana, 266

Reyntiens, Adrienne, 38
Reyntiens, Guy, 10, 38, 78
Reyntiens, Major Robert, 7
Reyntiens, Ynes, 9
Riddoch, Dr. George, 119
Risquez, Dr. Fernando, 282
Rives des Prangins, 210
Roger, Père, 323
Roomes, Miss, 92f
Roosevelt, Mrs. Eleanor, 218
Roscher, Iris, 301f, 305
Rudolf Steiner School, 210
Rumke, Dr., 243f, 253

St. Augustine's Hospital, 199
St. Christopher's Hospice, 201ff
St. Clere, 76, 96, 98f, 105, 144, 121
St. Elizabeth's Hospital, Boston, 222
St. Mary's Hospital, 118
Salzburg, 312
Sardauna of Sokoto, 242
Saunders, Dr. Cicely, 201
Schacht, Hjalmar, 104f
Schutz, Brother Roger, 296f
Scott, Dr. Peter, 132, 237, 243
Scottish Association for Mental Health, 149
Scoville, Mildred, 237
'Sesame', 197
Sex, discussions with Mary Stocks, 172
Singapore Association for Mental Health, 274
Sivadon, Dr. Paul, 249
Skillern, Eileen, 190
Smieton Dame Mary, 110
Smith, Dr. The Hon: Honor, 119
Smuts, Rt. Hon: Field Marshal Jan, 124, 161, 308
Socrates, 250, 252
South African Council for Mental Health, 302
Spanish 'flu, 30
Spock, Dr. Benjamin, 312
Springhead Park, 146
Stapleton, Professor, 269
Stephenson, Sir Arthur, 271

Stewart, Walter W., 216
Stocks, Baroness, 171f
Stoller, Professor Alan, 269ff
Strachey, Mrs. St. Loe, 60, 114
Stratford Festival, Ontario, 227
Stürup, Dr., 237
Sunner, Miss Shelagh, 146
Suzman, Mrs. Janet, 305
Sydney Opera House, 272

Taizé, 296ff, 319
Talbot, Edmund, 35
Talbot, May, 20
Tara Psychiatric Hospital, 122, 237, 301
Teilhard Centre for the Future of Man, 327f
Thailand, 262–265
'The Torch', 250
Thompson, Mary, 283, 288
Tigani El Mahi, 245
Thompson, Rev. Ian, 288
Tower Hill Psychiatric Hospital, 303
Towneley Estate, 45
Towneley Family, 324
Towneley, Mary, 320
Towneley, Simon, 43, 48, 56, 115, 120, 166, 320
Tozer, Mrs., 172
Trevelyan, Mr. John, 162
Tsung-Lin Professor, 302
Tun, Dr. Jesus, 265

Uganda 292–7
Ugandan Association for Mental Health, 293
U.N.E.S.C.O., 154, 162
United Nations, 154
United Nations building, 220
University of Nigeria, 246
U Thant, 220

V.A.D.s, 27
Vaughan, Cardinal, 15
Venezuela, 281f
Venezuelan League of Mental Hygiene, 281

Verrière, La, 249
Versailles, 249
Vevey Conference, 209ff
Vickers, Sir Geoffrey, 226
Victoria Hospital, Sydney, 270
Victoria Mental Health Authority, 270
Vienna, 229
Vincent, Lady Kitty, 7

Wagdi, Dr., 272
Wakehurst, Lady, 239
Wall, Dr. W. D., 163
Warren, Dr. Wilfred, 146, 249, 261, 274, 291
Watson, John, 131
Wedding in 1933, 84
Wellesley Human Relations Service Centre, 224
Western Nigerian Association for Mental Health, 246
Westminster Abbey, 285
Whitchurch, Lilian, 169f
Wiltwych School, 218
Winchester General Hospital, 27
Women's Group on Public Welfare, 113
Woodcock, Mr., 295
World Congress of Faiths, 325
World Federation for Mental Health, 154–7, 163, 189, 207, 212ff, 224ff, 228, 235, 253, 258, 260, 264, 272, 276–281, 290ff, 311ff, 319
World Psychiatric Association, 257
Worsthorne, Peregrine, 47f, 56, 115, 120, 191, 303, 320
W.V.S., 109f, 112

Yap, Dr. P. M., 255f, 261
York University, 146
Younghusband, Dame Eileen, 248, 325f
Younghusband, Sir Francis, 325f

Zeppelin raids, 26
Zulu War, 304